THOUGHT LEADERS

THE SOURCE CODE
OF EXCEPTIONAL MANAGERS
AND ENTREPRENEURS

THOUGHT LEADERS

THE SOURCE CODE OF EXCEPTIONAL MANAGERS AND ENTREPRENEURS

Shrinivas Pandit

Management Counsellor

Tata McGraw-Hill Publishing Company Limited

NEW DELHI

McGraw-Hill Offices

New Delhi New York St Louis San Francisco Auckland Bogotá Caracas
Kuala Lumpur Lisbon London Madrid Mexico City Milan Montreal
San Juan Santiago Singapore Sydney Tokyo Toronto

Tata McGraw-Hill
*A Division of The **McGraw·Hill** Companies*

This edition can be exported from India only by the publishers,
Tata McGraw-Hill Publishing Company Limited

ISBN 0-07-040308-2

Published by Tata McGraw-Hill Publishing Company Limited
7 West Patel Nagar, New Delhi 110 008 and typeset in Goudy at
The Composers, 20/5 Old Market, West Patel Nagar, New Delhi 110 008
and printed at Rashtriya Printers, M-135, Panchsheel Garden,
Naveen Shahdara, Delhi 110 032

Cover Design: Kam Studio

RZZCRRDLDLLXL

To my father,
Damodar Gopal Pandit,
who instilled in me the value of fairness.

Preface

Our chief want is someone who will inspire us to be what we know we could be.

Ralph Waldo Emerson

The original thinking processes of exceptional industry leaders—managers and entrepreneurs—are captured in this book. I call this achieving tribe 'thought leaders'. They are role models; they influence others through their powerful thoughts. But they are after all men and women like you and me; what is it that makes them different? In an attempt to uncover this secret, this treatise succeeds in identifying nutrients for the development of your core competencies and business growth.

In the *first* part of the book, I have profiled 22 thought leaders—20 men and 2 women. Each sketch describes: their nurturance syndrome. i.e. their characteristic upbringing, mentors' influence and turning points in their lives; and their special traits, thinking processes, competencies and differentiating elements in success. In short, the quintessence of each personality.

In the *second* part, I have collated the common elements in the nurturance of these leaders; identified common traits; and attempted to draw up the 'source code' that makes for exceptional business people who reach the heights of their field through reflexive search, leveraging their domain, and value-added branding. Finally, I validate the source code through my decades of experience as a successful, though not exceptional, human resources professional.

I have deliberately chosen to collage the less-known, for example Sartaj Singh, with the well-known, like Narayana Murthy. The resulting canvas has seven *entrepreneurs*—Bhavarlal Jain, Deepak Kanegaonkar, Ravi Khanna, Kiran Mazumdar, Prakash Ratnaparkhi, Ronnie Screwvala and Manoj Tirodkar—who took a risk and started on their own; six *entrepreneur-managers*—Humayun Dhanrajgir, Verghese Kurien, Deepak Parekh, Pratap Pawar, Sartaj Singh, Sudheer Tilloo—who have been entrepreneurial in building the organizations in which they work; three *manager-entrepreneurs*—Pramod Chaudhari, Narayana Murthy, Ashok Soota—who began their careers by working for some organization before branching out on their own; three *family entrepreneurs*—Rajabhau Chitale, Bhausaheb Kelkar, Vikram Tannan; and finally, three *exceptional managers*—Anu Aga, Dhananjay Bakhle and Raghunath Mashelkar. A data sheet on the 22 subjects is given in the annexure. Except for Dhananjay Bakhle, who is a functional head (medical director, Novartis), all the others are in the top leadership position.

After years of closely monitoring the careers of over 2000 managers, accountants, engineers, vice-presidents, general managers and directors in dozens of functional specialties and general management, which included interviews of over 3500 people, I felt the urge to codify the components of exemplary performance. These components do not belong to one individual alone. Thus was born the idea to undertake a study of outstanding managers to gain insight into their thought processes.

In August 1998 I wrote to 40 professional friends explaining the theme of the book. I requested them to recommend the names of successful entrepreneurs and outstanding managers, applying the following criteria:

- A minimum of 10 years of progressive performance on the job and/or in business;

- Demonstrated excellence in any functional area, general management, technical breakthrough, or chosen business activity;

- A clear potential for further advancement in their organizational or business career;

- Proven influence over others to innovate and give a higher performance by demonstrated results, and an infectious, positive mindset; and

- Creativity.

I specified, "It could be an employee in any category or an entrepreneur, in any business or service who is seen honouring commitment to her/his vocational calling. Such a person may have yet to achieve celebrity status. Spot a pathfinder, an innovator who you think could be considered for inclusion in the book. The turnover, PBT, share price (if it's a listed company) and such other indicators of sound organizational health shall be assumed to be excellent. I am looking for inspiring role models who have turned out splendid results. Personal knowledge of achievements and opinion about the person are of utmost importance. Apart from the criteria given above, I think you would apply your own personal litmus test."

My friends suggested 82 names. After discussion I contacted 30 of them and a further shortlist led to the 22 people profiled in this book. The collection is neither a representative sample nor a comparison of peers based on company performance ratings. I have deliberately mixed leaders from various industries and different backgrounds. Although I am aware of many more excellent role models, for this work I have depended upon the gut feel of my friends and my own impressions. Some of the participants felt a bit shy to be included with celebrities.

A structured questionnaire was sent to them. Interviews were conducted during 1999. They were audiotaped and transcribed verbatim. The interviews generally lasted about four hours over two to three sittings; some more, some less. The interviews were supplemented with clippings of speeches, articles, company balance sheets and house magazines. My interview schedule had a number of common questions but the priority was to keep the flow of the conversation natural. I wanted the dialogue to develop around the themes for reflective answers. It did.

The small size of the sample, therefore, or its lack of representativeness, was no impediment to deriving solid conclusions. The participants' self-assessment was marked by candour and humility. These leaders follow specialised practices, peculiar to their occupation of business management. Their framework of exceptionality is constructed around business work which leads to enhanced value to the customer in the product and services he receives.

The same belief framework provides meaning to them and to their fellow workers in their 'work' environment. They have acquired an intuitive and ineffable knowledge to spot, create and convert opportunities into commercially viable business ventures which provide employment, service and products to society. The elements of their sustained performance have provided me with insights into their thinking processes and result-producing practices. The set of attitudes and competencies used by them for achieving outstanding results are recorded. They are simple to follow, easy to absorb and apply.

I call these people exceptional because of their sustained performance, predictability in achieving success, durable influencing capacity and use of the source code. They have high credibility, use vivid language with compelling evidence, and they connect emotionally.

These men and women are not paragons of virtue. They do not lay claim to great wisdom. They readily acknowledge their shortcomings. They deeply revere their sometimes humble beginnings. They are aware of the invisible influence of coincidence and serendipity. They are somewhat reluctant to speak about their achievements, and more so about themselves. This is because of the sincere belief that their teams have contributed to their success. Their spiritedness is infectious. Reading about their experiences, you will find yourself getting charged. The structural shift in your consciousness will enable you to leverage your strengths. All those profiled are learners, so are you. Your domain skills will sharpen. You will proceed to draw on your untapped reservoir of skills to become an influential thought leader yourself, if you are not one already. When in need, refer to the practices of these business sages. They will unfailingly provide light.

Gender is no bar to leadership. So in the course of this book 'he' applies to 'she' and vice-versa. The words 'manager', 'entrepreneur', 'executive', 'participant', 'subject', 'role model' and 'leader' have also been inter-changeably used. The thought leaders are presented in alphabetical order.

Gift a copy of the book to your friends, business associates, clients or customers; they will remain ever grateful and you will earn tonnes of goodwill for your organization. Don't be surprised if you occupy the pages of some such book to inspire others one day soon.

Mumbai   SHRINIVAS PANDIT
December 2000   .

Acknowledgements

For almost three years, this book has dominated my life. I am hugely indebted to the 22 leaders who agreed to be featured. These extremely busy people were generous with their time and freely shared their views; their active participation and encouragement made it possible for me to write on this novel theme. A million thanks.

Without the help of the secretariat staff of these executives and the public relations and communication managers working in their organizations, I would not have been able to get convenient appointments and the relevant material. My thanks are due to all of them, particularly R Anand of HDFC, Ahmed Bunglowala of Thermax, P A Joseph of NDDB, A G Pandu of Infosys and Rufina Fernandes of Global Tele-Systems.

It's somewhat difficult to look back over three years or even earlier and thank all those who have cajoled, prompted or helped me to write this book. For starters, let me thank my son Nitin Pandit and daughter Vrinda Kirloskar for their humorous persuasion, "Dad, please don't tell us about leaders and careers. They sound like snakes and ladders to us, where are the ladders? Write a book that someone will hopefully read and we will be saved."

Jayashri Patwardhan, an able trainer who associated with me in a number of workshops I designed and conducted for my clients, deserves special thanks for constantly nagging me to give shape to my ideas in the form of a book.

I also wish to thank my friends Jayant Kher, financial consultant, and Nishigandh Deshpande, managing director of Gilbert Maxwell Electricals Pvt. Ltd., Baroda, for giving useful suggestions on the first draft. Journalist Parimal Chaudhari deserves thanks for making meaningful comments on some sample profiles and chapters of the book. Thanks are also due to Atul Deshmukh, executive director, *Business India*, and Mahesh Vijapurkar, deputy editor, *The Hindu*, both of whom put me in touch with good editors. With her penchant for "less is more", Ulka Bhadkamkar fleshed out the drafts, for which I thank her.

Thanks also to 40 professional friends, particularly BR Sabade, former secretary of the Maratha Chamber of Commerce, Pune, for introducing me to some of the leaders, and to Ashok Pradhan, vice chancellor of the Yashwantrao Chavan Maharashtra Open University, Nasik, for giving a useful lead.

I also want to thank the ever-helpful Premanand Shenvi, manager, Strand Bookstall, Mumbai, who did a candid appraisal of all the publishing houses and helped me select Tata McGraw-Hill Publishing Co Ltd (TMH). Special thanks to Madhav Naware, former regional manager, TMH, and the TMH team of Deepa Varadarajan, Nidhi Sharma, PL Pandita, Tamojit Roy, Roystan

La'porte, headed by managing director N Subrahmanyam for the interest they took in my first literary project.

Thanks to Dolly Nazareth who meticulously worked on my PC for the last one year, typing innumerable drafts and taking out as many copies as I wanted without getting fed up even once. Moreover, she responded to my impatience and occasional irritation with a smile. I am indeed grateful to her for her sincere input. Thanks are also due to Anant Yellonde, my multipurpose assistant for office work, driving and domestic help, and to Ganpat Alim for similar assistance.

All members of the close and extended family and the large circle of close friends have shown commendable understanding for my paranoid involvement in this project. They have all pardoned me for my inattention to them during these three years—a big thank you.

Like most wives, my wife Anjali has learnt to patiently live with my oddities. This time, I owe her a basket of thanks for being a helpless witness to her entire house being turned into a writer's studio.

My apologies to those whose names I might have inadvertently failed to mention; I thank them nonetheless.

Thought Leaders

▲ *Verghese Kurien, Chairman, IRMA.*

◄ *Narayana Murthy, Chairman,*
Infosys Technologies Ltd.

▲ *Kiran Mazumdar, Chairperson, Biocon India Ltd.*

▲ *Pratap Pawar, Managing Director, Sakal Papers Ltd.*

▲ *Dhananjay Bakhle, Medical Director, Novartis India Ltd.*

▲ *Rajabhau Chitale, Partner, Chitalebandhu Mithaiwala.*

▲ *Vikram Tannan, Managing Director, Banner Pharmacaps (India) Pvt. Ltd.*

◄ *Deepak Kanegaonkar,*
Chairman,
Vishudha Rasayani Ltd.

▲ *Deepak Parekh, Chairman, HDFC Ltd.*

▲ *Pramod Chaudhari, Chairman, Praj Industries Ltd.*

◀ *Ashok Soota,*
Chairman, MindTree
Consulting Pvt. Ltd.

◀ *Bhausaheb Kelkar, Chairman,*
S H Kelkar & Co. Ltd.

Bhavarlal Jain,
Chairman,
Jain Irrigation Systems Ltd. ➤

▲ *Prakash Ratnaparkhi, Executive Director, Electronica.*

Manoj Tirodkar, ➤
Executive Vice-Chairman,
Global Tele-Systems Ltd.

▲ *Sartaj Singh, Country Manager, FMC India Ltd.*

▲ *Humayun Dhanrajgir, Managing Director, Kodak India Ltd.*

▲ *Ronnie Screwvala, Managing Director, United Television Ltd.*

▲ *Ravi Khanna, Chairman, Controls & Switchgears Ltd.*

▲ *Raghunath Mashelkar, Director General, CSIR.*

▲ *Sudheer Tilloo, Group Chief Executive, DGP Hinoday/DGP Windsor Ltd.*

▲ *Anu Aga, Chairperson, Thermax Ltd.*

Contents

Contents

xviii

Part II

The Source Code

Part I

THOUGHT LEADERS

Anu Aga

"Acknowledging a customer in 24 hours is a religious endeavour."

Known as the '3M of India', Thermax, the energy and environment major from Pune, is a successful group (turnover Rs 700 crore) which is known to value ethical standards. The chairperson of the group is the gracious and compassionate Anu Aga (58).

*A*nu Aga's father, the entrepreneur and industrialist Ardeshir Bhathena, established the company, then known as Wanson (India) Pvt Ltd, in Mumbai in 1966 with a capital of Rs 3 lakh and a team of 40 people. Initially the company manufactured coil-type packaged boilers and thermic fluid heaters in technical collaboration with a Belgian company, Wanson. Due to lack of space for expansion, the set-up was moved to Chinchwad, an industrial suburb of

Pune. Today, Thermax is a multi-divisional company involved in the design, manufacture and marketing of products, systems and services in the areas of energy and environment. There are now six subsidiaries and four joint venture companies in the group. Thermax's core business is boilers, heaters, waste heat systems, vapour absorption machines, boiler revamp, energy services, and waste management, air gaseous, pollution control, water and waste water treatment and recycling.

CATAPULTED TO POWER

Anu assumed charge as executive chairperson of Thermax in 1996 two days after the sudden death of her husband Rohinton Aga, who had nurtured the company. A graduate of the Tata Institute of Social Sciences, Anu was at the time heading the human resources division of Thermax after having worked there for several years. Three years later, she created a sensation (and stoked rumours that the family was selling its stake) by handing over all operational executive responsibilities to managing director Abhay Nalawade, who became the chief executive officer (he has since left the company). Anu's daughter and son-in-law both work at Thermax, but they were not given charge. This was highly unusual for a family business; owners are usually unwilling to give up any kind of control. But, as we shall see, Anu is a highly unusual lady, an evolving person who maintains that "The organization will continue to be run by professionals who are the most capable. An organization cannot take success for granted."

Interestingly, this complex business in engineering and environment was built by three non-engineers—Anu's father, Rohinton and Abhay Nalawade. The architect of its phenomenal growth was Rohinton.

LIVING A MISSION

After obtaining a masters in economics from Cambridge University, Rohinton returned to India. He was working in the multinational oil company Burmah-Shell when his father-in-law Ardeshir asked him if he would join his infant company. Rohinton jumped at the opportunity. Says Anu, "He wanted to show what he could do, rather that follow some company. He was influenced by his uncle and mother's idea of a successful person, one who flourishes through risks. He had a risk-taking ability. My father's call spurred him into action." With a degree from the prestigious St Catherine's College in Cambridge and a job in Burmah-Shell, Rohinton could have carved out a glittering career in the then most sought-after MNC. But his entrepreneurial instincts made him quit his job to build a respectable value-based company.

Rohinton was a charismatic leader and the backbone of Thermax. He nurtured it, gave it direction and brought it to its present level of competence and presence in the industry. Then, in February 1996, Rohinton died of a sudden heart attack. The organization was able to absorb this shock only because he had groomed and trained a team of dedicated and committed professionals who would carry on his work, and thus, built an institution which would survive beyond an individual.

Of course, when Thermax started, it did not have a winning product, brilliant people or financial muscle. It was Rohinton's ability to attract and retain a large number of talented people, offering them a culture where they could innovate and make things happen, that helped the company achieve its present growth. Since its inception, Rohinton gave tremendous importance to research, development and training. Here's a list of the breakthroughs achieved by the company:

- 1973 was the year of the oil crisis. In response, the R&D at Thermax worked day and night and developed the Multitherm, India's first packaged water tube boiler for Indian coal and other solid fuels.

- Rohinton realized that water treatment was critical for the smooth functioning of a boiler. So in 1975 Thermax branched out into the manufacture of water treatment plants, initially for captive use, and later into large systems for power stations, fertilizer and petrochemical plants.

- The logic of Thermax's diversification and growth has been to move from the familiar to the not so familiar. Surface coating started in 1979 with a Thermopac adapted for paint drying. In due course, this activity was extended to include pre-treatment plants and ovens; and later, turnkey painting systems.

- As a natural extension to the pioneering efforts in thermic fluid heating, in 1985-86 their R&D developed the first fluidised bed boilers.

- In 1987 the heat recovery division introduced steam-fired vapour absorption chillers for the first time in the Indian market, in technical collaboration with a Japanese firm. Today this product is a market leader.

What was the core ideology? In Rohinton's words: "Understanding the market in depth, stretching it to the fullest potential, creating new unfulfilled needs, putting one's talents and those of the entire team in clear focus, being obsessed in the process, and emerging as a leader—this is living a mission. This is the role and heritage of a value-added society. It is exciting, it is rewarding and it is never-ending." He also believed that though they were in business to make profits, "Profit is not a set of figures, but of values." Anu adds: "It has been our endeavour to live up to this core ideology."

ROHINTON GROOMS ANU

Initially, Anu did not work, but spent her time socialising and taking care of her children. She says, "It was my husband who pushed me back to my profession, encouraging me to take up a career. He constantly told me how much more interesting I was as a partner when I was working." Assessing her potential to grow as a person and become a professional companion, Rohinton steered Anu towards an area which significantly influenced the direction of her career.

Anu recalls, "My husband invited me to a two-day programme on transactional analysis (TA) conducted by an American in

Mumbai. This workshop kindled an appetite to know more about TA and pushed me to learn more and get back to a professional career. I found that TA had the components of theory (learning), self-development and scope for effective counselling—it seemed to satisfy all my areas of interest. I studied TA under experts in India and went abroad to learn under Bob and Mary Goulding, who were the then authorities on TA. Through TA I got interested in many other branches of psychology, that helped me to understand myself better and become a consultant."

Anu's liking for TA led her to become a consultant to various companies, teaching the concept of TA from the late 1970s to the early 1980s. In 1986 she joined the HR division of Thermax, and became its head in 1991. In first taking Anu along with him to a TA workshop, allowing her to gain experience of teaching those concepts in other organizations, and then putting her in the HR division under a professional, Rohinton consciously sutured events and people on the canvas of Anu's growth. He displayed a rare sensitivity in grooming his life partner for handling much more demanding responsibilities, as if he intuitively knew what was in store for her.

I ask Anu what were the other influences that shaped her to become the person she is. She tells me, "I picked up my love of reading from my father. He encouraged me to be independent and to take up higher studies. I enjoyed reading and learning Indian dancing. I got my sense of humour and the ability to laugh at myself from my mother. I learned from her to be natural and unpretentious. As a child, I spent a lot of time with my immediate family and my extended family of cousins and aunts. The extended family met often for meals, going on picnics and vacations. I find that throughout my career I have been fortunate to be exposed to stimulating experiences which have triggered growth in me. Without the love and encouragement of my husband and children, I would not have had the energy and strength to venture out. My son's honest feedback and critique very often brought me in touch with reality and truth. He constantly pushed me to think outside the old maps.

"My eldest brother was also extremely nurturing towards me and helped me to have confidence and faith in myself. He made me feel that with my abilities I was capable of doing anything that I chose. My first boss in Thermax, Prasad Kumar, gently pushed me into being a career person and invested a lot of his time in helping me pick up the necessary skills. He introduced me to the Indian Society for Social and Individual Development (ISSID), which again has been important to my development." That Anu is an evolving person is evident by the way she has responded to triggers.

Enlivening Human Resources

In management circles, Thermax is known for its informal and open culture. Some unique aspects of that culture are:

- The ability to accept mistakes;
- The ability to manage and encourage executives with a wide range of styles and varying approaches; and

9

- The legitimisation of forums, such as staff meetings and open forums, to openly audit and check whether they practice what they preach.

I ask Anu to identify her contribution to the development of this culture. She says, "It evolved through discussions and consensus. Rohinton had a strong personality and HR was his most ardent critic." I probe, "But tell me, in the whole gamut of HR, where do you think you contributed innovatively?" She elucidates:

(a) "In improving team work processes;

(b) In inducting more humane treatment e.g. when we had to do mass-scale transfers from Pune to Khopoli while shifting some operations, we called families and listened to their requirements;

(c) In attracting and retaining trainees—I got several biodatas through our own employees; rather than rely only on placement agencies, I found that our own people are great sources;

(d) We used psychology tests at the engineer level, but we relied on a series of in-depth interviews; for higher-level posts we took as many as 10 or 12 interviews;

(e) In the energy and water treatment divisions the morale was low. I turned it round; and

(f) I brought in a lot of openness and sharing, which included confrontations and facing up to vulnerabilities, to bring out the authentic person or build one in the process. This involved conducting exercises in image sharing."

From my experience in human resource management, I consider this to be a substantial contribution. Its impact on building a wholesome organizational ethos is quite therapeutic. Rare is the compassion and humility required. Anu earned her promotion on merit. Rohinton developed a professional partner and with it gave Thermax a competent executive.

LEADING THROUGH PERSONAL TRAGEDY

Losing Rohinton was a terrible personal tragedy. The death of a spouse is a life changing event. The very next year came another enervating loss, the death of her son Kurush in a car accident. Anu poured out her heart in _Fireside_, Thermax's house magazine. The excerpts reveal a learned lady of courage trying to find meaning in death.

FIRESIDE—April-June 1997

In the last one year and two months I have lost my husband, my son, my mother-in-law and my pet dog. Some of you may ask how a topic like death has any relevance to an organization. To me an organization is made up of people and a topic which has to be faced by each and every individual is relevant ... our views on death will determine the quality of our lives.

Ever since Rohinton passed away I have read extensively on the topic of 'death'. The intellectual input is helpful and has given me an opportunity not to shy away from the reality of death. My husband died at 60, at the peak of his professional career. My son was 25, with life ahead of him. All my wealth and position could not prolong his breath for even a minute. Death is a great leveler and God is not partial to anybody.

There is some part I can play in shaping my life and there is an element of uncertainty. It is this unknown factor that makes me realize my vulnerability and tempers my arrogance with humility. If I become very negative and judgmental towards a person I pause and ask myself—what will I think and feel if that person dies today? I am not aware of a single instance when I have not realized that I am harping on the negatives and have taken the good for granted.

A lot of people wonder what will happen to Thermax now that my son has passed away. I am both amused and saddened by this. Thermax is an institution. My shares will go to my family, but *the organization will continue to be run by professionals who are the most capable—it could be someone from my family or someone who is not a member of my family.* One thing we in Thermax can learn from my experience— we cannot take anything for granted; *an individual cannot take life for granted and an organization cannot take success for granted.*

I interviewed Anu in August 1999 in her office in Pune. I asked, "During those traumatic days in 1996-97, what did you contribute to your job?" In a composed manner, she replied, "_I managed transition; I managed ambitions;_ Abhay and I clicked. The group did not split or splinter. I kept the group together unpretentiously, affectionately."

The unitive culture survived. The work done earlier by Anu on team processes bore fruit. Undoubtedly, her colleagues must have empathised and put a protective cordon around her. But her sublime response-ability (responsibility) is certainly inspiring Anu managed not only her personal transition but also adroitly handled her company's change-over. She took recourse to reading books to understand the meaning of 'death', a major transition point. Anu used the transition of Rohinton's death as the impetus for a new kind of learning. The result? She grew emotionally and spiritually and recognized the characteristic shape of transition. Her candid sharing of the inner alchemical process is awesome. This is pure leadership in action.

NEW ROLE

On July 1, 1999 Anu took a bold step. She handed over all executive responsibilities to Abhay Nalavade (who is, however, no longer with the company). Anu remains the chairperson. This major change, coupled with some top-level moves, reveals the powershift towards professionals rather than family members. Anu did not put in charge her daughter Meher or son-in-law

Pheroz Pudumjee, who both work within the group. And why did she relinquish operational charge? How does she see her new role? The excerpt below throws light on Anu's thinking:

FIRESIDE—April-June 1999

The reasons for my decision to discontinue being the executive chairperson are both professional and personal. As we all know, Thermax has not done well in the last three years. For public consumption we can keep giving reasons such as a slowdown in the economy and lack of new investments, which has affected the capital goods sector. These reasons are valid. However, I am convinced that even in this difficult market situation, we could have done better if we had served our customers better and improved our quality. From the letters I get from our customers, from the repeat orders lost, I know that we need to improve our act.

I am also the chairperson of Thermax Babcock & Wilcox (TBW) and I've been involved in the appraisal of the performance of the company through board meetings. I found that in this model, the managing director has clear-cut authority, responsibility and accountability. Every year the MD presents a budget with all relevant information, which is reviewed at each board meeting and at the end of the year, he has to deliver what he had promised.

In Thermax I found a lack of such accountability. One reason could be that the board did not feel comfortable

---

about asking questions, since I was the majority shareholder as also the executive chairperson. I, thus, felt the need to have clear-cut authority lines. Hence, Abhay will now be the MD and CEO of Thermax with autonomy, authority and responsibility for the results of the company and the board will expect the company to perform as promised.

When you get involved in the day-do-day running of a company, here and now issues take up your time and a macro-level perspective is often missing. In my new role, I will not be looking after the daily operations of the company, and I would like to look at issues which would have a long-term impact.

My son Kurush was very keen that as a family we should contribute directly towards the well-being of society. He always told me to find a social cause that was worthwhile and then direct my energy and resources towards it. I had kept postponing this. But I now feel the urge to fulfill my son's wishes and devote some of my time towards finding a cause and working towards it. There is another personal reason. Being an executive chairperson is a full-time job and it leaves me with very little time to read, reflect, meditate and be with my grandchildren.

Has it been an easy decision for me? I had got used to my role as a full-time working person. It filled my life, and there was no time to sit back and think. Maybe a part of me needed this busy schedule so that I had no time to dwell on the loss of my dear ones. However, I am aware that unless I pause and reflect, I can fill up my time and yet my life would lack meaning.

For growth to take place, I too need to shed my protective, secure shell. I also realize that *there is no permanent compatibility between a chair and the occupier* and that during the transition from one stage to another, I will be between two chairs—uncertain, scared but growing. Hence, though I have apprehensions and fears about how I would manage my new role and my changed life, I have decided to make this transition.

There are some rumours that the Aga family is withdrawing from business with the intention of selling their shares and settling down in the UK. In the past too such rumours have floated. Let me state that Thermax is a company that my father started and my husband nurtured and helped grow and flourish. I have a strong psychological attachment to Thermax and also the responsibility to look after the heritage I have been bestowed. I also happen to own a large part of the equity and hence it is in my own self-interest that I take care of this organization.

I have some broad ideas about my new role in Thermax.

- I want Thermax to be known as a company that genuinely cares for its customers and is proud of its quality. One of our Strategic Business Plan approaches for 1999-2000 is service orientation. I am its sponsor.

- We need to recognize and nurture new talent that will run this company in the future. I would like to find ways of discovering and investing in this group.

- Over the last three years Thermax's market capitalisation has eroded. Through greater accountability to the board, I would like the organization to change this trend.

- I will continue to write the quarterly 'Reaching Out' column for _Fireside_, to openly share my hopes, fears and insights with you.

- I represent Thermax at several external bodies like the Confederation of Indian Industry, the Mahratta Chamber of Commerce and Industry and the Mumbai Management Association. I will continue to play that role.

- I will be involved in major human resource and industrial relations issues and all key decisions concerning senior managers of M2 and M1 grades.

The reasons for delegating the operational responsibilities to the MD are logically thought out. Her concern for giving the organization a genuine customer orientation is reflected in taking upon herself this responsibility. She is also going to discover and nurture new talent and contribute work to external bodies like the CII. By removing herself from operational responsibilities Anu has made space, both for her personal growth as well as organizational growth.

REFINING THE INNER PROCESSES

I perceive Anu to be constantly refining her inner processes of growth and query her on this. She says, " Inventiveness is something to which I give great importance, and one of the methods is through regular meditation. I do give great weightage to the inner processes in my life. Personal advancement at this stage in my life means working towards greater peace and harmony within myself. After I realized that life is short and that death is inevitable and that status and wealth do not give long-term satisfaction, I am very interested in my personal advancement. I have all the independence I want. Nothing constrains me from the outside world. It is my own fears which are self-limiting. Ever since I learned *Vipassana* in November 1996, when I get agitated, the first thing I do is to sit and meditate, and very soon, I calm myself. It has had the most significant influence in my life." *Vipassana* means insight. It is an ancient meditation technique, and most executives who have attended *Vipassana* training say it does wonders.

Anu learnt transactional analysis (TA). In TA you realize that you have your rights, you are responsible for yourself, and you can't take responsibility for others. She became a member of the Indian Society for Social & Individual Development (ISSID). This institute makes you aware of your simultaneous responsibility towards yourself and the organization you serve. Both these developmental inputs *legitimise negative feelings*. You recognize their existence and learn to coexist with them. Subsequently she attended a *Vipassana* camp. This input provided Anu with experience at a still more profound level, the simultaneity of self, systems and others for which you are responsible. The fulcrum, you come to realize, is _compassion_. And compassion, I think, comes naturally to Parsis: Anu's heritage could not have conditioned her otherwise. Anu found _Vipassana_ to be a philosophical challenge, tremendously useful for facing life-changing events such as the multiple deaths of dear ones and the onerous responsibility of leading the company through the void.

Merely attending a programme does not produce results, the constant practice of techniques does. What Anu has done is to seriously practice what she has learnt. She swears by the results she is getting and that is what matters.

WORK EXPRESSES SELF

True to Indian tradition, Anu is most proud of her role as a wife and mother. She tells me she is not keen to leave her imprint as such on the organization. So I ask, "How would you like to be remembered?" She replies, "As someone who cared and continuously worked on herself to bring about improvements. I have found personal improvement energizing."

How do you bring about personal improvement, I enquire. "I find that meditation helps. Over time, my interest in work has grown tremendously. Not having any family responsibilities has helped. Early in my career I often had a need to impress; but with age, _I use work as a way of self-expression_. I am not a very good listener, but I am learning to be a better one. I am not strict about

19

time, I'm lazy and not very systematic. But I am disciplined about exercise, yoga, and meditation. Probably out of desperation because of my backache!" This inner journey has made her bold and given her solace.

"I am experiencing a certain amount of tranquility or wholesomeness. One thing above all has helped, and that is meditation. As Satya Narayan Goenka, the *Vipassana* guru, said, 'other things do fall in place'. There is a lot of trash but I am able to clean it, I am able to manage my time. I have been able to organize substance and form." Renunciation comes easily to an Indian because it supports meditative non-doing, not laziness. Although each individual has a choice to lead his life, *I feel the withdrawal of capable people from the result-producing materialistic world contributes to social loss*, and creates a void ordinary mortals cannot productively fill.

She adds, "I am serious about my task—customer care. *Acknowledging a customer in 24 hours is a religious endeavour.* I am employing innovative ways to improve awareness and skills. I gather a group of people and build a consensus, a lab experiment. Part of it is emotive enticement. The reward system will change. I am using pictures to provoke action. I am changing our heros from sales bringers, fire fighters etc. to identifying heros who align themselves with customer care."

I tell her, "If you are successful in the most difficult venture, customer care, it would be quite an achievement." Her reply: "I had a successful father, but I did not have a need to be successful." Without a burning desire to put her footprints on the sands of Thermax history, Anu has taken upon herself to improve customer care. This is because she is completely centered in her beliefs and practices. It shows that everything is not inherited. Individuals have a choice. When we look at from where she has come, her leadership appears truly transcendental. Being modest, Anu is not prepared to accept that she is a role model. "Role models have their own deficiencies. Push the IQ to develop your EQ."

Helen Palmer records in *Inner Knowing*, "The reduction of compulsive craving is said to result in a corresponding reduction in intrapsychic conflict and suffering, a claim now supported by studies of advanced meditators. As motivation becomes less scattered and more focused, the things desired become more subtle, more internal; there is less emphasis on getting and more on giving. Desires gradually become less self-centered and more self-transcendent."

It is this uncommon transcendental route that Anu has mapped for herself as well as for Thermax. Anu's domain discipline is social work. Her roots are in human resource management. The humanistic philosophy is moulding her personhood. The compassionate Anu is becoming more profound.

Dhananjay Bakhle

"I constantly challenge the way I work."

Dr Dhananjay Bakhle (41), medical director, Novartis India Ltd, blazed a trail in the Indian pharmaceutical industry in the early 1990s by pioneering the use of computer applications in medico-marketing. As the dapper and smiling Dhananjay speaks articulately about himself and his work, it becomes obvious that he is indeed a pioneer, constantly in search of solutions.

*D*r Dhananjay Bakhle has been in search of solutions ever since he can remember. It is this search that prompted him to turn away from the beaten track and become one of the first medical professionals to pursue a new career—medical informatics. His strategy was two-pronged: On the one hand, as an academic, he went into medical colleges and trained hundreds of doctors in computer applications; on the other, as a pharmaceutical industry man, he encouraged companies to recognize the strength of medical informatics, and field personnel to enhance their knowledge of products, to enable both groups to effectively reach medical professionals.

ACADEMIC LEVERAGE

With his academic background, Dhananjay initiated a new era of 'academic leverage' in the pharmaceutical industry. Where other companies sent sales people to camp patiently outside doctors' clinics to offer incentives and push products, he sent out the sales force equipped with 'troubleshooting cards'. All that the doctor had to do was fill in his queries or doubts about any disease and its line of treatment. He promised and delivered a solution in two days. This was a unique and forward-looking strategy. In the process he got his company and products positioned firmly in the minds of doctors. He prepared the ground, and the battle was half won. The rest was left to the efficacy of the products.

MISSION TO SERVE

Dhananjay grew up in the company of doctors—uncles, aunts and cousins, but not his parents: His father was a rubber technologist, while his mother was an active social worker. His mother influenced him to a great extent. From his early childhood, Dhananjay says, his mother had articulated a certain value base of integrity and transparency in personal ethics. Her communication skills were impressive because of her involvement in social work. She encouraged Dhananjay to read Marathi and English literature. Her example, coupled with reading, developed Dhananjay's cognitive and conversational skills. His exposure to literature on spiritual topics provided answers to some of his philosophical queries.

"As a manager, do you find this of relevance?" I ask Dhananjay. "Yes," he says, "in fact, today managers are not able to handle a number of critical situations because they look at things outwardly. We are on a certain plane, earth, but if you have a little spiritual orientation and inclination you can look at things differently. On the plane of spiritual thinking _there are no limits to achievement._"

Given this background, he chose to study medicine with the aim to serve humanity. Dhananjay narrates an illuminating incident: In his second year at Mumbai's Grant Medical College, he saw the movie _The Poseidon Adventure._ It was about passengers trapped in a sinking ship; Dhananjay identified and empathised with the experience of feeling trapped and suffocated.

The experience set him thinking about the dance of life and death, about life after death—an event that he had been witnessing as a medical student too. He thought about the innumerable patients trapped by incurable diseases, fighting for survival. This feeling of being trapped and suffocated has been a recurring motif in his life, and has spurred him to look for answers and to find solutions. As a young student it prompted him to ask: "Why not look for answers to the questions of life through drug discovery and better cures?"

This thinking led Dhananjay to a career in sustainable research, although this was not a popular option in the 1980s. He became involved with research when he was still a student by participating in the pharmacology department's chemical trials in new drugs. And after graduating, he decided to go in for an MD in pharmacology rather than in surgery. The search for solutions had begun in right earnest. Another aspect of medicine that he was drawn to: "Doctors don't have cures for all diseases. Why not bridge the gap between ayurveda and allopathy?"

Dhananjay's teachers taught him how to study methodically. His maternal uncle introduced him to the art of professional thinking. He learnt his leadership skills from his mother and uncle. Dhananjay liked to draw and he played chess, but he did not participate much in team games. Most of his free time was devoted to reading. In recent years he has read a vast amount of management literature, has a commendable collection of reading material, and is himself a veritable storehouse of data. His reading habits have served him well, leading him to refine his techniques.

Dhananjay feels that he happened to be doing the right things at the right time; and that the right type of people have entered his life, particularly his wife Nanda, who has a masters in pharmacology. "Our coming together was a cortical marriage of sorts," he says with a smile. Their synergistic relationship led to a joint venture in planning careers and sharing professional paths. He says Nanda has supported his career like a pillar. She has backed all his career moves and has provided emotional, moral and technical assistance. She moved from the industry to academics and shared many pressures at critical junctures in his career. Dhananjay feels that both Nanda and their daughter Vallari have provided him with the mental strength to reach new milestones.

CRAFTING A CAREER NICHE

Dhananjay made very intelligent and strategic career choices to position and market himself in the unlikely role of research head of a pharmaceutical company. His background as a doctor from a middle class Maharashtrian family, where reticence and aloofness are traditionally valued, makes his career moves seem all the more path-breaking and dynamic. Dhananjay's well-thought-out positioning is a shining example of the creative crafting of a career niche. His career growth has been vertical and rapid.

Dhananjay started his career in the clinical pharmacology unit of the German pharmaceutical company Hoechst as a research officer in Mumbai. He was also moonlighting as a lecturer in pharmacology at the Grant Medical College and at the JJ Group of Hospitals. He gained ground-level experience in various areas of pharmaceutical medicine in industry-sponsored research for five years. In 1988 he joined the British multinational Glaxo as an executive in clinical research. Within a year he was promoted to head their clinical pharmacology and information services, a position he held for three years.

Dhananjay moved to Fulford when he was 33 as vice-president of its medical division. He was probably the youngest VP in a well-entrenched pharma multinational in India. His MNC

27

journey has been interesting: His first experience was with the German Hoechst, then the British Glaxo, and later Fulford, which had a collaboration with Sehering Plough of the US.

He then joined Lupin Laboratories as director of medical services. After working for 16 years in MNCs, it was quite a change to work in an entrepreneurial organization. But he took the culture shock in his stride. He explains the difference: "Lupin has the typical approach of an entrepreneurial organization. It does not have the systems discipline of Glaxo. We were engaged in basic research in drug discovery. Lupin had a better team than Glaxo, but without the sheen. Glaxo had highly motivated but mediocre people, whereas Lupin had talented and motivated people who did their best. Lupin's image at one time got battered due to a financial crisis; now there is an urge to professionalise." Lupin's shrewd promoter, Deshbandhu Gupta, inspired Dhananjay to search for unique formulations.

However, Dhananjay got an offer from Novartis India Ltd that he felt he couldn't refuse, and joined as medical director in May 2000. He was asked to spearhead a special task force on e-commerce on behalf of Novartis India, and assigned trouble-shooting in the entire Asia-Pacific region. He has also been nominated by Novartis International as global technical resource person for tuberculosis, and is the Rockefeller Foundation's convenor for the South Asian region of the global alliance against tuberculosis.

At all his jobs, Dhananjay's technical competence in understanding brands and analytical skills in determining their Unique Selling Proposition (USP) have helped him convince the field force about the rationale of product launches. He has applied market positioning techniques with tremendous success. Dhananjay's _Horse Sense_ sharpened as a result of studying Al Ries and Jack Trout's book by that name, and their earlier one titled _Positioning_. The pharmacology fraternity of doctors, product managers and field personnel was treated as one homogeneous constituency to improve sales. Later he learnt the techniques of repositioning of brands in a world of fierce competition.

STAYING GROUNDED

At Glaxo, Dhananjay realized that it would take him many years to reach the position of vice-president in their tall hierarchy. As he describes it: "Fulford moved fast. They sent me to Singapore for an interview. Their speed and action were motivating. When I put in my papers, Humayun Dhanrajgir, Glaxo's managing director, was in England. He telephoned me from London and offered me a position at Glaxo's head office in the United Kingdom. Although two years in that country would have given me a UK rubber stamp, it would not have been a challenging experience, I don't think I would have learnt anything new. In contrast, Fulford offered an interesting learning opportunity. I took the right decision, as it proved later. I developed contacts in India with the Drug Authority and I gained precious medico-legal experience." Dhananjay's clear-headed thinking is evident. While most people would have jumped at the offer of a foreign posting, with its sterling allowances and cushy living at an up-market address, he did not lose sight of the nature of the experience he was looking for.

ORIGINAL CONTRIBUTIONS

Dhananjay's contributions in his rather unusual career are unique. He undertook original research, improved communication with the doctor fraternity through medical journalism, and has been deeply involved in the medico-legal aspects of the industry. It is intriguing that legal wrangles would interest a brilliant doctor and research fellow. But Dhananjay dug in his heels and helped the pharmaceutical industry move to have several regulatory hurdles removed and to fight difficult court cases.

Although during this time he was holding a brief for his employers, Fulford, he also had a power of attorney from Wyeth Laboratories, a sign of how much confidence other companies placed in his ability to handle complicated legal battles. He says: "I spent six years in the Supreme Court, where I enjoyed working with lawyers. We got some products registered on the fast track." Asked to specify what skills he used in this process, he says: "Analytical skills and rationality of the product. The product has certain inherent qualities, a *raison d'etre*. I used my analytical skills to discern and define these qualities and bring them into focus." Dhananjay enumerates his special contributions:

- *Original research:* He developed various research models for the evaluation of new drugs in humans; created an instrument for measuring the pupil size, the 'pupillometer'; filed a patent for a new anti-migraine drug derived from fruit extracts, which is under clinical evaluation; filed an American patent for a new drug for sexual dysfunction; he is presently working on many ayurvedic and herbal medicines to be introduced as mainstream medicines, and not alternative medicines; and he is pioneering a new area of 'improved chemical entities' in India for cost-effective research in the new patent regime.

- **Medical journalism:** Dhananjay introduced a medical bulletin, _Future Medicine_, to update Indian doctors about the latest advances in different fields of medical science; and initiated an on-line journal and discussion group on the internet.

- **Medico-legal battles:** He provided medico-legal support for court cases fought by the pharmaceutical industry against the government; and spearheaded a quasi-judicial marketing battle for a multinational pharmaceutical company in India.

CONSCIENCE-KEEPER

A good example of Dhananjay's ability to zero in on a product's viability is his contribution in 'tailing off' products. He explains: "Every product has a certain age. There has to be euthanasia. When you 'tail off' a product, you have to give an alternative systematic product plan. At Fulford we tailed off two out of 30 products; at Glaxo 15 out of 65-70; and at Lupin four to five out of 70. I killed certain products right at the concept stage, arguing it out with the marketing people. The risks involved to the consumer have to be reckoned with. The marketing potential of a drug and its medical rationality are two different things, at opposite ends. The medical director must act as the conscience of the company."

From creation of a drug to its patent to its marketing and finally to its launch is a long journey. In the end, research and development (R&D) will decide the future of companies, Dhananjay observes. According to him, there are two types of pharmaceutical companies: Those that are generic, such as those which market aspirin, paracetamol, etc, and those that are research-based. "We now have a critical mass of both trading companies and research companies. As a result of globalisation and competition, the structure of the industry is changing. Research in new products will be a critical determinant of growth," he says. This is a reality that Dhananjay had identified and invested in over 15 years ago. Wherever he has worked, he and his team have undertaken detailed product analysis. "One needs the ability to see, right in the early stages, which project should be advanced and which should be killed, rather than waste time churning out voluminous, unproductive reports as many laboratories do. One requires a high level of decision-making competency to pursue useful research," says Dhananjay.

THE WISDOM OF RESEARCH

In his search for synergies between allopathic and ayurvedic treatments, Dhananjay has been in touch with yoga teachers of repute like Jitendra Chikare Shishya, who runs the Prempuri Ashram in Delhi. Meeting Jitendra Yogi was a turning point for Dhananjay, providing him with an insight into how ayurvedic products were conceived and herbal formulations made. He also came in contact with Swami Omanand in Rohtak *gurukul*. That meeting put

Dhananjay in the research mode on ayurveda. He feels that the scope for new product introduction and product innovation is phenomenal.

Dhananjay concedes that he had a lot to learn in ayurvedic medical research after joining Lupin. "You need mastery in more than one area, a kind of towering competence in a multidisciplinary approach. The distinction has to be made between knowledge and wisdom. We have tremendous spiritual wisdom, a lot of knowledge, but _we don't have the wisdom of research._"

Speaking earlier about his work at Lupin, Dhananjay said: "Although I spent 15 fascinating years in medical research, I had a rather narrow approach. Today, I have advanced not only materially or spiritually; I have a better world view. I am using analytical skills and existing wisdom; but the important differentiating skill I am using is the application of modern techniques to unearth ancient wisdom." Dhananjay is in the process of discerning which out of hundreds of existing therapies will stand the test. He is putting his medical informatics competency to good use by converting data into knowledge.

He keeps his ear to the ground, and is today a veritable storehouse of information. For instance, he makes it his business to know that a certain American company has been formed to derive an anti-cholesterol drug from Chinese herbs. He studies where the venture capitalists are putting their money, what kind of product research they are backing. Such intelligent forward analysis of competitors' movements and capital flows develops strategic thinking and a sixth sense.

33

AMBITION TRIGGERS

I ask Dhananjay what triggered his powerful ambition. He says the first trigger was when he was given charge of the Drug Information Centre at JJ Hospital. Computers were new in hospitals in 1985. The Computer Research Society had asked what kind of computer configuration the hospital would need. Dhananjay was asked to put up a proposal, which he did on the basis of some theoretical research he had undertaken. When the proposal was put up to the society, the treasurer asked: "What do you know of computers? Have you used a computer at any time?" Dhananjay replied: "No, I have never touched a computer." The treasurer shot back: "Then what authority do you have to recommend a particular computer or system? If people who have used computers or are knowledgeable about them recommend something different, what would your answer be?"

This caustic question was the first trigger: Dhananjay felt that all his work on the proposal had been in vain. Since he had no access to a computer, his opinion was not considered valid. He decided to master computers; within a year, he was completely computer-literate. When Dhananjay was put in charge of teaching doctors at various medical colleges in Mumbai, he took it as an opportunity to learn various software packages in use around the city, and concurrently created a voluminous database for JJ Hospital.

The second trigger came in 1989 at Glaxo. Dhananjay had realized that information was the lifeline for the effective functioning of medical departments in the pharmaceutical industry. He tapped various databases for information. He came to the conclusion that data entry was the bottleneck. Here again the feeling of being at an impasse, a feeling of being trapped, was the driver. He knew that databases were available on CD ROMs. He approached Philips and induced them to sell CD ROMs in India. Glaxo became the first pharmaceutical company to have a medical database on CD ROM. It became a great in-house source of information not only on Glaxo products worldwide, but on competitor products as well. This access to vast data helped Dhananjay come up with many innovative research and marketing ideas.

The third trigger for his ambitions came at a meeting with the chief of Sehering Plough, who showed Dhananjay a small product that was not doing well in India. He pointed out that the precise reasons why this product was not doing well would have to be communicated to the press, lest they carry a story on the company with incorrect information and paint the company in a bad light. This brought home to Dhananjay the impact of information on marketing strategy, image and the share price, leading him to a new level of awareness: "That meeting changed me. I decided to read more on _product positioning in the customer's mind_. I realized the sale is made there, not on a shelf in a drug store." This applies at the individual level as well: In the era of 'Me Inc', each one will have to strategically position himself in the minds of his customers to advance his brand.

These triggers indicate that what spurs Dhananjay is any indication of a bottleneck or dead-end, any feeling of being trapped or blocked. The challenge pushes him to search intensely for answers. *The search skills he uses are data scanning, analysis and the discipline of scientific enquiry.* This provides useful clues for creative career management. Dhananjay does not accept problems as irresolvable. He sees obstacles as opportunities and immediately begins to equip himself to find answers. This is solution-mindedness.

CHALLENGE YOURSELF

What goes into the making of this solution-minded mould? Dhananjay says: "I have always believed in God. There is some force up there that has helped. I believe in meditation. It is a vehicle through which I have obtained strength. In moments of despondency, I find the confidence to take up the challenge." But how does he harness these forces and make them operational? Dhananjay explains: "I analyse any issue that confronts me. I identify tasks, apply project planning techniques, and then work smart, not hard, to complete them within the deadline that I have set for myself."

Dhananjay takes a moment to gather his thoughts. "I have gone by the differentiation concept. I was able to do something that others have not done, even in navigating my career, in the application of technology to the medical profession. I continuously look for a paradigm change; *I constantly challenge the way I work*; I am continuously experimenting. My colleagues used to initially get confused and upset by this, but later, they saw the advantages in experimentation. The ability to function in a most orderly way and take a structural approach in the most chaotic of situations helped me immensely."

GIVE THE DEVIL HIS DUE

I ask Dhananjay how he manages organization politics, an unavoidable aspect of work. With a mischievous smile he says: "The top management spends a third of its time in managing politics or solving related issues. They are involved players. Being young is a problem in a hierarchical organization. Some of the top management encourage you at first, and then try to sabotage you. Initially I used to tackle these issues head-on, but this created a furore. My father's example was at the back of my mind. He had suffered at work because of his straightforward, blunt nature."

Over the years, Dhananjay has learnt to get around this problem. "I have come to realize that it is better to feign ignorance at times, because there is a limit to corporate transparency. I've learnt not to make acerbic comments, however valid they are, and to keep working. In the face of conflict, many managers withdraw completely; it is easier to do so. But the result is that work doesn't move and careers come to a halt. Today, instead of regressing in this manner, I prefer to make digressionary moves, defuse the situation. After all, you need sponsors for your projects, so you need to give the devil his due! Of course I've been lucky, I have met a lot of good people too."

ENTREPRENEUR-EXECUTIVE

Dhananjay doesn't think much of security or complacency. "It is the cozy, cushy middle class that makes people mediocre," he says. "*Adversity stimulates creative faculties.* Immune systems do not develop unless they are stretched." Dhananjay mentions several top people in the US who arrived in that country as dispossessed refugees. He says that if you are a middle level manager, you had better read the writing on the wall. You have to innovate. Become entrepreneurial. It is a battle for survival, and only those who apply a differential approach will prosper.

In the pharmaceutical industry, Dhananjay is hot property. He is also a role model in medical colleges, encouraging doctors to fan out in different career directions. He is a thought leader who has expanded his vision from the operating theatre to the very concept of healing. We need more Dhananjay Bakhles to create new solutions and to show us how to creatively build an exemplary career.

Pramod Chaudhari

"The customer must prosper as a result of taking my solutions and project."

Praj Industries Ltd, Pune (turnover Rs 60 crore) focuses on supplying alcohol and brewery plants and equipment from concept to commissioning, as well as fruit processing plants. Pramod Chaudhari (51), founder-chairman and managing director, is a perfect example of a manager-turned-entrepreneur, blazing his trail with his eye on the larger goal.

A graduate in mechanical engineering from IIT, Mumbai, Pramod Chaudhari joined Bajaj Tempo in 1971 as a trainee and, by choice, worked on the shop floor. This was an uncommon choice; most engineers are unwilling to sweat it out on the shop floor with workers, soil their hands and acquire real experience. But as Pramod says: "I wanted to see how workers actually work with their hands and try it out myself, and I did. *It was hands down learning*. I could mix with them, share jokes in their lingo, understand their feelings and listen to their grievances. I thought it was important for me to get schooled like this at the start of my career. I made the choice because I considered it *necessary grounding* for becoming a real manager of men and machines." Pramod's career is self-made, the milestones being distinct choices, as we shall see.

A SELF-MADE CAREER

Pramod did not want to graduate through the factory hierarchy to become a general manager. He realized that a general manager of an organization must get groomed in all functions, like production, sales, marketing and commercial. So he made another conscious choice. In 1975 he joined Widia India, a cutting tools company, as a technical sales and service representative. He did not angle for the coveted marketing division at that stage. He opted for another kind of fieldwork; from the factory to the market place.

The rush in the 1970s was towards marketing, corporate planning, finance, design and other such corporate office jobs. Those who had taken a management degree from the Institutes of Managements (IIMs) had no compunction in saying that they had forgotten their domain discipline, say engineering; and would like to talk only about marketing. Managements could not, therefore, rely on their knowledge of domain subjects. For the technical components of the job, they had to turn to specialists. As much as the workers were not prepared for multi-skilling, managers gradually lost multi-disciplinary proficiencies because of their lack of interest in their domain disciplines. In this atmosphere, Pramod's choice to get experience in different positions was highly unusual. He got rapid promotions in Widia, rising from sales engineer to area sales manager and then regional sales manager in just six years.

To gain experience at a senior level, in 1982 he joined Rapicut, another cutting tool company, as vice-president of marketing. Despite a promotion as marketing director, he became restless. I ask, "Pramod, I appreciate your focused approach in acquiring all-round experience, but what was your ultimate purpose, the goal?" The reply is prompt: "I had decided that whatever experience I wanted to get in service, I should get it in a maximum of three jobs. By the age of 33 or so I should be free to start something on my own." Mind you, getting a job was difficult and no 'alimony' was paid for voluntary separation in those days!

Moreover, Pramod did not have entrepreneurial genes; nor was the climate favourable for entrepreneurs in the control and licence raj. And yet young Pramod, coming from a middle class rural background, made conscious choices on the kind of experience he would obtain, the changes he would make on the way, and how he would unchain himself at a particular age to venture out on his own, without any financial backing. What powered these highly independent and focused decisions?

CLINCHING THE DEAL

Says Pramod: "My father encouraged me to take an independent jump; he used to say, be curious. He was quite supportive. Freedom is required if you are to achieve something. He was an agricultural graduate engaged in sugarcane cultivation and harvesting. I spent my childhood in the sugar factory area of Koparwadi in Phaltan, Maharashtra. So I grew up in a rural background. I had seen my father, farmers and factory workers working with their own hands." What then prompted him to opt for the shop floor? Pramod explains: "Although I graduated from IIT, my rural background made me keep my feet firmly on the ground. I was not very clear how to build a career, but one thing came to me naturally, to work hard where things happen."

At Bajaj, his role model was M K Firodia, "a tough taskmaster who took the company from three-wheelers to two-wheelers. Firodia had an eye for detail, and a tremendous memory. He was excellent at inspection, and used to ask all the right kind of questions. He instilled confidence. Firodia guided me through difficult periods."

To gain experience in sales and service, Pramod later moved to Widia. What was Widia's contribution to his development? Says Pramod, "Widia sharpened my commercial negotiation skills in specific aspects like contract negotiation, payment terms, convincing the customer, and market development. Over there I acquired leadership skills by getting the engineering staff to adhere to stringent work norms. The German director, Mr Rentrup, was a role model. He instilled the killer instinct in me. This meant *not to return without making a deal*. It required more application engineering to provide customised tools. He took added interest because the MNC Sandvik Asia was the competitor."

At Widia, his engineering background combined with his shop floor experience proved invaluable. Pramod tells me why: "Telco was a major battleground for us in Widia. Jakatdar, their MD, was a visionary, who was bringing in modern technology in machining. He relied on Widia for their every need. So, special tooling was becoming a major issue. My advantage was that I could stand by the product, demonstrate it; whereas the Sandvik guy had to take an assistant with him. I was able to mix freely with workers, machine tool design engineers, managers, talk in their language and convince them. That impressed Telco's hierarchy. We retained the customer."

Thus a relationship grew, with display of technical competence and deft handling of human relations. Says Pramod: "Although I was in sales in Widia, I clicked with the Widia and Telco technical personnel. We convinced Telco to use new technology for equal drilling for crankshafts. I was the only expert in the country in this technology. I didn't do the designing, but the application part. They used to tease me that I was getting a double salary, one from Telco and another from Widia!"

Why then did Pramod leave Widia? "Well, I wanted to do something on my own; I did not know exactly what. When I got an offer to join as co-promoter in a medium-sized company, I took it. But it didn't work out. I realized I was 33 and had enough experience. The craze for independent creation was so strong that I could not be held back by a job any longer." And that is how Praj was born.

THE VOYAGE BEGINS

Says Pramod, "The elders in my family had reservations, but my wife Parimal, a Fullbright scholar and a journalist, was very supportive. I put my car away in the garage and started moving around on the two-wheeler. I studied the distillery business, which was dominated by three players from Gujarat. With the help of my father's contacts, I undertook an analysis of the needs of the distillery units, talked to a few people to find out to who and how licences are issued, and contacted a few parties. Siddeshwar Mill in Sholapur district showed interest. I established my technical competence. I must say help came rushing in. The then Pune commissioner, V P Rane, Mr Late in Delhi, and some others offered help." I cannot resist asking: "Corruption, contacts, what?"

Pramod hastens to clarify: "No, not a *naya paisa* was given, nor asked. There was no previous connection, nor any recommendation letter as such." Then how did he obtain the necessary permissions? "I suppose it was their response to our sincerity of purpose. They probably thought 'Here are young people doing something new on their own, fresh air, so let's give them a chance'. They had a genuine desire to help people like me." How did he approach them? How did he impress them?

Pramod continues, "I approached them up-front, and impressed them with my straight dealing. I would dash off to Delhi, or wherever. I presented exhaustive technical data. *I used techno-commercial language to convince them.* I gave them clarity of thought, an IIT background, and I was very persuasive; but above all, the substance of our proposal was appealing. We wanted to create a technologically effective, better-engineered plant, in contrast to the traditionally manufactured and technically weak plants. We provided a better economic package with lower capital costs and cost of production, and other benefits to the mills. We created an image of a professional team on the basis of our approach. Also, we could relate better because of our rural background. I changed my look; I wore Indian clothes rather than a suit; speaking in Marathi and Hindi helped. We got the permission."

Another opportunity was provided by Vikram Singh Ghatge of Shri Shahu Sugar Mills in Kagal. He had a pollution control problem in his unit and advanced Pramod and his colleague Shashank Inamdar Rs 1 lakh for them to go to Vienna to bring in technology. They had to execute a bank guarantee. Mr Gokhale, Bank of Maharashtra's general manager (credit), pitched in, and off they went to Vienna where they signed an MOU with Fogulbush. They also got two contracts from Malegaon Sahakari Sakhar Karkhana. Both these sugar mills were cooperatives. So in the birth of Praj, the cooperative sector played a major role by providing it with an entry point.

To consolidate his position, Pramod scouted for private sector customers. He saw an ICICI advertisement offering venture capital assistance for technological development. He approached them and some of the officials were very helpful. A real mentor emerged in N Vaghul, their legendary chairman. Pramod says he inspired the power of visioning, in terms of raising finance and expanding, and by painting a vast canvas of unfolding opportunities. There was an element of nationalism in his talk.

By the mid-1980s, their hard work had begun to pay off. Says Pramod: "In 1988-90 we became equal to the MNC Alfa Laval. By 1992 we had an edge over them, and in 1995 they had to phase out their biostil division!" Praj experienced a boom period from 1991 to 1995, with 120 per cent growth boosted by exports. The focus on alcohol and beer technology was intensified in 1996-97 under the leadership of Shahank, the technological anchor of Praj. Pramod's dreams had been realized.

REFERENCE POINT

It has been a good journey, with satisfactory progress and achievements. What are his ambitions now? Is he working towards a quantum jump in turnover, say to Rs 500 crore? "Frankly speaking, a high turnover or the numbers game was never my focus. My main idea was to do something different, which I did. Second, I had no Ambani model. Third, achieving a turnover of Rs 50 crore, from scratch, was a major milestone for me. My ambition was to create a platform, a stage for various players, actors, actresses to come and perform." I ask, "But Rs 60-65 crore, isn't it a mere drop in the ocean when you are going global?"

Pramod defines his objective: "Sheer size does not matter. Today, whenever somebody thinks of putting up a distillery, they think of Praj first. Understanding the project, the technology, quality and overall vision are important. I may not get each contract, but _Praj must be the reference point_. I wanted to be at the high end of technology, where value addition is higher, and that's where I am. The entire contract need not be in my name, there would be many local subcontractors." So has Praj emerged as a reference point? "Yes," Pramod says. "We have a successful track record of supplying multi-feed distilleries in tropical countries."

Pramod is clear about his goals. He is not going for growth in size. He wants Praj to matter as an organization internationally recognized for quality supply of alcohol and brewery plant and equipment, with service that satisfies the customer. For a person with a rural background and service experience, to make such determined progress is not easy. He has been able to build an enterprise that matters because he made himself hospitable to receiving suggestions, ideas and new thoughts.

SOUND CHOICES

To make a choice means you elect to act for an option; you select a course of action in preference to other courses that may be available. The choice is a point of decision. In electing to work on the shop floor and then in the field in sales, Pramod exercised his will to gather ground-level experience. The former led him to participate in converting raw material to finished products, the latter in deal-making and securing contracts.

The decision to be free at 33 for venturing out on his own was like diving into unknown waters. A choice he exercised at every step was in creating goodwill and asking for help for creation, whether from his wife Parimal, Firodia, Vaghul, Rane, Late, etc. It was a choice to expand the customer base from cooperatives to the private sector and then to the world. And so is the decision to make Praj a reference point, rather than pushing for bigger volumes and higher turnover.

The theme in all these choices is clear, to grow into a healthier, stronger and self- actualized individual in search of new high-tech challenges. This is manifest in Pramod's current addiction: To rev Praj into "a company bubbling with enthusiasm and joy". What is the kind of thinking or approach required to develop such an enterprising spirit?

FOCUS ON THE CUSTOMER

"_Curiosity is at the heart of the growth model,_" says Pramod. "You have to be curious to understand an enterprise. When you join an organization, explore its dynamics and trace your area of aptitude and vocation. Ask non-hurting, intelligent questions. Be curious, not inquisitive. _Go to the source, not only wanting to know 'how', but to get to know 'why'._ Remember, ambition is the driver of achievement. I also feel achievers should spend some time with prospective managers or entrepreneurs, like Firodia did with me."

"It's true, Pramod, but how do you get them to do that? These are busy people," I say. Pramod shows that _in the art of obtaining mentors, it's again dedication and persuasion that count._ He says: "You must follow up gently. Seek an appointment, ask for just half an hour. Make your point. Show what you are doing. Get them engaged in your endeavour, brief them. As I did with Firodia, I did with Vaghul. I requested Vaghul to come and inaugurate Praj House. He obliged me. Everyone felt inspired. Such people influence you by their presence and thought. I had no frustration in following up. I had good support from high-ups; I met people of a helping nature."

Pramod is obviously a man of action, not a mere talker. "I do not merely articulate. I did not get caught up in the 'MAFA syndrome' (mistaking articulation for action), when you go on speaking about action, but do not actually act. You engage yourself in convincing others of action, but have you actually done what you are articulating that you have done or are going to do?"

How does he know that those who are talking to him are not engaged in MAFA? Says Pramod, "Well, your marketing expertise lies in assessing that. When you visit, don't talk about your product, talk about different things that are of more interest to the customer and his business or areas of concern. Just chat about what is happening in his sphere of activity. Lead him to speak about his area of work, chosen topic of interest, business, the markets they are entering, technical problems, and get him to focus on them. Gradually you are able to see the truth. Get relevant information on energy consumption, their bottlenecks, needs, approach, organizational politics, everything. You must not be nosy, though. You must show genuine concern and help the managers, engineers, whoever. You slowly gather evidence of 'doing'. If something has not been actually done, you realize it is mere articulation."

Talking about his customer skills, Pramod further explains: "You have to percolate the customer system, infiltrate the organization right down the line. Without hurting the concerned functional manager's ego, cite him the benefits of your package, your offer, and how it would strengthen him. Show him the advantages to resolve his problems. You try to build up the network through such individuals, right through the decision-making tree, from the bottom to the top. *It is para-technical talk sprinkled with lots of persuasion.* Getting the first order is okay, but I must ensure I get the repeat order. Such searching enquiries help to cultivate an entrepreneurial mind. In the end *the customer must prosper as a result of taking my solutions and project.*"

Praj's name comes up whenever anything is happening in the sugar industry, and Pramod's connections are wide-ranging. As he says: "I don't mind helping a customer even in personal matters, even match-making for his daughter or son, if that gets me closer to him to understand his business need." Pramod indeed has tremendous energy. He continues, "I am a robust optimist. I like to dabble, implement ideas, touch a chord, make a difference. You have to find the zones which are evocative, easily aroused. _You must have pills for the ills of the customers._ That helps you become a businessman."

ADDICTED TO THE CAUSE

This voyage of a manager-cum-entrepreneur is thrilling and motivating. It's a heady combination of skills—determination, clarity of thought, concomitant choices, a focused approach, drive, an unstoppable receptivity to learning, unflinching 'followership' (the willingness to follow, which leads to becoming a leader), and the ability to convince the customer. How Pramod escaped the mindset of an employee to adopt that of an employer is a lesson in mindset change. How he transposed the skills he acquired as a corporate employee to an entrepreneurial setting is worth imitating. It is a transplant that skilled surgeons would be proud to watch. Pramod had observed while working at his corporate jobs that consensus decision-making had to be affordable. In Praj he came to realize and put into action the fact that risk decisions are to be made instantly and singly. No guts, no glory, as they say.

Pramod's story proves that skills can be learnt. It is not a road map. It is a six-lane highway of definite goal setting, targeted experiencing, specific learning, masterly negotiating, skillful convincing and genuine caring. The path less travelled is now made so familiar by leaders like Pramod that there is little scope for fear of the unknown. He has demonstrated that entrepreneurship is do-able. You have to be addicted to it, like Pramod is.

Rajabhau Chitale

"The customer's hunger for tasty products motivates us."

Chitalebandhu Mithaiwale, Pune's producers of quality Maharashtrian mithai, milk and snacks, have an enviable brand image in the niche western Maharashtra market. The family group, Chitale Udyog Samooha, has a turnover of Rs 125 crore and employs 500 people. Rajabhau Chitale (68), sweet like his mithai, leads the pack of illustrious Chitale brothers who, by dint of sheer merit and hard work, have built this unrivalled quality brand image.

Rajabhau, the first graduate of the Chitale clan, never considered seeking a job: Business was in his genes. His father, B G Chitale, had started distributing milk in Mumbai in the 1940s. When Rajabhau was in college, he would help his elder brother Raghunath sell milk in his spare time. The excellent groundwork laid by his father and elder brother resolved Rajabhau to join the family business.

RESURRECTION FROM DISASTER

In the 1950s, the *mithai* business was largely the preserve of Rajasthani and Punjabi businessmen. In 1954, Rajabhau opened a shop on Deccan Gymnkhana, Pune, selling milk and milk products. A year later he got married. Just as his business venture was taking off, disaster struck in 1961 when the shop was destroyed in floods. Rajabhau showed his mettle by setting up shop again within 10 days. The present premises near Vishrambag Wada, in the heart of Pune city, were acquired in 1964 because the growing business needed more space. The location was well chosen as it brought the marketplace closer and increased sales.

The erstwhile milk-vending family has evolved into the Chitale Business Group (Chitale Udyog Samooha) specialising in the production of milk, sweetmeats and milk products. The credit undoubtedly goes to the pluck and foresight shown by Rajabhau. However, he constantly mentions the contribution made by his brothers and other family members in his forays, and the wholehearted support of his wife of 44 years.

GUJARATIS TEACH HOW TO SWEET-TALK

Rajabhau intersperses his talk with grateful acknowledgement of his elder brother Raghunath's great help and significant influence in the conduct of business, particularly in dealing with customers. Raghunath learnt how to keep customers happy as a result of a four-year-long association with the Gujarati business community while living in Mumbai and in Gujarat. Thus Raghunath equipped Rajabhau with the tricks of the trade and the key to retaining customers.

"What lessons do the Gujaratis have to teach, Rajabhau?" I ask. His answer is like a primer in customer relations: _"Never tell the customer he's wrong._ If he _is_ wrong, tell him politely that you'll look into his complaint; that although product quality is generally good, maybe his particular point needs to be looked into." This later got translated into the Chitale motto: 'Customer satisfaction guaranteed one hundred per cent'. "We Maharashtrians are infamous for our rude talk and trademark impolite treatment of customers, with exceptions to prove the rule. That's why I was curious to know how the Gujaratis dealt with these issues," Rajabhau adds.

He proceeds to encapsulate what the Gujaratis told him: "We don't carry a sword. We talk politely because it is the customer who gives us business. It is in our interest to be cordial and sweettongued. We have, therefore, no labour problem. In fact those who work with us, in workshops or sales counters or as assistants in bazar shops or department stores, possess the same mindset. Each employee wants to start his own small business as soon as possible. We have to work hard to retain our employees, whereas yours is a permanent service mentality and you have to find ways to drive away the work shirkers and recalcitrants. The trading characteristic—'how do I create business?'—is inherent in our genes." Rajabhau feels his education in commerce was greatly enhanced with such practical wisdom from Kutchhi shopkeepers.

He continues, "Of course, our Marathi customer is not particularly polite either. Of late there is a perceptible change, but inherently he too is curt; he comes to the shop in a querulous mood, although the problem may be minor. The body language and tone of voice are insulting. However, we as businessmen and owners have to change the mindset of our employees because 'the customer is king'. We are imparting training. Our polite behaviour and diplomatic handling will build our service image, which in turn will eventually cause the customer response to change. It's a cyclical process and we are doing our best."

Another important lesson that he learnt was that the *first customer* who enters the shop *must not be allowed to go without buying* whatever he has come to buy, for whatever price he is willing to pay. "The first four years, I took tips from a helpful Kutchhi neighbour on how to ensure that customers repeat their visits to the shop. He's the one who told me about the importance of the first customer, who inaugurates your business day."

Another factor, Rajabhau says, was that "I was a novice in a business dominated by the Agarwal and Punjabi communities. If I could not satisfy my customers, they had a wide choice. It was a buyer's market, not a seller's market. Moreover, it was essential to exercise care in maintaining quality, considering the fact that our products are perishable commodities. It involved careful monitoring of each process, from the raw material to the finished product. I was guided at every step by Raghunath and soon learnt how to tackle problems arising from the special nature of our business."

There are special lessons provided in this transformation of a non-business mindset to a successful business growth mindset:

- One must be eager to listen and learn from traditional business communities the art of commercial talk, manners and deportment, be they Sindhis, Marwaris, Gujaratis, Jains, or Punjabis. Individuals must take the initiative to learn from successful business neighbours and cultivate a mindset tuned to making good careers.

- Customer care, which is at the core of management concerns, needs to be inculcated and nurtured in employees. Managements have to step forward to propagate such practical learning.

EXPOSURE PROFITS

I ask Rajabhau what else influenced his thinking and business growth. He says: "I attend at least four conferences a year and visit some exhibitions. You meet good people, hear new things, see good products, and come across well-written product literature and company reports. All that helps. I have also attended seminars organized by dairy institutes in Anand and Bangalore— that was quite profitable. _I read whatever book or literature I pick up from the angle of its utility for implementation._"

Rajabhau feels the Japanese have a lot to teach, and exposure to their mode of business has been a significant influence. With his elder brother's encouragement, in 1970 he was part of an export delegation of the Mahratta Chamber of Commerce to Japan. He was impressed with their systems and technology. Rajabhau's vision expanded from the village to the city, and from the city to the international level. The Japanese work discipline and the reverence with which they treat their customers made a deep impact on him. "Their hospitality and treatment of customers is far superior to that of the Europeans. If you ask for a second carrier bag, they'll willingly give it you; elsewhere it will be pointed out that you've already been given one. Their business dealings are clean and their marketing strategies tenacious," Rajabhau says admiringly.

The Japanese system influenced him to introduce product-wise accounting. Rajabhau has always been fastidious in keeping his accounts white. Both Chitale units, at Bhilwadi and at Pune, have won awards for paying high income tax and they are none the worse for it. He believes the company works better by being transparent in all dealings. Thus, the Chitales have built up a sound reputation by marrying old-fashioned values and a distinctly individualistic approach to a modern and professional business style.

ACHIEVEMENTS *PAR EXCELLENCE*

The group has consistently modernised and innovated, whether in the dairy, billing systems, or product development. These achievements are noteworthy.

Dairy Modernisation

Rajabhau was in search of a new pasteurizing machine to replace his old 1947 model. In 1968 came the big opportunity. He saw an ad from Cadbury seeking the supply of 3000 litres of milk daily to their factory at Induri, 21 km from Pune. He contacted Mr Dalal at Vulcan Laval who helped with the machine, as well as with the customer by introducing Rajabhau to Mr Unwala of Cadbury. Later the Chitales also bought a chilling unit and other processing machinery from Alfa Laval. So the Cadbury opportunity gave the Chitales not only a boost in sales, but more importantly, modernised their dairy unit. Their horizons expanded.

Modern Billing System

The Japan trip in 1970 gave a definite direction to Rajabhau's vision. Impressed with the problem-free billing systems in the department stores there, he introduced a similar system in the two shops in Pune, which is in use even today. This unique billing system eliminates errors, theft and pilferage. It uses a special memory key system imported from the US which stores and collates information about a customer's purchases from the different counters of the shop. This key is handed over to the cash counter, which helps to automatically tally the number of items and the price. This saves time lost in computing and cross-checking.

Never behind the times, the Chitales will soon replace the bulky key with a sleek card. Rajabhau's fine grounding in customer management is reflected in the way the counters are managed. The owners ensure that there is no overcrowding, and that

59

the queues at popular counters move fast. Rajabhau's attempts are always focused on updating the methods of retail merchandising so that the customer feels relaxed.

Milk In Polythene Bags

In 1974, after much difficulty, an import license for a French milk-packing machine was obtained and the distribution of Chitale milk truly reached international standards. Milk was made available in polythene bags, increasing sales from 5000 litres of loose milk to 1.5 lakh litres daily.

Students of the Symbiosis Centre of Management and Human Resources, Pune carried out a survey of Pune's milk supply. They reported: "Chitalebandhu (supplies milk) through seven centres and a network of 300 wholesalers and about 5500 retailers. The success is due to consistency in quality. Being a small and flexible organization, it has been able to capitalise its position and achieve an unassailable leadership in the market."

Rajabhau's regular reading of professional and commercial literature on the dairy business helps him spot lapses and take effective remedial measures. He diligently follows the current developments in microbiology, although he has no foundation in the field.

Savory Product Development

Rajabhau's amazing business acumen and foresight is illustrated by the growth chart of the *bakarwadi*, a perennial hot favorite from the house of Chitales. In 1978, Rajabhau brought this traditional savory snack out of the confines of domestic kitchens and soon got customers addicted to it. In 15 years' time, the labour requirement more than doubled. Even then, production could not increase beyond 700 kg a day. However, demand was far higher, and increasing the number of hands made it hard to ensure quality.

Rajabhau thought of mechanizing the process and started reading all the available foreign literature on the subject. He sent his son Shrikrishna to Holland and Germany to check out machines which could be adapted for their specific use. After personally conducting tests, Rajabhau imported a machine from Holland in 1993. While automating the production, the emphasis was to mass-produce the item and at the same time retain the same crispness and taste as when it was made manually. This machine produces 1000 kg per batch and the sale of _bakarwadis_ has risen to 30 lakh kg per annum.

Similarly, the production of _pedhas_ has been completely transformed. The traditional _kadhai_ in the making of _pedhas_ was done away with and steam boilers were pressed into service. Yet another innovation in the process has been the introduction of a moulding machine imported from Japan in 1998, which eliminates the manual shaping of _pedhas_. To produce 45 kg of _pedhas_ would earlier have taken eight people many hours of work; now two people can do it in 45 minutes.

During a business tour of Europe in 1984, Rajabhau took some trials on a milk-condensing machine at Alfa Laval's factory in

Sweden. When he was convinced that it could be used in the production of *khoya*, a basic ingredient in many Indian sweets, he installed a machine in the Bhilwadi plant. As a result, a lengthy process was streamlined and premium quality *khoya* is now prepared at the rate of 250 kg an hour.

Rajabhau abhors stagnation; he believes existing strengths must be built upon, and therefore he increased the bandwidth of Chitale products. For instance, he started the production of edible gum *ladoos* with the long preserved secret ingredients of Marathi homes. Sales have increased to 150 kg a day. Similarly, *motichoor ladoos*, ginger sweets and many other delicacies are well-established items. They now have 76 products on sale. The Chitale group has carved a special niche for itself by producing traditional Maharashtrian sweets and snacks instead of going into competition with Rajasthani, Bengali or Punjabi sweetmakers in manufacturing their specialities. Rajabhau confidently says, "It is *not necessary to diversify in order to grow*. It is possible to keep growing within one's chosen line of business, and we are doing precisely that."

GO FORWARD TO EXIST

The Chitales have studiously captured and literally patented the quintessence of Maharashtrian taste, building an image and a niche market. Lakhs of people from other states who have settled in Maharashtra have acquired a taste for these products, helping the Chitales expand. This is the secret of their long-standing monopoly.

"What motivated you, Rajabhau?" I ask. He admits that in the early years, the chief motivating factor was, of course, to make money to meet the growing family needs. Apart from that, he says, his inspiration was wholly self-activated. He drew strength from the fact that other communities strove hard and moved ahead in this business; then why couldn't he do the same? He kept up his efforts, as he always believed in the dictum '*One who does not go forward ceases to exist*'. He had not imagined earlier that he would taste such sweet success; but by the mid-1970s, he knew that the group was meant for big things. Maintaining the status quo was never an option; his ambition was shaped by his father's philosophy, "If we can make 5000 *pedhas* in one batch, why can't we make 7000 in the next?" According to his father, there was nothing wrong in taking financial loans to achieve ever-expanding targets. This thought goes against the grain for Maharashtrians.

Competition with other manufacturers was another great motivation to excel. Coupled with this was the motivation to meet the growing demands of customers, especially the epicurean tastes of the residents of Pune. Not only the demands of customers, but also the pressure of their high expectations, provided the impetus to supply quality products. As Rajabhau says, "*The customer's hunger for tasty products motivates us.*" To meet the demands of changing tastes and for further expansion, the Chitales plan to soon introduce new products like soft drinks, snacks, ice cream, skimmed milk, cheese and flavored yoghourt. His mind ever active, Rajabhau has targeted another niche segment: "Since the number of diabetics is increasing, special products can be introduced for them," he says.

PROFESSIONALISATION DILEMMA

With a track record in overcoming hurdles of technology, the marketplace and the speed of growth, the group now wants to concentrate on developing better leadership and manpower. All the Chitale menfolk are involved in the daily management of their diversified business activities. Rajabhau, his son Shrikrishna, and Raghunath and his sons Madhav and Sanjay look after the *mithai* business; the dairy business is managed by brothers Parshuram and Dattatray and their sons. All are partners in the business and manage their respective units with a fair amount of independence. All of them have first-hand knowledge of what they produce; therefore there isn't undue dependence on managerial and production personnel.

Rajabhau proudly states, "If the need arises, we can make the best *pedhas* ourselves. We know exactly how much material is required for each item. We taste each batch before it goes to the sales counter. In short, *we have a finger on the pulse of the entire business.*" This kind of involvement leaves the family no time for frivolous pursuits. "We are not members of any club. We do not smoke or drink. We do, however, participate in functions which have a social bearing and, of course, being a large family, there are always family commitments. Apart from that, we take time off every year by rotation and go abroad," says Rajabhau. It is a policy that has stood the older generation in good stead and has been followed by the younger generation as well.

Now that the Chitales are in a leading position, maintaining the highest product quality and ensuring customer satisfaction with an unlimited market potential, everything seems to be in place. "So, Rajabhau, now you can relax?" I probe. The answer is no, in fact Rajabhau is not at all complacent. He shares his concerns: "Technology and market are not a problem for us; but the speed of growth and lack of professional management do worry us. Our weaknesses are that we cannot reach all our products to all shops; lack of refrigeration facilities; and lack of permission to use preservatives. _Ownership and management are topics of concern._"

Besides, the customer profile is changing. The demographics and city-scape are in flux, what with disco-going youngsters, the increasing number of diabetics, the exploding population of retirees, the wayward growth of Pune, the new trend of restaurants attached to shops, and eating habits in transition. How will this affect the Chitales? What is Rajabhau doing about it?

Rajabhau says frankly: "This is where we are falling short— future scenario building and marketing, strategies for growth. Without losing our traditional expertise, wisdom, goodwill and image, how do we grow? We require professional management, modern thinking, but with our type of 24-hour commitment, devotion and trustworthy behaviour. We are looking into this very issue of how to professionalise. We are aware of our limitations as well as of our competencies. We are also aware that the constraints of growth are within ourselves. I and my brother are constantly thinking, we have tried out some things but we have not yet found a solution that would work without unproductively disturbing the family management synergy."

I appreciate Rajabhau's dilemma. Most family organizations are facing it, one way or another. The fear is not only of losing family control; what is feared is loss of goodwill, brand image, family name and prestige that the patriarchs would have to face if professionalisation fails. The positive point is that patriarchs like Rajabhau are conscious of the need to professionalise, that Rajabhau wants to put proper leadership in place before hanging up his boots. The issue is not whether or not to professionalise, the issue is quality growth. In both alternatives, the level of competency will determine the future outcome. Awareness must lead to time-bound action. And as Rajabhau says, "One who does not go forward ceases to exist."

The Chitales deserve continued success: Mechanized milking procedures, introduction of new embryo transplant techniques to produce a better breed of buffaloes, empowering women with job opportunities in the rural belt of Sangli where the dairy is situated, and working on the concept of making villages self-sufficient—these are the many factors that merge to keep the Chitale flag flying high.

Humayun Dhanrajgir

"Create an opinion and pulsate with enthusiasm."

The handsome Humayun Dhanrajgir (64) could well have been in films, in politics, or in both, considering his parentage. Born to Raja Dhanrajgir, the head of a mutt in Hyderabad, and Zubeida, the beautiful actress of the first Indian talkie Alam Ara and the daughter of the nawab of Sachin in Saurashtra, Humayun presents a heady mix of lineage and looks. He recently retired as managing director of Kodak India Ltd after spending the bulk of his career at Glaxo, where he pioneered third-party drug manufacture.

*H*umayun Dhanrajgir's extraordinary career bears testimony to his soaring ambition and desire to tread a path untrodden by his ancestors. At the multinational pharmaceutical company Glaxo, Humayun rose through the ranks to become vice-chairman and managing director. Despite his aristocratic lineage, Humayun became a model professional thanks in large part to his down-to-earth up-bringing.

A VALUE-BASED UPBRINGING

Although Humayun's mother had been in films, she discouraged him from entering that line because she had a deep respect for education and believed there were better and more productive vocations than acting. Like most sons of aristocratic families, Humayun too was sent to a public school, St Lawrence, but unlike other privileged sons, he was taught to respect thrift in matters of money. "I was provided a small allowance and I had to manage on that, "Humayun says. "My parents taught me that it is wrong to flaunt one's wealth." He was made to realize that money was valuable, and should not be squandered just because it was available. He was struck by the contrast in the attitudes of middle class friends who practiced thrift, and friends from rich families who abused money and poked fun at those who were less privileged.

"What were the other values your parents taught you?" I ask. "Frugality, integrity, truthfulness, respect for elders and empathy," says Humayun. "My father always insisted on kindness and hospitality." Guests had to be honoured and treated with respect no matter what their background. At each and every interaction, it was mandatory to give greetings with folded hands and a smile. Coming from an elite family, it could have been expected that Humayun would put on airs. However, the value system imbibed at home and the interaction with schoolmates from different backgrounds had taught Humayun humility and compassion. At school, he participated in sports, debating, riding and acting, thus receiving the perfect training for becoming a good team member.

THE PROFESSIONAL PRINCE

Zubeida's desire to realize her childhood ambitions through her son ensured him the best of western education. After school, he was sent to the University of Loughborough, UK, for a bachelors in chemical engineering. Later he did his masters at London University. Zubeida followed him there and stayed with him for two years, ensuring that he put in at least two hours of hard work every day. Humayun has pleasant memories of his actress mother taking interest in his engineering drawings and making observations about them. "My mother used to say, you must know how to separate the wheat from the chaff," says Humayun. She managed to develop his powers of concentration and methodicity. Humayun's excellent college results showed that the confidence reposed in him by his mother was justified. On the solid foundation of rich Indian family values, Humayun acquired the western values of scientific inquiry and a disciplined approach to work, which made him the perfect professional that he is. He could well have been called a professional prince, had the princely states still existed. His career graph shows that he did become one, but of multinationals like Glaxo and Kodak.

DISTINGUISHED MENTORS

Whether in the UK during college, or in a remote place such as Satna in Madhya Pradesh where Burmah-Shell posted him, or later in Madras or Calcutta during his Glaxo days, Humayun had no inhibitions about mingling with people from backgrounds other than his own. Even when he was in the company of very distinguished people, he did not feel small or different. This facilitated easy interaction with and learning from people who mattered.

I ask him about the people who had an influence on him. He recalls several. At school, he says, he was impressed by the personality of K I Thomas, the headmaster of St Lawrence, who remained supportive even later in Humayun's life. Cecil Savidge, a former official of the Raj, was Humayun's guardian in England and later a director of the International Chamber of Commerce. Humayun says he was greatly influenced by his disciplined ways and value systems.

Narayanan, who was later managing director of Ponds, became a close friend in England. "Nari was brilliant and taught me valuable lessons. He taught me the methodology of studying in the best possible way. He demonstrated the importance of precision and speed at the drawing board. He used to say, 'No free lunches', in other words, there are no shortcuts to application," Humayun says. The lessons learned from him helped Humayun obtain six distinctions in college (Nari himself got nine). At university Humayun became independent, confident and capable. He forged strong friendships and developed good interpersonal skills.

Sir Raghavan Pillai, India's foreign secretary, took a liking to Humayun and honoured him with nuggets of wisdom. He told him: "Always put your best foot forward. You will be asked to do a job you may not like, but go ahead and get involved. Test the waters, do not become a rubber stamp, ask for information and data." When he was posted at Satna, Humayun tried not to be cowed down by the backward environment. He tried his best to understand the nuances of the job, immersed himself in it, studied the subject and took responsibility for showing results. He was guided through these difficult times by Sir Raghavan's advice, *"Try to develop a liking for the job, however distasteful it may be."*

Humayun's wife is a steady, down to earth woman, not one to get carried away. She provided a secure and close-knit family life to Humayun and his sons. Yet she was always ambitious for him and it was her father, a former governor of Maharashtra, who introduced Humayun to John Farrant, the managing director of Glaxo. They hit it off and thus began a long and enriching association. Farrant was a great thinker. He had tremendous skill in analysis and decision-making. He would say, "Let's look into the facts, let's get to the bottom of it." Farrant gave Humayun difficult assignments and demanded more and more information. *He always looked at data with an eye to converting it into a money-making opportunity.*

SMART CAREER MOVES

After completing his masters, Humayun worked for three years as a process design engineer with British Oxygen in London. He handled independent assignments and was the only Asian member of a key commissioning team for big projects in Scotland and Wales. He earned the prestigious membership of the Association of Chemical Engineers (London) on the strength of his qualifications and work experience.

In order to widen his professional horizons, Humayun changed his career course from engineering to marketing, and joined Burmah-Shell in 1964 as a covenanted officer. As part of his one-year training he had to work in different parts of India, often on his own. It included being posted to an inhospitable place such as Satna. It required enormous resilience on his part but it brought out the best in him. He relished the challenge of working in an environment far removed from that of the UK. His perseverance paid off; he passed the training with flying colors and was taken into the mainstream. Five years later, he made a conscious career change, this time from marketing to management, in a smaller company, Glaxo.

MANAGER *EXTRAORDINAIRE*

It was at Glaxo that his skills in handling people came to the fore. Farrant became his mentor and entrusted him with greater responsibilities as time passed. Humayun handled a crucial industrial relations (IR) issue in the Madras branch with the mandate to shut it down if required. Within a year he moved to the head office as special assistant to the managing director. A year later he was appointed as manager and took over the Mumbai branch.

At the time Mumbai was Glaxo's biggest territory and Humayun, at 34, was Glaxo's youngest manager. After 15 months he was asked to move to Calcutta as branch manager to handle a difficult IR issue. By now he had earned a reputation as *a problem-solver for difficult IR issues.*

FROM PERSONAL SETBACK TO PERSONNEL VICTORY

A major health setback slowed him down around this time. But Humayun fought back; he overcame the stress and trauma of cancer and resumed work with renewed vigor and determination. After successfully managing the Calcutta crisis, he returned to the head office to start a major management by objectives (MBO) exercise under the guidance of UK consultants Urwick Orr, with John Humble as a key associate. After two-and-a-half years he was shifted, against his judgement, to the personnel department, in the key post of chief personnel manager. He proved more than equal to the task and two years later, he was asked to manage the crisis arising from a lockout in the Aligarh factory, where the dismissed staff had gone on the rampage.

Humayun was elevated to the board as personnel director in March 1978 at the age of 42, becoming one of the youngest directors in the company's long history. His penchant for rejuvenating branches and bringing new ideas to fruition prompted the authorities to entrust him with yet another responsibility: At 45 he was made the director of the foods division, which was an independent profit center. With the freedom to take independent policy decisions, he brought in risk-taking investments in the face of opposition. He was instrumental in increasing the market share and the business of the center. His stature as a successful operating head grew and culminated in his being transferred as director of the flagship division of the company, pharmaceuticals, at the age of 48.

HARBINGER OF THE WINDS OF CHANGE

Humayun was poised on the threshold of the greatest achievement of his career when he took on the reins of the pharmaceutical division. He planned the introduction into the Indian market of Zinetac, an anti-ulcer medication. Although Zinetac was at the time fast approaching the world's number one position in anti-ulcer formulations, Humayun knew he would have to overcome countless regulatory hurdles before it could be introduced in India. The risk was high. An interdisciplinary task force headed by Humayun managed the project. The highly secret manufacture was entrusted to a third party, which was in itself a revolutionary step. A special 100-strong field force was handpicked and trained to launch a single product, a practice the company had never followed.

It took a breathtaking six months from conception to launch of a world-class product, a cycle time unimaginable in those days. Humayun had to struggle to bring about a change in group thinking in respect of the low transfer price of the bulk drug, which was selling in the international markets at $1000 per kilo. He managed to obtain the support of the group chairman, Sir Paul Girolami. The successful launch of Zinetac was a defining moment in the history of the company and of the pharmaceutical industry. Moreover, Glaxo was the first company to launch a new entity through medical symposia conducted by world-renowned doctors. Humayun's trend-setting enterprise was instrumental in changing the company profile from that of a vitamin purveyor to a serious seller of prescription medicines. Humayun used the same launch model to introduce a score of new Glaxo entities, which were world-beaters at the time.

THE GOLDEN ERA

Getting products manufactured by third parties acquainted Humayun with a group of highly talented entrepreneurs. He encouraged them to become partners of Glaxo, by manufacturing these products in their own facilities built to match Glaxo standards. This was another revolutionary trend. On the marketing front it created tremendous excitement in the field-force, which attained its highest potential. The company further increased its market share, outperforming the so-called Indian tigers.

On being appointed deputy managing director in 1989, Humayun took responsibility for the production of formulations. There followed a period of intense investment in these facilities to upgrade them to world class. Spanking new facilities were created for injectables at Nashik and an aerosol facility was also started. It was pay-off time now as volumes were large and Zinetac also was made in-house.

Humayun was appointed managing director in 1990—a natural choice. He welded the top management into a coordinated team. It was a golden era as their products enjoyed widespread support from the medical fraternity. From 1992 to 1994 he was president of the Organization of Pharmaceutical Producers of India (OPPI), the apex industry body dominated by the multinationals (Humayun, however, managed to persuade Ranbaxy to become a member). He led many delegations to Delhi on pricing issues and patent laws. After reaching the pinnacle of his career, he retired as vice-chairman and managing director in August 1994.

However, his professional expertise could still be put to good use and he was invited to join Lupin Laboratories as their first-ever managing director. There too he implemented many new ideas for the growth of the company.

FROM PHARMA TO IMAGING

His reputation as a top achiever prompted Eastman Kodak to offer him the position of managing director of Kodak India Ltd for a five-year term from October 1995. Four years of exceptional growth followed, with concentration on team building and consolidation. The first challenge he successfully handled was that of selling India to Eastman Kodak. The turnover shot up from around Rs 200 crore to nearly Rs 600 crore. The Indian subsidiary currently enjoys strong backing, in terms of technical expertise as well as avenues to market its products.

Humayun has always tried to extend the boundaries of his job responsibilities. He loves the challenge of achieving difficult targets and scaling unprecedented heights. This desire manifested itself once again when he first thought of starting a Kodak unit in Nepal. He saw that as a very significant dimension for changing the company's wealth creation strategy. He saw that they were too dependent on input, with low margins and falling prices (because the Japanese yen was falling). Moreover, local distributors were playing tricks with customers, evading sales tax and so forth. Kodak needed a strategic weapon to combat this situation. He knew that Nepal was keen to industrialise. If Kodak set up a unit in Nepal, an added benefit would be that they could bring these films into India without paying duty because of trade agreements with the Himalayan kingdom. Humayun's foresight and persuasion paid off once again; the approval took eight to ten months, but the Nepal unit is now a 100 per cent subsidiary of Kodak India. The Nepali bureaucrats were impressed by Humayun's transparent dealings and sincere efforts. There were no bribes nor any middlemen, only factual information and expertise. It is a $6 million project and, if successful, will give Kodak a big competitive advantage, apart from a boost in earnings.

When I interviewed him for this book, Humayun was still with Kodak. Talking about his role there, he said: "At Kodak my role is more that of a facilitator than a doer. Strategic business units

(SBUs) are in place. My job is to resource them and their job is to achieve their end. The work is all to do with enabling, facilitating, shepherding. In Glaxo the average age tended to the middle or upper 40s, with 5000 people, a huge experience block and a relatively stable environment; whereas here I am the CEO of 500 people with an average age of 32 and a turnover of over Rs 500 crore."

The environment is different in one other crucial way: It's fully wired. Humayun said: "We are on the information highway with Lotus network, voice mail. My boss and other colleagues all over the world interact via the e-mail, faxes, and cell phones. We do not have the luxury of time. I get notes on Lotus and I have to respond quickly. I have to cobble together new things, see to the legal aspects and their complex series of requirements since multimillion dollar products are in the pipeline. One has to find a way to be able to do work in this vast wired network. *I discovered the art of giving an interim response, a technique to create space.*"

THE STRATEGIES OF OPERATIONAL SUCCESS

"*Create an opinion and pulsate with enthusiasm,*" Humayun recommends to those who want to launch an idea. After this come sincerity and determination which should shine through the presentation and body language. Humayun does not set forth any foolproof formula for success. Many variables such as luck, coincidence, timing and the coming together of good people play a part in any successful career. According to him, what is critical is the attitude you display and the way you wage your war. Over and above all this is, of course, a considerable degree of persuasive power. "Look at all the facts, analyse to death; but _don't overlook the human judgement factor_," is his advice to new entrepreneurs. This factor can be brought to bear on an issue with the help of persuasion. _Humayun achieved most of his successes by entering the area of persuasion, keeping in mind that he might not succeed. But he always persisted, he never gave up._

In the course of his illustrious career, Humayun has demonstrated the two most important facets of a good operating head. At Glaxo he was the 'doer' and at Kodak, the 'facilitator' and the 'assembler'. At Glaxo, he brought about a revolution through action. It worked well as there was autonomy, but at Kodak the requirements were different: It has world hierarchy. His role was to resource the SBUs, and it was their job to achieve their ends. He did not need to direct what others did because there was enough expertise, product knowledge, direction and market available. On the other hand, he had to shepherd, create the climate and make the team stay together. Whereas at Glaxo the work culture was more laid-back, in a company with a global network such as Kodak, speed is of the essence. Quick responses and rapid decisions were the order of the day and Humayun assimilated this requirement very well, when he was in his sixties, at that.

A MONARCH AMONG MEN

For a man who says "Work is my ethic", putting up his boots is not an option. Humayun's retirement plans do not include reducing his activity, only changing his subject area perhaps. Far from resting on his laurels, he looks forward to dividing his time between work and his aim to see his sons pursue worthwhile careers.

His motto, 'Never say die. If brought down, get up and go forward', inspired him throughout and will continue to inspire coming generations. The saga of Humayun's amazing spirit and resilience deserves a glowing mention; it has surfaced every time a threat presented itself. At the height of his tenure with Kodak, he suffered a second major health alarm when he was diagnosed with prostate cancer. He had to undergo surgery in London but returned within a month, his enthusiasm intact and raring to go. In this aspect, his story resembles that of his namesake, a Mughal prince who had everything but had to spend some years as a wanderer by a quirk of fate. That did not deter him from gathering support and regaining his past glory to bequeath a rich heritage for posterity.

Bhavarlal Jain

"Leave this world better than you found it."

Since its establishment in 1963, the Jain Group (turnover Rs 400 crore, 2200 employees), Jalgaon, Maharashtra has pledged itself to agriculture. Practically every activity it has undertaken, be it business or social, is related to this field. At the helm is an ideologue, founder-chairman Bhavarlal Jain (63), who dared dream to put Jalgaon, a quaint little district town in central Maharashtra, on the world map; and he did.

Jalgaon displays a rare 'work is life' culture. Through his deeds Bhavarlal Jain, popularly called Bhau (brother), has demonstrated that agriculture, the agro-processing industry and related business can be made profitable by educating farmers. Seventy per cent of our population is dependent on agriculture. It is our very lifeline, in which Bhau saw the opportunity to build a modern agrobusiness. He charged up sleepy Jalgaon with dynamic experimentation in farmers' education and progressive farming. When former agriculture minister Annasheb Shinde visited Jain's establishment, he wrote in the visitors' book, "If the central government and state administration put all their might behind Jain and a hundred other such industrialists, then our motherland will be industrialised in no time."

HIGH-TECH INTEGRATED AGRICULTURAL SHOP

The Jain group is India's unique one-stop high-tech integrated agricultural shop. The group helps the farmer to produce higher yields and better quality produce by providing genetically superior saplings, efficient water and fertilizer management systems and agronomical guidance. Jain then buys the yield and processes it at modern vegetable dehydration and fruit processing facilities. The group produces the finest quality dehydrated vegetables and aseptic fruit purees.

The group is engaged in:

- Cultivation of agricultural and horticultural products, nursery raising, agro forestry.

- Provision of agricultural services like agricultural R&D, demonstration, training and extension, turnkey agro-project consultancy and implementation, wasteland reclamation, soil conservation, and water harvesting, storage and conservation.

- Supply of agricultural inputs like micro irrigation, sprinkler irrigation systems, PVC and HDPE piping systems, tissue culture and greenhouses, water-soluble solid and liquid fertilizers, vermicompost bio-fertilizers and neem-based bio-pesticides.

All these inputs result in an increase in yield ranging from 30 to 230 per cent and a reduction in water consumption of 50 to 70 per cent.

THE HEADY BREW OF ENTREPRENEURSHIP

Jalgaon is a vibrant town with a surprisingly clean railway station (no wonder, it's maintained by the Jain group). Jalgaon's precincts are dotted with three manufacturing facilities where over 3000 people are constantly at work, despite it being the hottest place in central Maharashtra. This is an act of creation, an act of will of a visionary who, with three heart attacks behind him, still enthusiastically toils for 12 hours a day to bring prosperity to the Jain group, farmers and Jalgaon.

Bhau was born in a Marwari family, a community known for commercial acumen and hard work. His father was an agriculturist and small trader. After securing degrees in law and commerce and a coveted job as a state government officer, Bhau sought his mother's guidance. She advised him to go into business instead, since starting one's own business offered a greater challenge. Bhau heeded his mother's advice. With a meagre seed capital of Rs 7000, he took up a small kerosene and petrol pump agency, under the name Jain Brothers. The agency grew to become the Jain Group with an annual turnover of Rs 400 crore. Bhau says he owes what he is today to his mother's farsightedness. In the initial stages, the joint family provided reliable human resources and much needed emotional comfort. His wife submerged her identity in his aspirations, giving him unqualified support, cooperation and encouragement.

Buddy Handa and Subir Bose, executives of the American oil giant Esso, had an influence in aggressive marketing, while friend Shaikh *chacha* borrowed funds from the market to help Bhau tide over his difficulties. In addition, Damle of United Western Bank, Sethia of State Bank, D R Mehta of SEBI and Justice Dharmadhikari inculcated in Bhau the qualities of mind and heart necessary to conduct business with a certain value system. Birth in a business community, a supportive joint family network, contact with company executives, and the enormous possibilities of building a purposeful business based on agriculture were potent ingredients for Bhau's entrepreneurial success.

CREATION OF BUSINESS GOODWILL

Having opted for business, it is important to build customer goodwill. I ask Bhau how he did it. He says, "When I became a franchised kerosene distributor of Esso in February 1963, an opportunity presented itself. The budget increased the price of diesel from Rs 58 to Rs 85 per barrel. The day after the budget, there was a long queue at my shop. I chose to pass on the benefit of the pre-budget price to the customers. This laid the foundation for their goodwill at the very start of my business." If he owed any money, to Esso or to banks, he would go on the appointed day and repay whatever he could. He would apologise for not being able to pay in full and would ask them to forgive him. The point is that he would not avoid them, or miss appointments on false pretexts. The goodwill he created by such acts rolled over to build a network of contacts of substantial significance.

In the short space of three years, Jain Brothers became Esso's biggest diesel dealer in the Khandesh and Marathwada regions, bringing Bhau in close contact with hundreds of agriculturists and farmers. Sensing the link of diesel to the business of agriculture, Bhau redefined his focus. Instead of calling himself a diesel agent who was also selling some seeds and fertilizers, he advertised the Jain Group as suppliers of seeds, fertilizers, pesticides, PVC pipes and diesel for agriculture. The focus was enlarged and the emphasis was changed—from a mere agent of an MNC oil company to a self-made group which provided integrated inputs for agriculture. Esso went into the background and Jain pitchforked to the centre stage, in a creative crafting of a meaningful identity.

In pursuance of this widened horizon, the group made several breakthroughs. It:

- Purchased a sick dehydration unit; innovatively modified the equipment to produce refined papain instead of fruit powder; manufactured and exported ultra-refined papain from India for the first time and has been the largest exporter of this product since 1978.

- Pioneered the introduction of drip irrigation systems in India and introduced the concept of an integrated approach, bringing under one roof all the activities related to the agrobusiness.

- Established, primarily for export, one of the largest dehydration units in this part of the world to produce flakes, granules and powder of vegetables like onion, garlic, capsicum and ladies' fingers.

- Established one of the largest fruit processing plants with a rated capacity to process 100 tonnes per day, to make purees, pulps, concentrates etc.

JALGAON ON THE WORLD MAP

The Jain group's innovations are impressive. As Bhau says, "In 1963, Jalgaon had no special identity. I am proud of the fact that we have added value to so many lives and put this quaint little town on the world map. I believe this was achieved largely on account of my vision, supported by solid hard work." He continues: "Inspiring people by example is the method I followed for creating a committed and motivated team. We have received six state awards and 57 national awards for outstanding export performance, R&D achievements and entrepreneurship. To top it all, we received the Crawford Reid international award for 'significant contribution to the micro irrigation industry outside the United States'."

Bhau explains: "Micro irrigation is a scientific method of irrigation carrying desired water and nutrients directly to the root zone of the plant, drop by drop. Its advantages are early maturity, better quality and higher quantity. It is ideal for problematic soils and water, saves labour and up to 70 per cent water. It is successfully working on more than 40 crops covering over four lakh acres. Our market share in India is about 60 per cent. We export to more than 30 countries covering all five continents, with an export turnover of Rs 75 crore. We are recognized as world leaders in providing custom-made irrigation systems. Jalgaon is the first district town in rural Maharashtra, perhaps in India, to have had a company that raised Rs 100 crore in a Euro issue." This fine performance put Jalgaon on the world map.

But then the group faltered. With such a distinguished record of achievements, how did Bhau fail? His own explanation is an exercise in perfect communication and provides a case study for students to learn how to establish understanding and empathy by presenting facts and owning responsibility.

THE SAD PATRIARCH

On November 26, 1998, Bhavarlal Jain placed a half-page advertisement in _The Economic Times_ apologising to his shareholders, suppliers and creditors for his misadventure in diversification. It was probably the first time an Indian corporate had chosen this route to make a public apology for follies and bad performance.

The Economic Times
November 26, 1998

I am sad—that for the first time since our inception, we have fared badly. We ventured into unknown areas like finance, information technology and granite at the cost of our core business… I feel it is my duty to account for, to own up, to admit my misjudgments, to apologise.

I'm happy—that the greatest international recognition in the field of irrigation, the Crawford Reid memorial award, has been bestowed on me. I'm told that only 16 people have won it in the last 19 years and that I'm the only Indian and second Asian amongst them. I'm happy that though we burned our fingers venturing into unrelated areas, we didn't lose a single customer worldwide in our core business and our employees firmly stood by us, productive as ever. It has been a chastising experience from which we've emerged not unscathed, but financially disciplined, more mature, and certainly more focused.

I'm confident—that despite the hurdles, we can not only bring due recognition to this industry, but also bring about a second green revolution in this country. Because our fundamentals are rock solid. With our voracious appetite for growth and a policy of plowing back profits into our business, I believe there's a lot more we're capable of achieving. This is only the beginning. Work, hard work, continues to be an obsession with us. And hard work not only pays, but also brings honour and preserves character.

Such transparent communication reflects the sincere person that Bhau is, and aptly conveys the mixed feelings that he was going through. Bhau's confidence about the future is based on his tested fundamentals on the conduct of business and track record of performance. The Jain group went through three agonising years, but today it is almost out of the woods. If the customer is king, then dealers and distributors are kingpins. Bhau's master-stroke is his letter 'Eclipse Cleared' dated March 15, 2000 addressed to his dealers and distributors. The excerpts reproduced below show why.

ECLIPSE CLEARED

Our company has sustained colossal losses during the past three years. Every stakeholder bore the brunt of this loss—be they customers, dealers/distributors, general as well as core promoter shareholders, creditors, banks and financial institutions, or suppliers, associates, government and society at large. The atmosphere was agog with rumours, defamation, backbiting and calumny. It was a nightmare. During this period, we felt neglected, faced ridicule, deception, indifference and at times humiliation. We had to face situations not dreamt of before. Personal property, whatever little it was including family ornaments, had to be either pledged or sold. While doing all this, there was fleeting anxiety whether or not we will get through this ordeal.

There, however, was a reservoir of self-confidence and the great assurance of worthy deeds well done. Even during the weakest of our moments we bore malice towards none. Solace, therefore, became the source of strength. Soul-searching compellingly revealed that sorrow and sufferings are to be taken as part of life, never mind the minutes, days, months and even the years. The journey to light through darkness is long and painful anyway. Yes, there were moments of hope, but for a greater part there were dark clouds of gloom, a plethora of problems and at times crippling blows. A few acquaintances, relatives and friends volunteered help but by and large we had to fight our own lonely battle. Rock solid and sustained support did come from our dealers/distributors and our customers, both domestic and overseas. Notwithstanding the inconveniences experienced by them, they never turned their back on us. Associates also took their turn. However, the saving grace came, though belatedly, from banks and financial institutions. Amongst the banks and FIs, State Bank of India, United Western Bank, ICICI and SICOM did go an extra mile and took a conscious decision to assist the company in every way possible. Local banks and credit societies also extended their helping hand in their own way and within their limits.

Taking into consideration the good work done by the company in the past, the bright prospects for its future and unimpeachable integrity and foresight of the promoters, all of these institutions, within the limitations of their rules and regulations, have achieved an outstanding feat never before experienced even by most of them. The well-wishers and the sympathisers alike displayed their concern, vouched for us and did whatever they could. They even put to use their friendly influence and powers of persuasion. Similarly, the accommodation offered by some of the suppliers is unforgettable.

"Everyone brainstormed time and again and after prolonged deliberations finally came out with a restructuring scheme which was to be a 'New Deal' for the company. The implementation of the revival plan began on February 28, 2000, the day on which my business career commenced 38 years ago. I was overwhelmed by the coincidence. History was created; the organization was saved. Through the arduous passage, the founder-promoters, though distressed and pained, stood their ground resolutely. Those directors and associates who were directly responsible for making this happen, and those who heroically dared the odds day in and day out, heaved a sigh of relief. Obviously, it is going to take some time to complete the formalities and for things to be the same as they were earlier. Now it is our turn to perform. The eclipse has cleared. Let us forge our way with renewed vigour, zeal and fortitude."

Diversification Gone Haywire

What is Bhau's diagnosis of the group's colossal failure? He says, "Between 1991 and 1994, we diversified into unrelated areas like granite, computer hardware and software, and merchant banking. These projects were conceived based on instincts, and under the influence of the then euphoria in the economy. Businesses like information technology were found to require a high degree of technical leadership. The organization was not ready to provide it and the professionals who were relied upon did not measure up. The granite business was acquired and expanded out of personal preference, rather than as the result of an in-depth study of the business or any market survey. The merchant banking business was headed by a professional, who was good at marketing but failed in documentation and securitisation."

This must have affected the working capital, I probe. Yes, says Bhau. "All these investments went bad and led to a large-scale diversion of working capital funds. The interest burden increased and in due course even the core businesses like pipes and irrigation suffered for want of adequate working capital. Setting up sizeable food processing facilities with an investment portfolio of Rs 125 crore, without realizing that by its very nature food processing can take longer than envisaged to generate positive cash flows, also adversely impacted shareholder value."

Honest if defensive, he says: "We bit off more than we could chew and diversified beyond our horizons, we tried to diversify into businesses without building an organizational base for them. This cost the company something like Rs 100 crore in a short period of three years. Most of them were not errors of judgement, but were the result of an indomitable will and spirit which said 'we can do everything'."

I am blunt. "Bhau, you are sugarcoating the pill. You went beyond your knitting. You did not assess your in-house core competencies. Thinking that 'If MNCs can do it, why can't we?' led you into a trap. The shrewd businessman in you gave way to the idealist who courted disaster. What have you to say?"

Bhau frankly admits, "In a way, you are right. The nationalist got the better of me, the nationalist with a thirst for diversification. 'If professionals can do, it why can't we?' I thought, and the innovator in me won out. I am never shy of making mistakes, let us try, whatever the cost, because the cost has never been a criterion in my life. MNCs are money-driven. _Money was not my motivation, mover, driver, or originator, I have created wealth as a consequence._

"These three differing thoughts tore me apart—integration, diversification, professionalism. I had a craze to put an Indian organization on the international scene. I got carried away. I started 11 projects to be implemented in a period of two-and-a-half-years. I had no organization. If I don't know, I thought, I'll do it by hiring someone. Integration—original thought, and diversification—borrowed thought. Ideology got the better of me, so I don't call myself a successful businessman. I will do very well as an author, philosopher, writer. I am going through terrible pain because of that."

PROFESSIONALISATION FAILS

I ask, "But Bhau, you hired professionals, didn't you?" He becomes pensive: "The professionals I selected were good people, but not efficient. In business, if goodness is at the cost of efficiency, you cannot survive. Some were talkers and not doers. Most of them were failures in life. _Whatever you do, you must make a mark. You must do something which nobody has done, or do some-_

thing uniquely. My selection was based on ideology. I did not behave like a professional, I behaved like a patriarch. I am now a changed man. Now when we recruit, apart from assessing the candidate's philosophy, I want to assess his thinking methods, his competence and his values. What we need today are persons to turn round the group. I want my company to be a blue chip."

Like many business patriarchs, Bhau is convinced of an urgent need to induct professionals. He is a changed man after experiencing failure. His selection criteria were not professional. To professionalise a family-run group requires a wholehearted commitment from not only the patriarch, but all family members. Issues of organization culture, image in professional circles, key results areas, authorities and the support due to outsiders require serious application. Professionalisation is an issue of synergistic match-making. That is the direction Bhau and his sons are probably moving towards.

However, the fact remains that Bhau is creative, built a meaningful agro-industrial enterprise in a town away from industrial belts, developed a purposeful group from his family members and some professionals, and showed performance despite setbacks.

SOCIAL COMMITMENT SKILLS

What skills did he use to realize his dreams and achieve productive growth when he was not a 'professional'? How did he conceive, promote and build the edifice brick by brick? Bhau details the essentials:

The firm belief that given an opportunity every man has an ability to rise to the occasion and produce results;

Everything becomes routine after six months. So what you really need is not technical competence beyond a limit, but thorough planning and original leadership;

Social commitment is itself a skill which we utilised. Basically society will feel that these people will be doing more good than others. It's a great technique. And if you use it genuinely, it will lead to great results. Most people forget this. In their total attachment to bottomline results, in their pursuit of creation of wealth, they neglect this particular agenda of social commitment. If we do not participate in anything happening in Jalgaon, say in a conference on ayurveda and so forth, then I am no one. I should be a part of it. I used people skills.

"The 'work is life' formula was seen in action. It had a tonic effect. With this skill, we created extraordinary work out of ordinary people."

I have visited the Jain group's facilities in Jalgaon several times. All the plants are modern. Appropriate technology induction and skill upgradation has taken place during different growth phases. The skills he used provide a clue to his astounding success.

I have observed Bhau using social skills to mobilize action.

- Connecting: Bhau connects through his hospitality system which works with German precision. It expands his network of contacts. His staff at Mumbai and Jalgaon are ever ready to serve you. They book tickets, arrange transport and look after you with affection.

- Bonding: In his conversations, Bhau never says 'my company'; he always says 'our company', whether he is talking to a supplier, creditor, banker, stranger or journalist. With the use of affiliative words like 'our, we, let us' he establishes a bond on the emotional level.

- Sharing: He communicates his ideology, values, beliefs, philosophy, results and actions to his employees in Marathi, the regional language. He shares his personhood, without the veneer of personality. His transparency allows him to appeal directly to his interlocutor's conscience.

Through skillful rhetoric Bhau evokes a positive response to his obsession, 'work is life'. People do work for him. He does not talk of profits, probably because 'profit' is a bad word in our country, yet he has made profits. If asked, he admits that profits are essential. But he believes that profits follow work. He also has the social skill to skirt that which is not palatable, without losing focus. Bhau is a skillful communicator; more so a pathfinder.

Deepak Kanegaonkar

"I am an indefatigable optimist, difficult to demoralise."

Established in 1983, the DK Group (turnover Rs 50 crore,150 employees) consists of Phoenix Alchemy, India's largest suppliers of pour point depressants vital to the oil exploration programme; Vishudha Rasayani, manufacturers of speciality and performance chemicals; and Gandh Sugandh, which recently launched two up-market perfumes: 'Lata' in Mumbai and 'Urvashi' in Paris. Promoter Deepak Kanegaonkar (46) is a restless entrepreneur, who thinks non-stop of how to make 'big money'.

*W*hen I meet a person who says he wants to make big money, I am mightily pleased. In India, such a breed is rare. 'Making money' has an unethical connotation in our society. We are conditioned to think that it is sacrilegious to become wealthy and virtuous to remain poor. We are shocked if someone uses positive vocabulary to express the desire to become wealthy, make money, become rich, or live in style. The renowned philosopher Ayn Rand, a Russian immigrant in America, was thrilled to see that Americans had coined the phrase 'to make money'. They slogged to earn it. The Americans have made money. They have created wealth, haven't they?

When a middle-aged Deepak Kanegaonkar assertively and without a trace of guilt says he wants to make 'good money', I am impressed. I don't presume money can be made only through un-ethical practices, despite the prevailing ethos of corruption and distrust. I am curious to know how Deepak dares admit this frowned upon goal. What is his background?

HANDICAP RACE

Deepak grew up in Sholapur, a district headquarter in Maharashtra. His father Ramrao was an honest, if temperamen-tal, excise inspector; he did not get along with people and was promoted only once during his career. Kanegaonkar led a lower middle class life. Deepak was a naughty boy, so his father put him in a senior class in order to discipline him. Deepak's classmates were around three years older than him.

"The fact that my father put me in a higher class made me run the handicap race. I had to compete with older boys. I took train-ing in body-building. I became an athlete. The headmistress, Mrs Kelkar, influenced me. I overcame many hurdles to prove myself.

The family background did not help. It was not congenial. I swam against currents. Adverse circumstances built the confidence that if I struggle and work intelligently, good things will happen to me."

Deepak faced financial hardship while studying for a degree in chemistry at Sholapur and later for an MBA in marketing at Shivaji University, Kolhapur. He had no proper guidance. I wanted to find out if there was any further handicap. I probe, "Has there been a particular project or event that has significantly influenced the direction of your career?" Deepak narrates: "At my father's instance I entered into partnership with his friend and started a sugar factory in Sholapur. The partner duped me. After a bitter fight with him, I left for Mumbai with Rs 150 in my pocket. My father wanted me to work at a job. Meanwhile, I got married. My father-in-law followed me to Mumbai. He also appealed to me to take up a job, saying he would use his influence to get me one. I told him I didn't want help. I pleaded with both of them to trust me for two years. I was determined not to work for others. I said to myself I will create my own universe."

THE PHOENIX ALCHEMY

"Deepak, I understand you did not want to do a job. But how did you in the first place come to decide you should start a business, and that too in speciality chemicals?" I ask. He says, "My father was, as I told you, in central excise. So I used to hear stories of how people make money in alcohol, liquor, narcotics; alcohol is

99

good for cheap money for a short period of time etc. I am not a brilliant chemistry graduate. It is not the degree, it is the familiarity with chemical terminology that came in handy. I thought it was easy to sell pure chemicals. It is better to go into consumables, not durables. I made quick money in speciality chemicals."

There was a demand for pour point depressants (PPDs) in the early 1980s for the oil exploration programme. The Oil and Natural Gas Corporation (ONGC) was growing by leaps and bounds. The huge investments being made were to Deepak's advantage. "But how did you raise the start-up finance?" I ask. "I requested my mother and sister to give me their gold. They obliged. I collected about 2 kg of gold, mortgaged it and got Rs 1.50 lakh. I then took a plot of land on the Thane-Belapur road. I had come in contact with some government and bank officers while starting the sugar factory. In the meantime they were transferred to Mumbai. I used those contacts to get money from banks."

Deepak is a buccaneer. He took a closed unit and put up a proposal to banks to get a loan. He says, "I was literally reduced to ashes. I knew the phoenix rises from the ashes, and decided so would I. I have his alchemy in me, so I named my venture Phoenix Alchemy. I don't know the origins of this unbounded confidence in my capacity. But the alchemy worked. The turnover, which was Rs 9.5 lakh in 1984, was Rs 52 crore by 1998!"

ORDINARY MEN SOAR HIGH

Start-ups have a hard time hiring people: Few trust your abilities, truthfulness or sincerity; you have no credentials, no brand, not even a name. I was curious to know the selection methods used by Deepak to get people. He says, "I was lucky to meet good people, nice people. They trusted me, my word, the convictions I voiced. But I did not trust anyone, especially in money matters. In 1977, when we started the sugar factory, I had no capital, no experience and I trusted everybody. In 1982, I had no capital, five years' experience, and I did not trust anybody."

I probe, "But Deepak, trust is the foundation of building a relationship. It needs to be developed. If you distrust, unconsciously you evoke identical suspicion. Without people, you cannot start a venture, is it not?" He says, "You are right. I have not lost faith in humanity. In a situation where people find it difficult to get a job, some take a jump with you in your endeavour. You do things with them, work together, learn together. I had to conceptualize. It is the actual 'doing' and learning on the way. A sense of belonging, loyalty, emotional bonding takes place. As you incrementally grow in business, those who have started with you bring in their friends, having tested your sincerity and prospects. The chain builds up. I have 150 people, they are doing a good job. They are good at execution, not so much in concepts or seeing the big picture. I now need more professionals, and don't forget I did not lose those who joined me in the beginning. That means my track record of recruitment, retention and _getting extraordinary results from ordinary men and women_ is excellent."

LIGHT A CANDLE

From the success of Phoenix Alchemy, Deepak's spirit of enterprise led to the birth of Vishuddha Rasayanee in 1990. It manufactures a group of speciality and performance chemicals like glycol, ethers, poly glycols, emulsifiers, oil field chemicals, refinery chemicals, heavy-duty brake fluids and radiator coolants. This product range is much in demand in various industries like automobile, paint, leather, pharmaceutical, stationery, oil exploration, aviation and aeronautics.

In March 1996, the tank farm project of Phoenix was commissioned for storage of class A and B petroleum solvents. Situated in the hub of Navi Mumbai's industrial belt, the project has already captured a huge market. Phoenix has also acquired Ravi Antioxidants, a unit situated at Chiplun in Konkan which will manufacture ketonic resins for captive consumption for manufacture of inks. The excess capacity will be exported.

Phoenix has also recently joined hands with German-Ink Production GmbH. A new company has been formed by the name of German-Ink Productions Pvt Ltd to manufacture blue and black point ink. The German technology is the best in the world and assures a shelf life of six to seven years, as against Indian inks' eight to nine months. The ink will be sold in the domestic market and will also be exported.

As Alka Gune-Sane, director perfumes at Gandh Sugandh, put it: "We must admit with all humility that expansion and diversification have been possible because of the single-minded dedication of our highly motivated and inspired team. The group's emphasis on supplying quality products, our strong customer relations and of course Deepak's alchemical leadership are the main factors of success. His passion and sincerity have endeared him to our business associates within the country and abroad. He believes that it is better to light a candle than to curse the darkness. Going by this philosophy, he lit many candles of friendship and has built a fantastic network of friends, well-wishers and business associates throughout the world."

I SMELL MONEY

Modern synthetic perfumes contain more than a hundred ingredients. Chemicals called fixers, preservatives and stabilizers are used for making these perfumes. I thought Deepak's diversification into perfumes was a natural corollary to his main chemical business, but Alka said this was not so. "Fragrances and music are his two loves. It was his dream to pursue these intimate fascinations of his life. After gaining a firm foothold in the chemical industry and the experience to manufacture quality products, Deepak felt it was now time to chase his dream, which led to the birth of Gandh Sugandh with its two offsprings, Urvashi and Lata."

Gandh Sugandh was floated in October 1997 with the high aim of putting India on the international scene by creating and marketing high class, exotic perfumes. The world should know

India has the potential and the technical expertise to supply quality fragrances, and not just essential oils.

Alka Gune-Sane again: "Gandh Sugandh shall specialise in creating perfumes revolving around the exquisite base of sandal, the essence and incense of India. This distinctly complex essential oil, which is at times cool and spiritual and at others intensely sensual, is a perfumer's delight. All the perfumers in the world would love to use a lot of it in their fragrances, but the cost is prohibitive. Also pure genuine sandal oil is manufactured only in India from trees which are more than 30 years old. The export of sandalwood oil from India is banned. This treasured sandalwood oil is a gift of our rich heritage." Their slogan is 'Think sandal, think Gandh Sugandh'.

I say to Deepak, "You may love fragrances but you do not know about making perfume, you have no competence. How did you decide to enter the field?" Deepak narrates, "It is my hobby. For the last six years I have been collecting perfumes, smelling them, understanding them like Europeans do."

I knew perfumers need a 'nose' for it. The primary requisite to become a 'nose' is a keen olfactory sense. Mila Kahlon describes ('In Search of A Scent', *Jetwings*, July 2000), "It is not enough for the perfumer to distinguish blindfolded between the fragrance of a rose and a tulip; his sense of smell must be so acute that he can detect, in a mixture of a hundred or more ingredients, the precise amount of the different substances that have contributed to the formula. He must not only be able to recognize various raw materials but must have the capacity and artistry to blend them harmoniously. He must be able, for instance, to tell whether a certain lot of _labdanum_ is from Greece or from Corsica, whether the oil of _ylang-ylang_ comes from Madagascar or Manila. He should be able to tell the difference between oils of the same species of plant cultivated in different countries, and which type will achieve a particular result. The nose has his counterpart in the wine industry, where the skilled expert can tell in an instant the region, type of grape and vintage of the wine he is sampling. Each perfume is composed of a top note, the refreshing, volatile fragrance that is perceived immediately; a middle note, providing full, solid character; and a base note, which is classified according to one or more identifiable dominant smells."

Deepak comes straight to the point: "_I learnt to distinguish smells so well that I smelt money in it, as I had in speciality chemicals._" The scented voyage had begun.

MUSIC HAS FRAGRANCE

"Tell me the story Deepak, it appears romantic: Making a business out of a hobby!" Deepak narrates, "I had accompanied a couple of foreign tourists to South India. The ladies in the group were smelling _attars_ in antique bottles at a roadside shop. They exclaimed, 'Wow, this is quite exotic, sensuous'. It had a sandalwood base. We discussed what European women liked, what notes they adored, what moods glued them to a particular brand, etc. I instantly sensed that there was a great global market for sandalwood-based perfumes for foreign noses. I then bought motifs and Indian *attars* and studied them. I found out that pure sandalwood extracts are available in Bangladesh, Sri Lanka, and South India. Then I wondered how I could get the feedstock. Finally I made an agreement with the Tamil Nadu government and ensured a supply of sandalwood oil." After all this groundwork, however, Deepak admits that "the initial trials flopped".

But the initial setbacks only led to further vigorous efforts. It was somewhat surprising to learn that only four people worked on the project. They made 200 samples and shortlisted 20 of them with the help of Charles Caruso, a nose from France. After they had completed 17 months of work, a celebrity joined the voyage. Deepak narrates, "One evening I met Adinath Mangeshkar, nephew of the nightingale of India, Lata Mangeshkar. While discussing the perfume business, the subject of celebrity brands and perfumes in the name of film personalities, etc. came up. I expressed my opinion that unless the celebrity had a consistent, steady and ever-growing career graph, there was no chance of he brand becoming a success. Also, there had to be a synergy between the characteristics of the product, the name of the celebrity and the personality. I also felt that unless the celebrity was actively involved in creating and promoting the brand, success would be difficult. Then came the idea of branding Lata Mangeshkar, the world-renowned playback singer. A perfume in the name of Lata in the premium segment would be a perfect marketing idea, I thought.

"Moreover, Latadidi is a connoisseur of perfumes with a passion for high-class perfumes. We had the expertise, culture, exposure, logistics and resources to promote such a brand. Everything fell into place and 'Lata _Eau de Parfum_' was launched in October 1999." Lata is promoted as "a fresh floriental, with a top note that is spicy, sensuous; giving way to the delicate floral heart note of jasmine and rose, culminating in a divine, lingering soul note of sandalwood enveloped in musk, vanilla and amber." Says Deepak, "The unique selling proposition (USP) for the product is Latadidi's melodious voice, which has always given a class of songs that has soothed the audio senses of millions for nearly 50 years. Now, with an exquisite perfume associated with her name, she will please the olfactory senses as well. Now music has fragrance."

FROM SPIRITUALITY TO SENSUALITY

Deepak calls himself an '_opportunity looker_'. This is how he came to spot the opportunity to make an entry into the Mecca of perfumes, Paris, in September 1999. French perfumers were well aware that sandalwood creates a serene spiritual mood and also evokes an exotic sensual ambience. It has the potential to create thousands of versatile fragrances with other components but the French are frustrated due to its scarcity. Deepak decided to encash this opportunity, making Gandh Sugandh a unique perfumery house. Being an Indian and having a strategic tie-up with Tamil Nadu Forest Plantations Ltd, Deepak was ensured a steady supply of high purity, authentic sandalwood oil.

It is not easy to penetrate the long established world renowned French perfume market. One can spot opportunity but it is a long journey from the birth of an idea to a finished product on the shelves of stores like Galeries Lafayette, Printemps, Sephora, BHV, Le Bon Marche, Empreinte Parfums, Passion Beaute, La Samaritaine and Marionnaud.

India has been famous for thousands of years for spices, essential oils and raw materials for fragrances. However it is totally unknown in the world market for premium, finished perfumes. The Western manufacturers have always made exquisite products using Indian ingredients. To break the monopoly, Deepak decided to float Gandh Sugandh in 1997. In Sanskrit, *gandh* means 'nice fragrance' and *sugandh* means 'very nice fragrance'.

The ambition was to put India on the world map of high-class perfume manufacturers. India makes *attars* which are no doubt pleasant but are relatively simple formulations with few ingredients, rarely exceeding five. Whereas *eaux de toilette*, *eaux de parfum* and *parfums* are highly sophisticated products, with as many as 50 to 400 ingredients. Add to this the strict and stringent guidelines of IFRA Geneva, Switzerland, monitoring the good practices of perfume manufacturing throughout the world.

Gandh Sugandh's first product, Urvashi, was launched in Paris on September 16, 1999. It has been well received and has grossed a turnover of Rs 1.75 crore since its launch. Described by Deepak as "very exclusive and the most expensive fragrance on the Paris shelf", Urvashi is sold in a silver flacon with cabochon in 24 carat gold with a retail price of $123 (FF 760 or Rs 5412).

Reaching this level of success and appreciation in Europe was not easy. To create a product of international class, one must work with only the top French professionals. Says Deepak, "Being an unknown Indian, getting an appointment of even a few minutes was a Herculean task, forget about convincing them that I meant business and that I could be the best in the market. The process of creating a product with an 85 per cent acceptance level in France, Switzerland, Germany and Italy took more than 15 months. It involved innumerable product modifications, market surveys and opinion polls with the assistance of hard-core professionals of the French perfume industry. Not only the perfume, but also the brand name and design of the flacon have been test marketed, increasing the likelihood of success. To gain technical know-how and to meet quality control parameters, a team consisting of the technical director, Mr Cahndratre, the director perfumes, Ms Alka Gune-Sane, as well as myself underwent rigorous training for 15 days in the most renowned perfumery school of Grasse ASFO, Grasse, Prodarom.

"The components for Urvashi like the actuator, the bouchon, the flacon, the emballage and the thermoformage have been tailor-made to our designs and specifications under zero-error strict quality control procedures. These are vendors who are also suppliers to Christian Dior, Cartier, Guerlain and Chanel. It goes without saying: Whenever you give your best to any project, God is always merciful and generous, showering bountiful success and satisfaction on you. Money of course follows. In our case, dollars, French francs and euros."

To get an actual feel of the French market, Deepak made over 60 trips to Paris over two years. European legislation mandated production of an anti-poison certificate along with irritation and allergy data. Registration of the brand name, logo, and bottle design throughout Europe was also required. "The French Customs department was amazed at the exquisite silver flacon because never in the past 100 years had they seen such a fusion between jewellery and perfumes. Gandh Sugandh is the only company registered in a special category of goldsmiths and silversmiths as perfumers," Deepak says.

Note the meticulous preparation involved. It is inspiring to see an ordinary man take up an ambitious international venture and aim for perfection in manufacturing a class product—its presentation, packaging, procedures, systems, stringent formalities et al. Deepak knew that god is in the details and he invoked his presence by working tirelessly on each tiny part of the campaign. With his perfumes, Deepak invokes the base note—the dominant smell of Indian sandalwood—to arouse the basal instincts of spirituality and sensuality. The choice of which chord to tap is left to the aesthetic sense of the connoisseur.

THE INDEFATIGABLE STRUGGLER

Like all successful entrepreneurs, Deepak has a fair composition of motivational drivers such as money, power, curiosity and the desire for fame and recognition. Entrepreneurship, initially born out of the survival need—to make a living without recourse to a job—has graduated to fulfill a creative need—to earn recognition from the international connoisseurs of perfumes. He believes that "What I want to achieve is possible," and therefore knocked at the doors of veteran noses in Paris.

As any classical entrepreneur, Deepak speculated on his chances of success. He took a calculated risk in his hobby horse adventure. He is a born struggler with a phenomenal drive to overcome obstacles. These included a devastating fire at the Phoenix factory in 1988, an excise case, and floods at Pali in 1989 which affected the local factory. Says Deepak: "I am happy that from 1991, due to liberalisation, one is not required to adopt any shortcuts to circumvent the law."

Deepak is proud of his optimistic outlook, capacity for monumental effort and non-stop thinking. "_I am an indefatigable optimist, difficult to demoralise._ I spend a lot of time in situational analysis and then my hunches are usually correct. I follow up consistently and tirelessly because I am restless until the work is done. But I am scared of failure and of making the wrong decision. I have nobody on my conceptual wavelength with who I can share my inner anguish, problems and goals. I have to make accurate decisions." I could empathise with his dilemma, as I have seen Deepak driving his staff to get things done.

Successful entrepreneurs aim high. They are not content with what is. They always want to improve and modify. Deepak came to Mumbai in 1983; we know how he started out. I was at his house on the first night of Diwali in 1999. The restless struggler was at peace. He said, "I have returned from office after distributing a bonus to 150 people. These fellows work hard and sincerely. Their families depend on me. I owe it to them to pay well and to look after them with love. And I do that religiously." Behind the hard taskmaster, there is a deeply sentimental soul.

While delivering on time his speciality chemicals or producing a perfume of exacting standards, Deepak extracts extraordinary performance from his employees. But he feels duty bound to look after his people and is ruthless with himself, working almost non-stop. Deepak is a first generation entrepreneur spreading his fragrance across the seven seas with his age-old Indian values intact. Although he is in his mid-forties, he is not bent on preserving the status quo, as most of us usually are by that time. He is vibrant, almost always in an upbeat mood. He is breathing fresh life into Indian sandalwood—an aromatic inspiration in the quest for inner knowing or sensuous living.

Bhausaheb Kelkar

*"We have to create the best original fragrances and
reach them to the customer in record time."*

*S H Kelkar & Co (turnover Rs 150 crore), acclaimed by global
majors for its quality and reliability, leads the fragrance industry in India. Bhausaheb Kelkar (68), a connoisseur of perfumes,
is the chairman and managing director of this flourishing enterprise.*

Listening to Bhausaheb Kelkar talk is like sipping a
mature French wine. There is a flow of measured
words and speech that is precise, quick and straightforward, and effortlessly displays a vast knowledge of
the perfumery business. This brilliant son of '*attarwale Kelkar*',
makers of traditional *attars* (traditional fragrances), has stimulated thousands of olfactory organs here and abroad. The
leader of the fragrance industry in India, S H Kelkar is ranked

eighteenth among the world's top 50 perfume companies. Satis-fied connoisseurs have placed him in the Paris hall of fame.

S H Kelkar & Company shifted in 1952 from Dadar to a new marshy 35-acre plot in Mulund. That very year, Govind Damodar Kelkar, known as 'Bhausaheb', joined the company after graduating in chemistry from Bombay University. At that time, the staff consisted of only 14 people and the turnover was Rs 10 lakh. Today the Kelkar enterprise employs 400 people and the turnover has crossed Rs 150 crore; it has a perfumery in Mulund (a Mumbai suburb), an aroma extraction plant at Vapi in Gujarat and a research centre at Hyderabad.

ATTARS' GLOBAL SPREADSHEET

Traditionally, *attars* were bought only during Diwali, Moharram and other festivals; beauty care was restricted to ordinary cosmetic preparations and consumers were content to apply hair pomade and brilliantine. Further in the past, the world was borderless for fragrances. Ethnicity had not arrested their spread. Today, peoples' attitudes towards fragrances have changed dramatically. Fragrances have become an essential part of the modern lifestyle, cutting across class and demographic barriers. Cosmetic and consumer products that were considered a luxury just a few decades ago have now become a necessity. Varied fragrances entice the olfactory nerves of multi-ethnic communities around the world. Creative perfumers have stepped in, conceiving fragrances to meet evolving tastes.

In the fast-expanding world of perfumes, the Kelkars have chosen to remain wholesalers. Explains Bhausaheb: "We had chosen
to take the agency route for growth as it adapted better to the
prevailing business environment. We did not get into retail because we would have been required to compete with our clients,
and that's something we didn't want to do." Wholesale perfumers
may not have contact with retail customers, but that doesn't
make the names of their fragrances any less fancy. Fancy Boquet,
launched in 1922, has had phenomenal success, often compared
to that of Chanel No 5, the international endurance legend.
Other fragrances introduced in the 1920s were Navakusum,
Fougere Extra, Otto Rose No 1, Jasmin XXX and Fulbahar. Later,
Nightqueen B (1948), Royal Boquet (1956), Fantasia (1962),
Fasli Gulab, Firdaus (1965) and other such new products went on
to consolidate the Kelkars' tryst with aromatic destiny. Jasmin
(1974), Chariot (1977), Paragon (1980), Superstar and Sylvie
(1982), Arabian Nights Chararat (1995), Aquilaria (1996) and
Velvet (1997) made their presence stronger. New fragrances
rolled out of the Kelkar refinery with religious regularity.

The decade 1974-84 was marked by numerous hits and re-
sounding successes for the company. A host of new segments
opened up for them—functional and household products, personal care products, cosmetics, toiletries, hair care products,
zarda, agarbattis, edible products. They seized the initiative by providing outstanding fragrances. The Kelkar success story was re-
peating itself, on a much larger scale this time.

Their customers, whether multinationals or local producers, depend on them to come up with unique creations that would keep their users happy, and gain market share for their products. "We combine marketable creativity with consistent quality to give our customers a powerful edge in today's competitive marketplace. Perhaps that is why since 1955 there has not been a single year when the turnover was lower than the previous year's," says Bhausaheb.

SWADESHI SUBSTITUTION

Fragrances are deeply personal, and Bhausaheb's discerning talent led to the creation of new fragrances. Bhausaheb's uncle Dadasaheb asked him to work on some aromatic chemicals that were being imported, with the challenge to find a substitute within three years on a budget of a mere Rs 10 lakh. Kelkar and his enthusiastic team worked round the clock and ended up producing quality products like Hydroxycitronelal and Yara Yara, products that were better than their imported cousins.

I asked Bhausaheb whether there was a formula that characterized his method of work and found that he has followed certain immutable principles of discipline: "*Hard work, meticulous attention to detail and quality, customer acceptability and honest dealings,*" he cites. There was *a priori* confidence that they could do better than the foreigners. He showed the way to do it with indigenous raw materials and local intellectual capital. Bhausaheb's analytical abilities and blending skills satisfied the discerning and

116

differing requirements of various noses. Bhausaheb has no other ambition than to continue doing what he was programmed to do—create perfumes.

In 1960, the desire to be self-sufficient drove Bhausaheb to search for effective substitutes for western 'delta 3' components. The audacious idea of using turpentine was as much a creative leap as it was fuelled by nationalistic fervour. Bhausaheb brought to bear his knowledge of chemistry on the research conducted to make the new chemicals acceptable to consumers. Having ensured that constancy of smell was maintained, they got better results. In 1965 the Kelkar Group won the prestigious Sir C P Ray award. The Indian Chemical Manufacturers Association gives this award for pioneering research in the development of fragrance chemicals from Indian turpentine oil, using novel methods.

Bhausaheb realized that imported fragrance compounds did not satisfy local tastes, and set up his own aroma extraction plant at Vapi. In 1978, 90 per cent of the ingredients were imported. Today, the figure has come down to 20 per cent. Although the government was encouraging indigenous product development and was ready to ban imports, Bhausaheb did not lobby for such a ban. He was confident of success.

The Kelkars experimented, manipulating variables such as temperature, catalysts, pressures and delta 3 components, to produce special blends. They offered products of the same quality as the imported products and successfully edged out many of them.

A Swiss company wanted to enter into collaboration with the Kelkar group but their offer was politely declined. The group maintains this fiercely independent streak even today, when foreign collaborations are the in-thing.

Self-sufficiency has always been the guiding principle of the Kelkar Group. It led to backward integration in the early 1980s. They started cultivating critically important essential oil-producing plants such as geranium, *patchouli*, citronella, etc. Then they established a research station at Hyderabad in 1989. It was a conscious step to break free from the dependence on imported sources, which were scarce. They now regularly impart agricultural know-how to farmers and have built a reliable resource pool to meet their essential oils requirement.

PROFESSIONAL MANAGEMENT

Throughout, the motto that motivated Bhausaheb and the rest of the group is *"We have to create the best original fragrances and reach them to the customer in record time."* His infectious enthusiasm pervades the entire factory like a fragrance. Bhausaheb's brothers Suresh and Ramesh joined him in the 1960s. Suresh is their 'organization man'. With his formidable management skills and studious bent of mind, Suresh built the sophisticated Vapi plant, which supplies reputed manufacturers throughout Europe. The Kelkar export arm, Keva Fragrances, was set up in 1981 to tap the exploding overseas market. Ramesh excelled in creating fragrances to suit international tastes, and his keen nose for trends steered this 100 per cent export-oriented company from strength to strength. Today, Keva has a distinguished presence in the markets of South-East Asia, Europe and America.

Bhausaheb has run the family and business on traditional management lines. The three brothers synergised their strengths to expand business and conquer new territories. Says Bhausaheb: "We celebrate the birth of every new fragrance. The group's strength lies in _traditional professionalism._ Instead of increasing the business beyond a reasonable limit and losing efficiency, it is our continual effort to keep efficiency and business hand in hand. We would like to maintain our exclusivity, guard the formulations and not go into collaborations and unwieldy expansion. We will keep the family capabilities in mind and the family alone will retain the secret code of fragrance creation. Only part of the business would be carried out by trained professionals, so that they do not stand in competition with the group."

That the family stayed together was no accident. Says Bhausaheb, "It is imperative that the family stay together and I have taken care of this aspect as astutely as I have nurtured the business part. A lot of thinking has gone into it. We brothers discuss everything but as the head of the family, I have the final say. In working together, we have the discipline to work as a team. Nobody refuses to do any work. _All the people do all the work._ They have complementary skills. The decision-makers have professionally allocated functional responsibilities. I provide the leadership. I have avoided sibling rivalry by neatly distributing the shareholding. The three of us, with our technical acumen and

119

managerial competence, motivate teams to perform jobs of outstanding quality."

There is nothing inherently objectionable in keeping the business within the family and building a solid modern organization. A number of their employees have been with them for generations; if a business house is a trust house, then the Kelkars, like the Tatas, have earned that reputation amongst their clients here as well as abroad. What did Bhausaheb do to cultivate such a result-producing, committed culture? "Close personal attention and deep personal involvement at every level set us apart, engendering trust and loyalty. Over the years, we have fostered a unique organizational culture that recognizes individual merit and integrates it into the collective talent pool to achieve our objectives. *Our commitment to those who work for us goes beyond the boundaries of the workplace.*"

SOCIAL RESPONSIBILITY

To pay their dues to society, the Kelkar group has funded educational institutions in their hometown, Devgad in Ratnagiri district, and the Vaze College in Mulund. The college proposes to offer a diploma course on perfumery and cosmetics whose syllabus will include the development of smell memory, combinational skills and entrepreneurship. The course will produce more organoleptics—professionals who make a living by using their senses of smell and taste. Apart from employment in the tea, coffee and cosmetics industries, organoleptics also assess the aromas of products as varied as liquid floor cleaners, incense sticks and perfumed erasers.

PATHBREAKERS

There are few examples of corporations making an enduring contribution to the very structure of their industry. The growth of the Kelkars, however, has been part of a larger canvas. Their people have grown with them; their customers have progressed and the fragrance industry itself has matured with inputs from the group; and they have contributed significantly to the advancement of several professional bodies such as the Fragrances and Flavours Association of India, the Essential Oil Association of India and the Basic Chemicals, Pharmaceuticals and Cosmetics Export Promotion Council (CHEMEXIL). Industrialists and entrepreneurs who shape the structure of the industry are called pathbreakers. The Kelkars are pathbreakers.

Close personal interaction and attention to detail have marked their association with industry bodies. Bhausaheb and Suresh both held office as president of the Fragrances and Flavours Association of India. On the anvil are futuristic projects such as a creative center for enhanced perfumer-customer interaction and a state-of-the-art biotechnology research center. The Kelkars have shown that their model is eminently adaptable in India where 'family' is the oldest revered institution. Applying the criteria of professional excellence, the Kelkars come out with flying colours, whether on quality, delivery, service, trust, growth, technology upgradation, original R&D, market reach, import substitution, group branding, industry strengthening, or their contribution to society.

FRAGRANCE HUNT

In their effort to create special blends, the Kelkars adhered to the adage 'different strokes for different folk' to conceive fragrances that would appeal to peoples' evolving choices. Bhausaheb maintained a focused long-term approach although he was constantly thinking of, and resolving, the problems at hand. He has a passion to overcome hurdles and the zeal to find solutions.

There is always a feverish search for solutions and innovations. Competition with the self leads to unrivalled progress. Moreover, when the path is less traveled, the traffic is negligible. There wasn't much competition. Detailed preparation and knowledge of analytical chemistry and blending technology helped to produce enchanting mixes for different tastes. New fragrance varieties pleased and enticed customers. They were sensitized. They placed more orders, which led to new products.

Producing fragrances, which create moods and action, and catalyze an appealing sensation, became a second habit. Aromas that would recall memories of pleasant sensations became the hallmark of the Kelkar brands. Blending skills are at the root of the chemistry of associational recall. The customers' set needs were met through established connections under a durable brand.

Then they went on to produce new formulations for segmented tastes. Creative perfumers such as the Kelkars were able to create new tastes.

ALCHEMIST PERFUMER

James Bell, vice-president of the perfume firm Givaudan Roure, trained his sense of smell to identify 5000 different smells. He believes that natural ability is a prerequisite for maximizing one's sensibilities. According to him, "You start with a superior sense of smell, but then you must train it, like a concert pianist. Perfume is like music. It has a base note, a midnote and a topnote. You smell the topnote initially, the midnotes enhances the topnote, and the base note brings it all together." Bhausaheb's base note is strong. That is why he has been able to bring together the topnotes of Parisian noses and the midnotes of Indian noses to make good perfumes.

Our conversation ranged from culture to values, the status of family management, education and social responsibility. Bhausaheb did not speak in modern management jargon, although he is familiar with it. He used simple words and phrases to convey substance and profound meaning on business practices and the serious discipline of management. Bhausaheb and his team of brothers and nephews have worked systematically to retain middle class values, and yet walk into the hall of fame with grace. He has not allowed his Indian values to be compromised while doing business in the plush offices of the international fragrance industry.

123

The Kelkar group authoritatively proves there is nothing inherently unworkable about family business management. With gumption and drive as their defining characteristics, Bhausaheb and his team have carved out a niche market for themselves. Family businesses may take note: A mere family visiting card does not guarantee a place in the hall of fame, though it might take you up to the visitors' gallery. You need the mind of an alchemist to convert smelly turpentine into a quality fragrance, and the expanding vision of your industry–universe. Bhausaheb is blessed with both.

Ravi Khanna

"Lack of resources makes you resourceful."

Ravi Khanna (60) is the chairman and managing director of the Control Group, with nine companies principally operating in electrical switchgears, power generation, control equipment, connectors and industrial mail order services. His creative forays in identifying business opportunities are awe-inspiring. Tall and well-built, Ravi epitomizes madhurya, a certain sweetness and grace in tone, speech and manner. It is fascinating to see that this quality has permeated his staff too. They greet each other with Radhe Radhe, which means 'kindness, kindness'.

Coming from an illustrious and highly educated family, Ravi Khanna grew up with a legacy of family prestige, respect for elders and spirituality. As a child he was impressed with the success story of his uncle S N Talwar, who left Indian shores in search of a fortune and returned to become a successful and influential industrialist.

Deeply influenced by his neighbour Prof Rao, and two of his own professors, Ravi realized that technology was going to change the face of India. He wanted to be an instrument of that change. Thus he took his first independent decision—to become an engineer, and not a judge or lawyer like his father and grandfather. In 1962 he graduated in electrical engineering from IIT, Kharagpur with first class honours. He went to Germany, where he acquired experience and skills, and returned in 1965 to set up his own little unit in the garage of his father's house.

The Lessons of Childhood

Although he did not follow his father's footsteps, Ravi was deeply influenced by his resourcefulness, courage and spirituality. He was fortunate to grow up with diverse and enriching knowledge culled from the *Ramayana* and *Mahabharata*, as recounted by his grandparents on the one hand, and his father's readings from Swami Vivekananda and Dale Carnegie on the other. "What other influences were there, Ravi?" I ask him. He proceeds to narrate how another significant influence during his growing years came from an unexpected quarter.

In the aftermath of the Partition, thousands of refugees came to Delhi and Ravi was a witness to their resilience in the face of adversity. He saw how their incessant industry and innovation soon turned around their fortune. Most of them had been completely dispossessed, many had little education, but they would busy themselves in making whatever they could—torches, batteries, chemicals, soaps, and a host of other useful things. Their example of making do, of creating something from nothing, showed the young Ravi that determination and courage are assets in themselves.

DETAILS DO COUNT

In his first job as a design engineer with Metzenauer & Jung, then the third largest electrical company manufacturing switchgears and controlgear equipment, Ravi gained not only knowledge, but was also initiated into developing a _disciplined and thorough working style_. I question Ravi about this. He says, "My boss, Dr Kattner, personally trained me and inculcated in me the habit of maintaining a job register, which would contain separate entries for all the different jobs that I undertook. This facilitated quick retrieval of information and a ready means of reference, even without computers." The efficacy of this system is so deeply etched in his mind that, to this day, his staff members do not attend a meeting without their registers!

Another invaluable lesson learnt from Dr Kattner was the well-organized method of arranging the contents of a standard office table—a seemingly minor detail in the working of an organization, but one that instilled discipline and method in Ravi's working style. Moreover, he benefited greatly from Dr Kattner's lucid explanations of the workings of the company; this was a perfect transfer of know-how and know-why even before they became buzzwords. Within days many aspects of electrical engineering which had looked difficult to him as a student became crystal clear, and learning became a great pleasure. When he had left for Germany, Ravi had had only a dream; when he came back to India, he had the knowledge and the confidence to forge ahead to fulfill it.

GOING FOR THE GAPS

Ravi says the lessons learnt from the resourcefulness of the refugees whom he had seen in his childhood stood him in good stead when he started from scratch in 1966, with only Rs 500 in his pocket. Whatever money he had saved in Germany was spent on gifts for the family and on the weddings of his sister and brother. He had, therefore, no choice but to make the most of the meagre resources available. The wooden crates he had used to transport personal belongings, tools and so forth from Germany were turned into two large work-benches (for nostalgic reasons, he retains the work-benches at one of his workshops even today). He started out with just one electrician, whom he trained himself.

Seeing that in India the per capita consumption of power was much lower than in other countries, Ravi sensed a growth opportunity in the generation, distribution and control of power, for which equipment would be needed. Besides, advanced countries were unlikely to compete for this market on account of economies of cost and scale. Ravi started manufacturing control panels. Soon afterwards, his observant eye and business acumen provided him with a 'gap', an area waiting to be exploited. There was tremendous growth potential in manufacturing traffic signals. The knowledge of design and engineering acquired in Germany helped him in manufacturing the necessary sequential controls using relays and timers. He went a step further by also developing traffic signal poles and lanterns, as the ones used in New Delhi in those days were of poor quality. This first instance of correctly identifying customer needs and developing products amply demonstrates Ravi's *forte—gap analysis for business growth.*

Likewise, in 1974 he realized there was a gap in the supply of indigenously-built switchgears for use in warships. Before his competitors could convert their tenders into orders, his team had developed half a dozen components and got them approved by the Indian Navy. Consequently they achieved a breakthrough in marine switchgear indigenization and the company was awarded a prestigious contract for the first five warship frigates of the Indian Navy. In 1975, at the age of 35, Ravi received the *Tamrapatra* for excellence as an entrepreneur.

NEVER SAY NEVER

By 1980, his company had become the largest switchboard manufacturer in the small-scale sector. In order to grow further, he would have to start manufacturing vital switchboard components like circuit-breakers and contactors. Ravi launched a worldwide search for partners and zeroed in on Terasaki of Japan, one of the largest manufacturers of circuit-breakers. Initially Terasaki did not show an interest, so Ravi set out to buttonhole Mr Terasaki at the Hanover Fair in Germany. There he learnt that Mr Terasaki was attending a sales conference with European distributors at a golfing resort in Scotland. So determined was he to meet the man that he telephoned Scotland, booked himself into the same resort where Mr Terasaki and party were staying, met him, struck up a friendship with him over a game of golf and proceeded with him to Japan, where they signed an MOU and an agreement for technical collaboration! *This is indeed exemplary determination.*

His wife, who was travelling with him at the time, had expressed her doubts on what sounded like a wild-goose chase, but Ravi's instincts didn't mislead him. Ravi speaks in glowing terms about his wife: "My wife is a very intelligent and clear-headed person. She has immense faith in God; she comes from a large family; she is interested in gardening, painting, the scriptures, music and travelling. She has been ambitious for me. Even in our foreign travels, we meet our customers and collaborators together, making friends not only in business, but as families."

It had long been Ravi's intention to manufacture contactors. With that in mind he approached Telemechanique of France and General Electric of the US. Seeing there was no movement on those fronts, he decided to go ahead with the help of Simplex GE of the UK, although their product was not as good as that of Telemechanique. Within two years, his product had made good progress and the chairman of Telemechanique expressed his desire to join hands with him as a partner. Within a year, his company introduced India's only world-class contactors in the market, way ahead of the competition in terms of technology, adaptability and performance, at a reasonable price. Their presence gradually induced Siemens and others to change their designs.

These successes were soon repeated for other products which were not available in India. In collaboration with Stromberg of Finland, the group started manufacturing a full range of switches, switchfuse units and load-break switches. In 1991 they were approached by AVK SEG of Germany to manufacture alternators, 50 per cent of which would be exported to Germany. It was a totally unexpected opportunity. Ravi had never envisaged manufacturing rotation machinery for power generation. Yet when opportunity knocked he seized it, and became the third largest manufacturer of alternators in India after Kirloskar and Stamford.

These repeated successes were by no means just strokes of luck. As he puts it: "In business, _one has to be on one's toes_ all the time and not rest on one's laurels. It is common to see cash cows turning into dogs, but the inverse is almost impossible. Unless and until you keep on identifying and taking opportunities within the domain of your activity, you simply cannot keep pace with the competition."

AN INFECTIOUS ENTHUSIASM

Over the years Ravi has learnt that successful men are those who articulate their objectives with clarity and genuine excitement. He has perfected a technique to enthuse his people. First of all, he convinces himself about his objective and vision, and then he shares this vision with his friends and colleagues. The natural excitement with which his vision is conveyed and shared is highly infectious! His special brand of enthusiasm spills over to everything that occupies his attention, be it in the industry, or its development and diversification, or his duties as president of his residential area in Friends Colony, Delhi, or as a past president of the Okhla Industrial Estate Association. He firmly believes in the power of enthusiasm and spreads it among his colleagues, friends, relatives, customers and partners.

RESOURCEFUL PEOPLE MANAGEMENT

"What's the most important factor for a business to succeed, Ravi?" I query. Ravi proceeds to give me his *mantra* for successfully achieving the goals of his organization: "If you *choose the right men, initiate and motivate them*, then they build machines and capital. However, all the machines and capital in the world cannot build men." For him, the greatest assets of an organization are people with ideas and the excitement to actuate them. "Peoples' productivity can be increased through motivation, demonstration and celebration of successes. An innovative climate can be created through rewards, general praise, Kaizen and complete freedom to operate," he says. Ravi has managed to bring to bear on the internal dynamics of his organization the practices of German military training, on the one hand, and the principles of *Vedanta* on the other.

According to him, the best way to minimize conflicts among staff is to either get convinced or try to convince with patience, courtesy and dedication. He remembers what the Germans told him. It was said that when young German boys underwent compulsory military training, it was standard practice that whenever there was a quarrel or dispute, the parties concerned were not permitted to lodge their complaints with the senior officials before 24 hours had elapsed. Ravi saw the wisdom of this practice and adopted it among his senior colleagues. He has seen that conflicts are minimized when you are able to think over a controversy; it puts you in a frame of mind to try and analyse the other man's point of view.

As a student of _Vedanta_ for the past 10 years, Ravi has recognized that courtesy and love form the guiding principles of interpersonal communication; they help in smoothing rough edges and making the environment friendlier and more enjoyable. His experiment in shaping organizational behaviour on these five basic principles of _Vedanta_ may well find its way into the curricula of the IIMs and IITs some day:

- Do away with your ego, anger and hatred.

- Shun people who lie, cheat or scheme.

- Develop _madhurya_, a certain sweetness and grace in tone, speech and manner.

- Build and nurture relationships, sharing your joys, sorrows and excitement with your close ones. (Translated into corporate action, it means, for instance, that Ravi and his team try to share as much information with their staff as possible and run a transparent operation.)

- Strive for perfection in whatever you do, whether it is polishing the floor or making a cup of coffee.

Ravi's rationale for success in work is simple: *Start with hunches and instincts, then flesh them out with method and rigour.* Before starting out on a new venture, he thinks, and thinks alone. Then, he shares his thoughts with his team and works with them. Each one of his managers is an independent decision-maker, free to use his ingenuity to achieve his targets.

Ravi's analytical skills have been honed over the years. He did not acquire analytical ability in a business school; it is his business that has been his school, and he has learnt his lessons diligently. More importantly, he believes that one learns as long as one lives, and there are lessons to be learnt even from the most unexpected quarters. For instance, in the 1980s, his men were trying to perfect a draw-out switchgear system. Ravi, in the meantime, noticed the work of a Rajasthani carpenter, a master craftsman who was doing some work in his house. The fittings he used for drawers, though heavier, allowed the drawers to move smoothly. Such fittings were not available for switchgears, nor could they be imported at that time. The idea was enough: Ravi soon incorporated these features in a draw-out mechanism in switchgears, which proved far sturdier and more convenient than any of the others in the market.

SETTING HIGHER GOALS

Ravi attributes his amazing achievements to his constant urge to set his goals ever higher. He is not content with an ordinary performance but strives to be, if not the best, at least among the three best. This is true of everything that he undertakes. At one stage, for example, he had set himself the goal to play golf well. He realized that his game would not improve by simply playing with friends. So he took lessons and also practiced regularly at his own 9-hole golf course. He thus tackled a problem that no amount of coaching or books alone could have solved for him.

Similarly, when his company started manufacturing diesel generators two years ago, his goal was to manufacture a product that would be far superior to any other in the market. He and his team pitched for the highest standards in quality, noise attenuation, effluent control, etc. and soon carved out a niche for themselves in this field too.

Today Ravi's goal is truly global. "My most important task is that the conglomerate that I have built up should become world class in every way, so that we can call it a multinational Indian company where products, services, practices, designs ad quality excel and are on par with the best in the world".

Ravi believes that goals must be set high, whatever the field. "By higher goal, I mean a kind of desire and craving for betterment leading towards excellence. I am generally not satisfied with the level of cleanliness especially on the roads. The whole country looks unfinished, especially the urban areas. In my own little way, whether it is in or around the factory or my residence, or wherever I have influence, I try to motivate others and get involved in achieving a higher goal—even in the level of cleanliness expected."

For Ravi, setting high goals wherever opportunity exists, and achieving them, has become a habit. His *modus operandi* in solving problems is simple but unique. He says: "Concentrate on the problem, because *every problem carries its solution within itself.*" His favorite story is about two cats, an old cat and a young one. When a preacher in his discourse told them that ultimate happiness lay in the tail, the younger cat went round and round to get hold of his tail, and finally gave up exhausted. The older cat, however, merely walked straight ahead, saying that ultimate happiness was already within him and he did not need to go in search of it...

A True Change Leader

Ravi's natural urge for excellence, his innovative mind and environmental concerns have contributed to a complete transformation in the genset industry. Having manufactured alternators in a joint venture with AVK SEG of Germany since 1994, he happened to learn in 1997 that these were being sold to a large number of genset manufacturers who, like all others in the country, manufactured a sub-standard product which was noisy, leaky, inefficient and unreliable. What was more disturbing was that the industry was used to buying these unreliable machines.

Ravi's perfection-seeking mind immediately recognized a need to bring about a change in the industry's expectations, and he decided to build world-class silent gensets with sound-proof acoustic enclosures—an environmentalist's perfect solution to the problem of noise pollution. A further improvement was that in case of power failure, the genset would start automatically within a period of less than three seconds; and when the power returned, after waiting for the preset timing, switch itself off automatically. Thus, without going into competition with his own customers, Ravi _created a new segment_ altogether—a classic example of 'Only Me' versus 'Me Too' in marketing terminology. His product not only changed the industry's perceptions about gensets, but also influenced government policy. The Supreme Court passed orders banning the use of noisy generators, especially in residential areas, ordering that only noise-proof silent generators could be used. Thus, his company became a pioneer and market leader in this field. It is now manufacturing even larger sets, up to 1500 KVA, which are silent and can be kept in hotels and factories or public places for continuous supply of power.

Ravi's achievements and breakthroughs are a result of systematic innovation and an organized search for opportunities. His diagnosis of market gaps and disciplined follow-through to secure technology display ingredients of purposeful innovation. This is the man who saw refugees from Pakistan showing ingenuity in gathering together and harnessing all kinds of resources, and translated this into a profound observation: _"Lack of resources makes you resourceful."_

Ravi Khanna is an entrepreneur with vision, ambition and a deep desire to follow a dream with determination, hard work and team spirit; a true thought leader who leads by example. He is also a human being imbued with love and kindness for his family, friends, colleagues and all those who come in contact with him. As he puts it: "I would like to mould discipline and spread awareness to clean, beautify and enrich our otherwise endowed and cultured country—this is how I would like to be remembered."

Verghese Kurien

"We must build on the resources represented by our young professionals and by our nation's farmers. Without their involvement, we cannot succeed. With their involvement, we cannot fail."

Operation Flood, the largest dairy development programme in the world, ushered in the 'White Revolution' in India. The architect of this strategically networked and skillfully executed revolution is its fiercely competitive visionary leader, Dr Verghese Kurien (79). Having steered the National Dairy Development Board to success, he is now the chairman of the Institute of Rural Management, Anand (IRMA).

With an annual milk production of 70 million tonnes, India has displaced the US to become the world's number one milk producer. Nurtured by Dr Verghese Kurien, the Gujarat Cooperative Milk Marketing Federation (GCMMF) today has a turnover of Rs 2219 crore and a compound growth rate of 18 per cent. Kurien was for many years the chief of the National Dairy Development Board (NDDB), which has set up 175 dairies in 22 states in India. The Amul brand has made history, symbolising quality with its products like milk, butter and *ghee*. Let's go back to where it all began.

LANDMARK DAIRY DEVELOPMENT

The story of this landmark dairy development began in the crucible of the Kaira District Cooperative Milk Producers' Union in Gujarat. The farmers' inchoate need to earn better returns on their invaluable but perishable asset, milk, was met by a strategist, a leader and a visionary, setting in motion a White Revolution.

The late Sardar Vallabhabhai Patel was not only a great visionary but also a practical strategist. Born a peasant, Vallabhabhai had an inborn love for rural India and a deep-seated desire to transform it through rural renaissance. He recognized that the structure of a producers' cooperative evolved through farmers' wisdom was solid, based as it was on organic continuity.

Vallabhabhai's strategy gave equal weight to three components:

- Technology for the rural environment required setting up an institute of agriculture for the development of relevant skills, research into utilisation of suitable material, and for transfer of this appropriate technology to the rural community;

140

- Corresponding education of rural labour in a rural university, and

- Organization of producers' cooperative marketing institutions to augment rural incomes and develop local industry. The outstanding example was the milk producers' cooperative for the development of the dairy industry.

To make farmers' cooperation work required the skills of a leader, and the leader emerged in Tribhuvandas Patel. Vested interests such as those of middlemen had to be tackled diplomatically. Tribhuvandas was a Gandhian and a committed reformer. Kaira had a well-developed milk tract and an organized procurement system started by private traders. Under Vallabhabhai's guidance and with the Congress Party's backing, Tribhuvandas fought the government over its order favouring continuation of the Polson monopoly. He had the Kaira District Cooperative Milk Producers' Union Ltd registered on December 14, 1946.

Its transformation into a modern dairy was accomplished by the aristocratic Verghese Kurien, the most reluctant recruit to the cowsheds of Anand. Kurien, a Syrian Christian, is from Kerala. His father was a civil surgeon and his mother was the niece of Dr John Mathai, a finance minister in the Nehru cabinet. A mechanical engineer from Guindi Engineering College, Kurien obtained his masters from Michigan State University, majoring in metallurgy with nuclear physics as his minor. Kurien had gone to the US on a Government of India scholarship. Dr Mathai was keen that he join the Tatas and he also had an offer from Union Carbide. The government was, however, not prepared to release

him from the scholarship bond and posted him at Anand on a
salary of Rs 275 per month, as against the Tata offer of Rs 2000.

Before his stint in the US, Kurien had worked in the Imperial
Dairy Research Institute at Bangalore for eight months. But his
interests were in metallurgy or nuclear physics, certainly not dairy
science. Not wanting to be under the tutelage of his uncle, the
reluctant engineer, in a suit and felt hat, landed in god-forsaken
dirty Anand on May 13, 1949. In personnel management this
would be considered the most perfect mismatch between man and
job.

The foreign-trained *badasahab* (big boss) Kurien had to stay in
a garage next to the creamery, opposite the railway station, in the
company of flies, shrieking trains and their whistles. Kurien spent
his spare time patching up worn-out gear boxes, boilers, shafts
and belts. Once he bluntly told Tribhuvandas, "Get rid of this
junk and buy new equipment. You will save a lot of money in the
long run. And you won't give anyone a chance to return your
milk. If you don't do as I suggest in your own interest, you are just
wasting my time." Why did he say that? He explains, "I was
putting in my resignation every month; after eight months it was
finally accepted because I had made a nuisance of myself. When I
was packing my bags Tribhuvandas came and said, 'So you are
leaving, what about the equipment? You install it and go.' I asked,
'How long?' He said, 'Two months.' The salary would be Rs 600
per month i.e. Rs 1200 for two months. I agreed." Kurien recommended buying a plate pasteurizer, which was expensive.
Tribhuvandas borrowed Rs 40,000 from his brother-in-law, gave

it to Kurien and sent him to Mumbai. Kurien returned with a pasteurizer purchased from Larsen & Toubro.

Kurien himself has so far not fully dissected the precise reasons he stayed in Anand despite alluring offers from the private sector and the advice of Mathai and other family contacts. I asked him, "With your aristocratic background how did you reconcile yourself to staying in a garage?" Says he, "If I had had the benefit of background and infrastructure, success would have come rather easily and my independent contribution would not have been easily measurable. Here I knew there was so much to be done—how could I not try? I had a trained butler. Mumbai was close. The Mathais were there but I would stay at the Taj at Rs 50 per night. I could afford it because in Anand I had no expenses at all." The overwhelming motivation was his genuine friendship and regard for Tribhuvandas. He unconsciously started accepting him as a mentoring leader. H M Dalaya, an expert in dairy technology and a friend of Kurien's from Michigan, was inducted in April 1951. The triumvirate of Kurien, Tribhuvandas and Dalaya started working at full force. From their experience evolved a vision, articulated by Kurien, to build an institution—the Indian Dairy Products Marketing Board. It would build the market for milk products.

It became a reality ten years later when the National Dairy Development Board was founded. Other elements of the dream were realized with the creation of the Gujarat Cooperative Milk Marketing Federation, a federation of Gujarat's dairy cooperatives that is now India's largest food sector business. The dream is fleshed out; the rationale for the institution's existence gains depth and breadth through Kurien's growing commitment to placing the instruments of development in the hands of the Indian farmer. The duty of the professional is expanded to give life to a dream that is truly a dream of India's future; a just nation in which rural citizens have as much access to the fruits of progress as their urban sisters and brothers. *Kurien articulated what, decades later, has become the byword of development; only when those who are directly concerned with the results of development have control over its ends, and the means to achieve those ends, will true development occur.* Kurien's design of grassroot democratic institutions nestled in Anand, the milkmen's habitat, and run by professional and technical experts is the foundation of Amul's success. This came to be known as the 'Anand Pattern' which was later followed by other milk cooperatives under Operation Flood.

THE ANAND PATTERN

Kurien pioneered the Anand Pattern when he was the general manager of the Kaira District Cooperative Milk Producers' Union. It demonstrated that democratic institutions in villages, within a specific economic sector, could help an entire village community develop. He nurtured the union from a daily collection of 500 litres a day in 1948 to one million litres a day in 1990. He helped set up similar district cooperative unions in six other districts of Gujarat and these eventually federated under an apex body, the Gujarat Cooperative Milk Marketing Federation Ltd, which covers more than 2.1 million milk producer families.

The Anand model is essentially an economic organizational pattern for small producers who join hands to benefit from an integrated approach in handling their produce. The system enables them to obtain the efficiencies and economies of a large-scale business through professional management, the freedom to decide their own business policies, adopt modern production and marketing techniques, and provide those services that small producers individually can neither afford nor manage. The cooperatives under this model have progressively eliminated middlemen, bringing the producers in direct contact with consumers. In spite of opposition to these projects by middlemen and other powerful vested interests, Kurien has been able to make major breakthroughs in the dairy and oilseeds sectors because of the support he mustered for these projects at the highest government levels.

Devaki Jain puts it aptly in *Women's Quest for Power* (Vikas, 1979), "The Anand Pattern is more than a description of structures and activities.It is based on certain values, techniques and ideals."

Tribhuvandas, the leader, was held in high esteem by milk producers because of his high integrity and the affectionate manner in which he mobilised and convinced them of the power of cooperation. Dalaya, the expert dairy technologist, was able to find innovative solutions to all technical problems. *Kurien was the warrior, the risk-taker, the strategist and the tough-minded professional manager who put to use his redoubtable organization skills to set a mould, the Anand Pattern.* He put his protective sheath around farmers and Anand against political or foreign invasion and bureaucratic or even minor interference.

The troika synthesised their skills to produce a unique Anand culture. Bold, innovative initiatives in solving problems, pride of participation in the rural renaissance movement, integrity and pride in work are the defining characteristics of the Amul ethos. I ask, "How were you able to get professional managers to come to Anand and work for farmers at lower salaries than they could normally expect? You brought in management as another middleman." Says he, "I had six Ph Ds. Money is not the only reward once the belly is full. Such people that I required, I got. At that time the dairy industry was in its infancy. Glaxo, Nestle, were there. My prestige was an inviting factor. The farmers don't mind managers being paid higher salaries. *Quite a few things work because of the 'work' you do.*"

"You developed a different Indian professional here at Anand, a kind of a different mindset. What are its distinctive features?" I ask. Kurien reels out a list:

- "The ethic of mastering one's own subject;

- Focus on others' needs, whenever you are supposed to serve;

- Internalisation of the externals one serves; as far as my work is concerned, I must take others' needs into account;

- Constructive iconoclasm towards bureaucracy;

- Clarity of mind about seemingly small elements that go to make up great endeavours. The devil is in the details."

The beauty of the Anand mindset is that we have seen it work when simultaneously many other cooperatives, institutions and organizations have sunk neck-deep in a sea of corruption, nepotism, infighting and shameless ego-bashing. Anand stands like a lotus in the swamp of human decadence.

DAIRY STRUCTURES GAIN STRENGTH

Former prime minister Lal Bahadur Shastri's invaluable legacy to India is the National Dairy Development Board (NDDB) created in 1965. Shastri asked Kurien how the Amul dairy thrived when cooperatives elsewhere, barring Ajarpura in his home state Uttar Pradesh, were unsuccessful. Kurien cited the reasons: Anand's proximity to the Bombay Milk Scheme and an excellent growing urban market; and the fact that milk producers were managing unions at village and district levels—they were the owners of Amul dairy; also they ran it by employing competent professionals.

In a DO (demi-official letter) to all his cabinet ministers, chief ministers and governors of all states, Shastri wrote: "Apart from the technical efficiency of Kaira Cooperative's processing units, the most striking achievements have been in the socio-economic field. If we can transplant the spirit of Anand in many other places, it will also result in rapidly transforming the socio-economic conditions of the rural areas, and our achieving the objective of a socialistic pattern of society. We have envisaged a large programme of setting up cooperative dairies during the Fourth

Plan and this will, no doubt, be based on the Anand Model." Shastri approved the formation of the NDDB. Its mandate was to replicate Anand all over India.It would be headed by Kurien. He wanted it to be headquartered in Delhi but Kurien convinced him that it should be situated in the farmers' habitat, away from baleful political and bureaucratic influences, and that it would make a visual impact on villagers when it grew. And it did make a great impact.

The dairy industry had four sectors: Modern private (like Polson's); traditional traders and middlemen; state government departmental projects, and cooperatives. The first three were opposed to the entry and development of the fourth sector for obvious reasons. Kurien, ever on the lookout for paths of growth, devised a plan whereby the milk and butter surpluses of Europe would be gifted as commodity aid to the NDDB. The latter would regulate its flow into the Indian market while protecting the local industry against any possible harm arising from the conversion of foreign aid into trade. You needed balancing facilities which would enable you to carry forward the winter production and secure the market. Procurement was no longer the problem. This was the objective and methodology of Operation Flood.

Kurien conceived and launched Operation Flood in 1970. The innovative operation has been instrumental in helping the farmers mould their own development, reaching milk to consumers in 700 towns and cities through a national milk grid, reducing seasonal price variations and simultaneously removing the middlemen and rendering the activity an economically viable proposition.

Phase I of Operation Flood was financed by the sale within India of skimmed milk powder and butter oil gifted by the European Economic Community (EEC) countries via the World Food Programme (WFP). As founder-chairman of the NDDB, Kurien finalised the plans and negotiated the details of EEC assistance. He looked after the administration of the scheme as founder-chairman of the erstwhile Indian Dairy Corporation (IDC), the project authority for Operation Flood.

During its first phase, the project aimed at linking India's 18 best milksheds with the milk markets of the four metropolitan cities of Delhi, Mumbai, Calcutta and Madras.

Phase II of the project, implemented during 1981-85, raised this to some 136 milksheds linked to over 290 urban markets. The seed capital raised from the sale of WFP/EEC gift products and World Bank loans had created, by the end of 1985, a self-sustaining system of 43,000 village cooperatives covering 4.25 million milk producers. Milk powder production went up from 22,000 tones in the pre-project year to 1,40,000 tones in 1989, thanks to dairies set up under Operation Flood. The EEC gifts, thus, helped to promote self reliance. Direct marketing of milk by producers' cooperatives increased by several million litres a day.

Phase III of Operation Flood (1985–1996) enabled dairy cooperatives to rapidly build up the basic infrastructure required to procure and market more and more milk daily. Facilities were created by the cooperatives to provide better veterinary services to their producer-members.

While the demand for milk was rising, the cattle population remained more or less static. If milk production had to be increased, the buffalo and our own good milk breeds of cattle had to be upgraded; nondescript cows had to be cross-bred with exotic species to increase their milk production, to make them more efficient converters of feed. With this objective in mind, intensive research and development in animal husbandry was given a thrust. Today, animal breeding is an integration of three major areas—artificial insemination and quantitative genetic techniques; embryo transfer; and embryo micro-engineering. Optimal genetic improvement can be achieved by making use of developments in each of these areas.

Understanding the significance of embryo transfer in India, NDDB established its main embryo transfer lab at the Sabarmati Ashram Gaushala near Ahmedabad. Embryo transfer in the Indian context is primarily a tool to create a nuclear germ plasm pool to supply future bulls to artificial insemination centres for production improvement in cattle and buffaloes. The techniques have enabled India to rapidly multiply the elite donors among the cross-breeds and buffaloes and to produce superior bulls from them in adequate numbers. Production of buffalo calves using non-surgical transfer was achieved successfully in India, for the first time in Asia. Through a wide network of research laboratories, the transfer of embryos has already moved from the laboratory to the village, where embryos have been transplanted into cows in the farmer's home by specially trained staff belonging to the cooperatives. The NDDB has to its credit some significant results:

- The enormous urban market stimulus has led to sustained production increases, raising per capita availability of milk to nearly 200 gm per day;

- The dependence on commercial imports of milk solids has been done away with;

- The dairy industry and its infrastructure have been modernised and expanded, activating a milk grid;

- Marketing has expanded to supply hygienic and fair-priced milk to some 3 crore consumers in 550 cities and towns;

- More than Rs 5000 crore flows back annually to the 10 lakh members of the dairy cooperatives;

- A nationwide network of multi-tier producers' cooperatives, democratic in structure and professionally managed, has come into existence. Millions of small producers participate in an economic enterprise and improve the quality of their life and environs;

- Dairy equipment manufacture has expanded to meet most of the industry's needs.

The past 35 years of the NDDB have been eventful, giving birth to India's modern dairy industry. It helped to create what has become a model for other developing countries and the international agencies that are concerned with dairy development.

Imagine every morning and evening, some nine million farmers carrying potfuls of milk to their cooperatives, milk that will travel from remote villages to towns and cities throughout India. Today, these farmers own some of the largest and most successful businesses in India.

Their infrastructure has returned a greater share of the consumer's rupee to the farmer. It has built markets, supplied inputs and created value-added processing and products. All this has happened because the farmers' productive capacity has been linked with professional management in cooperatives. One big lesson learnt is that farmers must be respected and trusted. They may not be educated, or even literate, but they possess common sense and even wisdom.

What led to Operation Flood's success? It is not simply the application of science and technology, or the creation of farmer-owned structures; it was all of that, combined with the orchestration of all policies and programmes that affect production, that helped reach the goal.

Cost reduction and technology management, modernisation of process and plant technology, interventions for productivity increase, frontier technologies like DNA vaccines and genetically-engineered bovine somatotropin, embryo transfer technology and in-vitro fertilisation of oocytes are under way to update the technology available to rural producers and so further improve their productivity and income.

The success of the milk cooperative movement under the aegis of NDDB has had unexpected results. The government has brought other primary commodities like edible oils, fruits and vegetables under the board's care. The cooperative umbrella has been extended to the growing of trees and even to salt farming.

Launched in 1979, the Oilseeds Growers' Cooperative Project now links over a lakh farmer-members spread over 5,000 oilseeds growers' cooperative societies in eight states. In order to establish a direct link between the producers and the consumers of oil, thus reducing the role of oil traders and oil exchanges, NDDB decided to enter the consumer pack market for edible oils through its Dhara brand of refined rapeseed and groundnut oil. Within a short span, Dhara has become the market leader in branded edible oil because of its tamper-proof packaging and high quality.

THE AWAKENED WARRIOR

We had no dearth of visionaries or leaders with noble dreams, strategists with political acumen, civil servants with administrative expertise, business managers with a touch of everything, but very few awakened warriors. Sardar Vallabhabhai Patel was an awakened warrior. He was a visionary, a strategist and a warrior who fought for integrating India. Rural renaissance was not a beautiful and poetic description of a vision to be delivered at a convocation address. It meant fighting with the pyramid of vested interests entrenched at every layer of the local to global political-financial technostructure, right from the middlemen at the grassroot level to wily competitors, from jealous bureaucrats to foreign donors,and technical aid-givers. Kurien, the awakened warrior, fought to bring prosperity and dignity to the milkmen of India. Let us view some incidents in Kurien's pilgrimage of liberating the cowherds, their cows and buffaloes, to deliver what they were capable of delivering, and earn what they were entitled to earn and enjoy.

THE STRATEGIC MAP

Kurien wanted to secure exclusive rights to supply milk to the Bombay Milk Scheme (BMS) after a second plate pasteurizer, along with refrigerating equipment, was installed. This meant challenging Polson's monopoly. Kurien drafted his plans with meticulous care.

The minister, the late Dinkarrao Desai, called a meeting of representatives of Kaira, Polson, and D N Khurodi, the Bombay Milk Commissioner who was never favourably disposed towards the cooperative from Gujarat. The difficulty was that both Kaira cooperative and Polson could vary the price and divert the milk from Kaira depending upon the seasonal fluctuations in demand. Kurien suggested that the government should demarcate areas for milk collection for both suppliers. The minister was pleased with the suggestion. At once, Kurien produced his winning card, a map with the selected areas neatly marked. Dinkarrao closed the subject saying it was his government's policy to support the cooperatives and the division was fair.

Look at how Kurien mapped the strategy. Its elements are: First, identifying Polson's monopoly on supply as the bottleneck. Second, to use the political contact of Tribhuvandas to approach Dinkarrao. Third, to contain Khurodi. Fourth, to know that the government, even if committed to supporting the cooperatives, would need a convincing case. Fifth, the minister would like to play it fair. Sixth, from emotional arguments, it would be profitable to bring the discussion to facts, and for that a map with markings would be a good guide—it would be a master card. Finally, the immaculate timing of the presentation of the map. See the preparation, the sequenced moves, and adroit conveyance. *The conceptual mapping of the strategy is employed to annex the territory from a competitor through use of a strategic map. The warrior whisked away the territory.*

DEMONSTRATION IMPACT

Unicef had been distributing free milk powder in underdeveloped nations for many years. Its experience was that the recipient country's dependence does not diminish. Unicef therefore felt it was necessary to develop the local dairy industry. It offered a donation to the Bombay government (as it was then known), which would include milk drying equipment worth Rs 8 lakh, in return for which the government would pledge to distribute, through the BMS and Kaira Cooperative, Rs 12 lakh worth of free milk to undernourished children in Kaira.

The offer was conveyed to Kurien whose instant reaction was negative, looking to the cost of distribution. However, he put the proposal to the Kaira board. Kurien accepted the farmers' collective wisdom that rejecting the proposal would mean denying free milk to the cooperative members' own children. Unicef's regional director for Asia Sam Keeny knew that the terms were tough.

The Bombay government wasn't prepared to make good the financial burden. Milk conservation coordinators Donald Sabin and T G Davies were in charge of the project. They were supported by a New Zealander, Ronald Hill, a dairy engineer in Unicef's milk conservation program. In the discussions Khurodi, the Bombay milk commissioner, was trivialising the very idea of spray drying buffalo milk at Anand. Unicef representatives were, however, impressed with Dalaya's technical competence, and Kurien they thought to be "highly articulate and possessed of great courage in defense of his cause. *He brought the drive and ambition of an industrial tycoon to the management of a society of small peasant milk producers.*"

The battle between Khurodi and Kurien was about whether or not buffalo milk could be spray dried. It was fought with supporting evidence from experts in New Zealand and England. Cow's milk is easier to dry because of the low fat content. The technical issues were contentious, centred on the required equipment like a pasteurizer, refrigeration and milk drying plants, condensing plant, mojjonier tester, infrared dryer, etc. Kurien voiced his displeasure vehemently, saying, "We asked for a powder plant, we can prove it to you that buffalo milk can be spray dried." The Unicef team visited Anand. The visual impact of the Anand cowsheds was uninspiring. Hill, Davies and Sabin had to take a leap of faith in trusting the competence of the Anand duo, Dalaya and Kurien. They took the visitors to the backyard of the creamery to show a device they had constructed, consisting principally of a spray paint gun and an air-heater. Although most of the powder went up the exhaust chimney, it proved their point that buffalo milk could be spray dried.

Subsequently, Dalaya found out that L&T had a small experimental spray drying plant. Kurien called Axel Peterson of L&T, who told him that the plant had already been sold to Teddington Chemicals at Andheri. Undaunted, Kurien organized a trial. Khurodi, however, wouldn't even give them the milk they needed for the trial, saying "Get it yourselves". A can of skimmed buffalo milk was called for from Anand. Khurodi was asked to pour the milk. Lo and behold, the first snowy flakes of spray dried buffalo milk drifted down into the glass receiving chamber. Ron Hill took photographs to record that memorable moment. Unicef realized that Kurien and Dalaya were tremendously knowledgeable, were in command of the situation, knew exactly what they wanted and why, and could not be forced into any decision against their will.

Nonetheless, back home, Sabin and Hill could not get the engineering division at Paris to agree to send a Danish Niro plant; instead, they suggested a Dutch Volma plant. Dalaya had sound reasons for his choice. The Niro atomizer was the only spray dryer whose specifications were suitable for drying buffalo milk. And L&T, who had the agency for the Niro plant, would be able to service it through their Mumbai branch. Unicef cabled its displeasure:

UNICEF NOT ACCUSTOMED TO BEING TOLD WHAT PLANT IT SHOULD GIVE STOP.

Kurien replied:

KAIRA UNION NOT ACCUSTOMED TO BEING TOLD WHAT IT SHOULD HAVE STOP CABLE COMPLIANCE STOP

Kaira Cooperative got the Niro plant.

However, it should be noted that Kurien did not send off this missive before consulting H M Patel, who was the principal finance secretary in the Indian government. Patel had approved his action.

In this incident, we see a clear setting of goal: Getting a spray drying machine for preserving buffalo milk, thus putting to productive use the surplus generated by seasonal fluctuations. A tactical fight was with a known opponent, Khurodi, who had expert advice from abroad. But as they say, there are as many opinions as there are experts. Kurien's evidence would have been nullified by Khurodi's. Dalaya and Kurien knew this. They also knew that demonstration convinces. The Unicef officials would be won over only by practical proof. The final matching cable response was to prove to Unicef that the customer too was competent. See the language: 'cable compliance'. You require guts to say that and Kurien has guts in plenty. The warrior procured the material.

LOGISTICS VICTORY

At the cooperative's proposed new dairy, butter would be made from fresh cream extracted at the plant from the day's collection of milk. Consequently, it would retain the freshness of taste and the aroma that characterise fresh sweet cream. The foundation stone was laid by Dr Rajendra Prasad, the president of India, on November 15, 1954. Almost a year later, prime minister Jawaharlal Nehru would be invited to inaugurate the dairy on October 31, the birth anniversary of Sardar Patel, patron of Kaira Cooperative, who had died in 1950. As always there were delays, accidents at the building site and the usual uncertainties of machines arriving on time and so on. Undertaking to build a dairy in eleven months was a mammoth task. Kurien's consumption of cigarettes went up proportionate to the increasing levels of anxiety.

The order for boilers was placed with J N Marshall & Co, who were importing them from the reputed Scottish firm Cochran's. Kurien soon realised that the boilers would arrive in Mumbai harbour about 25 days before the inauguration. The harbour was always congested and the situation was made worse by a strike in the port. Ships had to wait for days to dock. Such a desperate situation called for an extraordinary remedy, and Kurien drew on his credit with Morarji Desai through Maniben Patel. Morarji requested L T Gholap, the ICS chairman of Bombay Port Trust (BPT), to help Kurien. Not even for the chief minister could Gholap break the rules; only the Port Trust could make an exception. Gholap called an emergency meeting of the BPT board and it was decided to grant Kurien's request. The ship jumped queue, offloaded only the two boilers and returned to its former place. Kurien had also spoken to his friend, the chief commercial manager of Western Railway, to keep four wagons ready for transporting the boilers straight to Anand from the dockyards. A day before the arrival of Nehru the first batch of powdered milk came off the production line. It was the first plant in India to make spray dried milk powder, and probably the first anywhere in the world to make it from buffalo milk. Before he left, Nehru embraced Kurien, saying: "I am glad there are people like you in this country to do the things that you have done."

Of course, there were many doubters. Khurodi had taken a bet with Kurien that this would be impossible to achieve, i.e. building a dairy in eleven months. See the determination, more so the anticipation of bottlenecks, appreciation of the connectivity of different organizations (the port, the railways, etc.), the nodal points, and skillful use of the appropriate contacts to work through the quagmire of logistics. The flow charts for smooth movement were in Kurien's mind. In the combat, tt was a victory for management of logistics. The warrior ensured that his supplies were not cut off.

THE NATIVE BULL FIGHTS

The government urged Amul to make condensed milk since there was a pressing need to conserve foreign exchange. In 1954-55 alone $1.5 lakh worth of condensed milk had been imported, 60 per cent of which was used by the armed forces. Manubhai Shah, minister for commerce, who was committed to the development of Indian industry, broached the subject. Kurien was initially not keen to make condensed milk on the ground that the demand existed only because of acquired food habits and tastes. He would rather concentrate on making cheese.

Nestle, the Swiss MNC, had approached the government for permission to set up a plant to manufacture condensed milk. Manubhai requested Kurien to go to Switzerland, which he did. Towards the conclusion of negotiations Kurien said, "You will, of course, replace your experts with Indian personnel, who will be trained by you to run the factory." The Swiss demurred. One of them exclaimed, "Condensed milk is a delicate product, difficult to manufacture. We cannot leave it to natives." The native from Anand exploded. Thumping the table, Kurien roared, "Are you suggesting to me that in my country there is no one who can do such things, including managing your damn company?" Naturally, negotiations broke off. Kurien returned determined to teach Nestle a lesson. The self-respect of a proud Indian _dudhwala_—as he likes to call himself—was deeply hurt. The swaggerer could not swallow the insult.

By now Kurien had acquired the commercial acumen of the Gujaratis. His latest survey of the market had shown that he could increase the purchase price of milk by say 20 per cent, and earn more profits as compared to butter because there was demand for the product. This was the business reason for changing his earlier unwillingness to make condensed milk. It took two years for Dalaya to make condensed milk out of buffalo milk. Buffalo milk has a higher lactose (sugar) content than cow's milk. When mixed with cane sugar (sucrose), it would form over-large crystals, giving the condensed milk a disagreeable sandy texture. But Dalaya's persistence paid off.

161

After successful trials Kurien took a tin of his new product to Manubhai with a request to curtail imports. The move affected Nestle and the MNC climbed down. It was now ready to put up a plant on terms stipulated by the government. The team from Switzerland included the gentleman who had offended our native. Manubhai asked the delegates to visit Anand, and Kurien got the opportunity to hit back. He gave them a cold reception and sent them at once to see the Amul dairy. After the tour, the Swiss returned to Kurien's office. He did not invite them to sit. Can you believe he made them stand like chastened schoolboys? With tight lips and a curt gaze, he questioned the offender: "Well, Mr Kreber, what do you think of the natives now?" Kreber, his hat in hand, submitted an unqualified apology. The chapter was closed, the relationship restored. Nestle later set up a plant at Moga in Punjab.

Amul's condensed milk cans reached army barracks. It was the first time in the world that buffalo milk had been used to make condensed milk. With Dalaya's technical expertise, the Indian buffalo had risen to a level of performance equal to that of its sister the cow. This elevation was due to the single-minded commitment of the duo of Dalaya and Kurien. The Swiss attitude turned the bull wild. It was an insult to Indian intelligence. An Angry Kurien took on the giant and mauled him.

You don't have to be subservient even if your need is greater than the global MNC's. You must garner the courage to go on your own, and you must innovate indigenously. What is inspiring is that Kurien did not indulge in licking his wounds, nor did he wallow in self-pity. He fought with his two horns, the technical brilliance of Dalaya and his own high self-esteem. A bull is a fighter, he saved his buffalo. A bull belongs to the warrior family. Our warrior won.

DEFIANT DONEE

In 1968 the EEC had a surplus stock of 306,000 MT of butter and butter oil. Skimmed milk powder was even being fed to European calves, causing them to suffer from an excess of protein. Attempts were also made to sell the surplus at less than production cost to Eastern Europe. Stored butter became rancid and unfeedable even to cattle. Kurien proposed that the surplus European milk products be gifted to India under the World Food Programme. Called a 'billion-litre' idea by one commentator, the proposal was accepted by Dr Adekke Boerma, the visionary and compassionate director general of the Food and Agriculture Organization (FAO). During a conference of department heads, the Pakistani representative Nazir Ahmed, wanting to have the last word, asked, "All the same, how can we be sure that your project is foolproof?" Kurien would not let pass such an opportunity for drama and mischief. With a stony face like a Buddha, all eyes gathered on him, he said, "I thought I had done my best to make it foolproof." Took a breath, shrugged his shoulders and added, "But I see that I have failed." Nazir was silenced.

The battle against the delivery of unusable commodities had raged between 1970 and 1973, the government's protests and pleas were ignored. The transmitting agency WFP's failure to maintain quality and the continuous inflow of food aid under Operation Flood also lengthened the duration of the first phase itself to eleven years. The delay caused a reduction in investments in a series of technical programmes and the conduct of the entire sequence of Operation Flood had become a nightmare. Kurien lost his patience. While addressing the economic committee of the 20th International Dairy Congress held in Paris in June 1978, Kurien castigated them, "When we complained, we were in effect told that beggars could not be choosers. And, finally, when I had to intervene in the matter, I simply had to reject the commodities in question, and declare that India was not a dumping ground for commodities unfit for human consumption. Surely, it should not have been necessary for me to say that?"

"The fact of the matter is that the agencies are often much more closely identified with the donors than they are with the recipients. They hold out their hands to the donors and accept whatever crumbs may fall from the table, instead of representing the recipients and insisting that moral commitments be adhered to. We are not supplicants. We are not beggars. And, I submit, the donors are not doing us any favour." Ruth Heredia, in her most readable book *The Amul Story of India,* says, "Never before had a delegate from a developing country spoken quite so frankly in that forum. The facts were incontrovertible. But he had to accept as an inevitable consequence the envy and malevolence of many."

Kurien fought with institutions manned by different nationalities and in a foreign land. The issue was the smooth flow of surplus butter and other food aid. Wherever there was a bottleneck, Kurien rushed in to remove, circumvent, or demolish it. What Kurien did was to demolish psychological fortifications with an abundant supply of facts. He first disarmed the *phoren* adversaries in their favourite obsession of playing with facts, information, data. When they became naked, the focus shifted to intentions, purpose and trust, and then his tongue waxed eloquent. Kurien was itching to take on the giants. It was a battle of wits and our warrior won it hands down.

An awakened warrior lives with courage, compassion and discipline. Kurien's courage is evident in all these episodes. His compassion for the Kaira farmers is unbounded, as it is for the underestimated buffalo. His disciplined thinking and authentic focusing help him channel his energies and wage dogged fights in pursuit of the noble cause he has willy-nilly got stuck with. As the wily warrior-sorcerer Don Juan said, "*The basic difference between an ordinary man and a warrior is that a warrior takes everything as a challenge, while an ordinary man takes everything as either a blessing or a curse.*" As a protector, the warrior's purpose is always outside of the self; so it was with Kurien. He was protective of farmers and Anand's potential. Kurien is undoubtedly an awakened warrior.

THE MIRACLE *DUDHWALA*

Kurien networked successfully at three levels. He used the protective umbrella provided by Congress leaders, starting with Sardar Vallabhabhai Patel, to exploit political contacts. To name a few, Jawaharlal Nehru, Dr Rajendra Prasad, Lalbahadur Shastri, Jivraj Mehta, Manubhai Shah, Indira Gandhi and Morarji Desai. Tribhuvandas was of great help in this political theatre. Secondly, he cultivated civil service contacts whether cabinet secretary Vishnu Sahai, industries secretary B P Patel, joint secretary K B Damle, agriculture secretary D D Sathe, finance secretary H M Patel, joint secretary K B Lal, cabinet secretary B Sivaraman, BPT chairman L T Gholap, or foreign experts like Donald Sabin, Ronald Hill, T G Davies of Unicef, Dr Adekke Boerma of FAO, Prof Michael Halse and many others. Kurien also networked with institution officials like Dr S C Roy, A K Roy Choudhari, G M Jhola, Dr R D Aneja, Dr Amrita Patel and Prof Tushar Shah, belonging to NDDB, IRMA, IDA and GCMMF. Kurien uses his vast network of contacts at all these levels and some 15-odd institutions and committees of which he is chairman or a member.

Kurien has not used these contacts for personal work. He has used them to protect and further the interests of farmers, cooperatives, dairy development and India. These contacts interact vertically and horizontally at different levels. They are spread far and wide within India and throughout the world. Kurien has a dozen doctorates to his credit. He was awarded the Padma Vibhushan in 1999. He received the Ramon Magsaysay Award for community leadership in 1963, the World Food Prize in 1989 and was named International Person of the Year by the World Dairy Expo, Wisconsin, USA in 1993, in addition to some 30 other awards. Kurien used keynote or convocation addresses for sharing his dreams on milk and related products, dairy and rural development, foreign aid and third world issues, the role of professional managers and women in societal change, and the marriage between professionalisation and farmers' wisdom. Kurien says, "*We must build on the resources represented by our young professionals and by our nation's farmers. Without their involvement, we cannot succeed. With their involvement, we cannot fail.*"

The speeches are flooded with facts, data, convincing arguments and pearls of wisdom. There is a fervent appeal to one's conscience. Kurien's mastery of macro-level issues and their impact on micro-level cooperative institutions is breathtaking. His book tells the inspiring story of the pursuit of his dream. Norman E Borlaug, 1970 Nobel Peace Prize Laureate, says in his foreword: "I consider Verghese Kurien to be one of the world's great agricultural leaders of this century. This collection of his speeches, so aptly entitled *An Unfinished Dream*, can help to light the way for those who must carry on the battle to ensure greater food security, prosperity, and peace to the world. I am honoured to commend this book to those future hunger fighters." The volume is a priceless addition to our home-grown management literature.

Among many other serendipitous encounters was that with cabinet secretary Vishnu Sahai when he visited Anand with agriculture minister K M Munshi. Realizing that Kurien was a metallurgy engineer and not a dairy engineer, Sahai arranged a scholarship for him along with practical experience in New Zealand. Kurien suspected that the products the New Zealanders were sending to India were adulterated. He collected information with the help of a friendly local driver and effectively stopped the practice. Michael Halse, a Harvard-trained Englishman, was a brilliant copywriter and adman working at the Indian Institute of Management, Ahmedabad (IIM-A) in the late 1970s. Kurien had met him through his cousin Ravi Mathai (son of John Mathai), director of IIM-A. Halse coined the winning expression, Operation Flood, for Kurien's billion-litre idea of using free surplus dairy products of the EEC.

I point out, "Although you came up against opponents like Khurodi, Polson, or Desai, you also met some helpful souls."

Kurien replies: "Of course, many. The hand of providence is certainly evident. Jagjivan Ram wanted a private dairy to be built in his constituency. I told him 'no'. I am here to build cooperative dairies. I didn't give the normal bureaucratic reply—I'll put up a note, etc. He ordered my transfer. Then I went to see Indira Gandhi. V Ramchandran, secretary in the Prime Minister's Office, said tell me about it. He put up a note. Within an hour, Mrs Gandhi's reply came: 'Don't touch him'."

Kurien is multi-skilled. He has networking and drafting skills, and is highly articulate. He makes high-powered presentations and more, he is a born tease with proclivities to play-act if you rub him the wrong way. I ask, "Where did you learn these skills?" This was his power-point reply:

- *Where you have the will you will have the skills;*
- *Study, search, practice, application;*
- *Healthy irreverence;*
- *Look for the kink in the thing, be curious.*

I argue, "But how can you change the mindset, transform the will?"

Kurien says, "The original coding of cast iron, heredity, cannot be forged beyond a point. Metallurgical treatment doesn't change that to stretch beyond a point, as the foundry men say. My thesis is that heredity is like cast iron. There would be some bit of transformation." Kurien believes in the Malayalee poet Kumaran Asan's saying, 'One Malayalee is good, two are bad and three are worse.' Change the laws or else they themselves will change you. *Our laws have made our mindset negative, dishonest, unproductive, obstructionist and indisciplined.* Kurien says we must liberate our resources. Economic liberalisation is aimed at liberating our material resources. We need to liberate our mental resources, viz. the mindset, from our anti-national and anti-work ethic labour laws.

The local *dudhwala* (milkman) is a familiar figure in Indian folklore and the current reality. The witty joint secretary K B Lall used to affectionately address Kurien as '*makhanwala*.' Kurien enjoyed these pet names. In fact, he has become a '*cooperative dudhwala*' who maintained astounding delivery schedules in the most difficult circumstances. One such occasion arose when the India-Pakistan conflict began in April 1965, escalating into a full-scale war in September that year. Kurien was summoned to Delhi in October. He met B Sivaraman, agriculture secretary, who was closeted with a group of defense services bosses. They came straight to the point—2650 MT of whole milk powder to be supplied on an emergency footing by March 31, 1966. Could Amul undertake the task?

169

Kurien made some quick mental calculations and agreed on the spot. The defenders of the nation looking for help from the native *dudhwala*! He was risking his and Amul's reputation. One of the generals, not knowing Kurien, expressed doubt that he would be able to honour his commitment. Before Kurien could open his mouth, Sivaraman said, "Gentlemen, this ministry has the highest regard for Kurien's word. When he says something will be done, we assume that it will." Sivaraman then offered Kurien any financial assistance he needed. Kurien got the opportunity to give an apt reply. "Sir, I thought you said there was an emergency. If Kaira Cooperative were to use a national emergency to squeeze money out of the government, it would be dishonoured." And he left the room gracefully.

From Delhi, he went directly to Ahmedabad and met the state minister for agriculture and cooperatives, Utsavbhai Shah. For supplying that quantity of milk powder to meet the emergency, he had taken into account powder manufactured at government-owned plants at Rajkot and Mehasana, in addition to Amul. He needed the minister's permission. Without hesitation, Utsavbhai gave it. Our logistics master, and his charged rapid action forces, burnt the midnight oil to honour the word given to the nation. It was a miracle, unbelievable! Dr Raghunath Mashelkar, director general of the Council of Scientific & Industrial Research, says, "Amongst the management leaders in India, Kurien is not only an icon, he is a miracle." With monomaniacal focus, Kurien the *miracle dudhwala* did his bit for the nation, and in style, bravo!

Raghunath Mashelkar

"Only protected usable knowledge can create wealth."

The Council of Scientific & Industrial Research (CSIR) is a lumbering scientific giant, with 40-odd laboratories and 80 field centres engaged in fundamental and applied research in the whole gamut of science and technology. With his 'patent, publish, prosper' motto etched in the mindset of 10,000 highly qualified scientific and technical personnel, director general Dr Raghunath Mashelkar (57), a Fellow of the Royal Society, has used his alchemical leadership to rejuvenate Indian science and create wealth from usable knowledge.

aghunath mashelkar the outstanding polymer scientist is an equally outstanding business manager. As CEO of CSIR, he has made India's laid-back laboratories commercially relevant. He has brought researchout of its ivory tower to participate in the wealth-creating process of the nation.

TOWER OF PERFORMANCE

Mashelkar's tower of performance is visible from Kashmir to Kanyakumari in the otherwise dusty ethos prevalent in government institutes around the country. Let us glance at the salient features of his voluminous credentials:

Mashelkar has made original contributions in diverse areas, from polymer science to engineering. His contributions cover scientific investigations on the modelling of industrial polymerisation reactors, molecular and convective diffusion phenomena in polymeric media, transport phenomena in swelling, superswelling and shrinking polymers and engineering analysis of non-Newtonian flows. The 220 research publications, 18 books and 24 patents to his credit show his intellectual sweep. Mashelkar does not forget to mention the contribution made by his co-authors.

He has contributed to industrial research with individual efforts on modelling simulation in the polymer and chemical industry and through the polymer engineering group at the National Chemical Laboratory (NCL), Pune.

In 1989 NCL did not own a single US patent, whereas up to March 1999 it was in the vanguard of filing patents amongst the 350 filed by CSIR, as against 95 in 1995. Funds spent on business-driven research grew from Rs 2,250 crore in 1993-94 to Rs 4,000 crore in 1998-99. CSIR laboratories earned Rs 125 crore from industry. Foreign earnings increased to $4 lakh in March 1999 from $1.8 lakh in 1995. The quantitative change becomes obvious with such figures, but they do not tell the full story of the qualitative process change.

When Mashelkar rescued _haldi_ (turmeric) from Western biopirates and got the patent, he became a popular scientist whose achievements led to tangible results. His leadership of the patent literacy movement has heightened the awareness of the scientific community toward patent-worthy innovations.

Mashelkar took over as director general in 1995. His performance index shoots up when you see the _mindset change_ he has wrought in CSIR. He made research user-friendly with economic benefits. This is path-breaking in the prevailing thicket of gloom and cynicism.

Mashelkar's tally of awards, honours and directorships numbers over 75. Three merit special mention. He was awarded the _Padmashri_ in 1991 for his significant contributions in the field of polymer science and engineering. In 1998, he was made a Fellow of the Royal Society (FRS), London, a rare distinction. And the same year, he was given the prestigious JRD Tata award for corporate leadership, which recognizes the business orientation that he imparted to CSIR. These three are signals on the terrace of his tower of performance. How did Mashelkar become such a luminary?

THE MOTHERING OF EDUCATION

"In what ways do you think your family background was special in helping you to become the person you are?" I ask. Mashelkar says, "Hardship at a young age taught me a few lessons. One of these was to *never give up*. The second was to *concentrate on 'what I have' rather that 'what I don't have'*. Poverty is not an abstraction or a statistic for me. I walked barefoot till I was 12."

Having lost his father at the age of six, Mashelkar worked on a casual basis in shops, providing sundry help. His barely literate mother, Anjanitai Mashelkar, brought up her son with great courage and determination. The hunger for education was planted in him by her. She drove Mashelkar forward at decisive moments in his life, when he could have easily succumbed to the overwhelming odds and given up.

Mashelkar and his mother lived in a one-room tenement in a chawl in Deshmukh Galli, Khetwadi, in Mumbai's Girgaum area. Young Mashelkar was a consistent topper in his Marathi-medium school. When he needed Rs 21 as entrance fee to enter the senior school, Anjanitai borrowed it from a friend who, like her, was doing odd jobs in nearby households. Mashelkar recalls, "When we had weekly tests in school on Saturdays, we had to carry our own answer paper, which cost three paise. One had to always wonder where that money would come from the next week." For this reason, he almost gave up his studies at the eleventh standard. Just then the Gomanthak Maratha Samaj came to his assistance with a modest scholarship.

Unable to have either privacy or space in the chawl, Mashelkar studied for his Secondary School Certificate (SSC) examination under the streetlights at Chowpatty, just as Bal Gangadhar Tilak had done.

His excellent grades led well-wishers to offer him the Rs 200 needed for college admission. He was also selected by the Sir Dorab Tata Trust for their prestigious scholarship. When he finished his bachelors in chemistry with flying colours and wanted to take up a job to ease the financial situation at home, his mother asked him a simple question: "What is the next degree in this subject?" Mashelkar thus started and completed one of the fastest ever doctorates in chemical engineering.

After his Ph D, his mother encouraged him to go abroad and excel in his chosen field. There followed an illustrious career at the University of Salford, UK, where he established a first-rate group in polymer engineering and carried out pioneering work in the field. The desire to climb the educational ladder was nursed by the barely literate Anjanitai. He says, "I owe it all to the supreme sacrifice and vision of my mother who, by doing odd jobs, nurtured me and motivated me to keep studying." Mashelkar recalls that when someone asked his mother why she wanted her son to get educated, she simply said, "If he had not been educated, he would have been forced to do menial jobs, like I was. I did not want that to happen."

GURUS MOULD

Mashelkar's mother motivated him for higher and higher studies. But surely, he must have met research guides on the way? He identifies them. "First of all my great *guru*, Prof M M Sharma. When I joined him, we worked on zero budget. There was an abject poverty of equipment. To survive, we had to think. He showed me the importance of idea-based research, and continues to guide and inspire me. Another eminent chemical engineering scientist, Prof R Kumar, has had a great influence on my thinking. Whatever I was doing, he would always ask 'What is new? What is different? What is said for the first time?' He kept a very high emphasis on innovation and creativity of the highest order.

"Prof C N R Rao, who to me is the most celebrated scientist in India, has been my mentor and had a great influence on me. He is so demanding, on both himself and others! To satisfy him is very difficult. The best you can get from him is 'not bad'! He continues to drive me to do my best. Dr B D Tilak, who brought me to NCL in 1976, continues to give me support and encouragement even today. Dr L K Doraiswamy, another doyen of Indian chemical engineering, encouraged me enthusiastically and relentlessly in the early years. Finally, Art Metzner of the University of Delaware, USA and the late Gianni Astarita of the University of Naples have also had a great deal of influence on my strategies in research."

When I grouped the input of these *gurus*, I found three clusters shaping Mashelkar's thinking:

- Creativity and innovation (Sharma and Kumar);

- Demand and supply—give encouragement, demand results (Rao, Tilak and Doraiswamy);

- Strategic research (Metzner and Astarita).

Based on an excellent academic foundation, Mashelkar's visionary advance was fuelled by these creative, demanding and strategic inputs. The fusion led him to make innovative forays at NCL and CSIR.

THE PATENT PILGRIM

During his stewardship of NCL from 1989 to 1995, Mashelkar launched his campaign to globalise Indian research and development (R&D). Instead of only producing a large mass of quality scientific papers (approximately 250), Mashelkar convinced his colleagues that to stake its claim in international knowledge markets, NCL must have patents. The global knowledge peddlers do not pay as much attention to pure research as they do to patented research. Although the output in terms of scientific rigour was excellent, its utility in dollar terms remained zero without US patents. Initially it was hard to convince the scientists, as research papers bring peer recognition. Mashelkar, however, finally succeeded in changing the mindset at NCL by bringing in the concept of patentable papers—novel, non-obvious and commercially exploitable.

I ask, "We consider ourselves intellectuals. We had the likes of Dr Homi Bhabha and Dr Vikram Sarabhai, and we still have a galaxy of renowned scientists like Dr Jayant Naralikar, Dr Abdul Kalam and Dr Swaminathan. These men have done yeoman service to the cause of their domain disciplines and respective fields. Where did we lose out?" Mashelkar replies: "Yes, these three are jewels of Indian science, and there are some more. However, India lost out on not having a strong intellectual property culture. *Only protected usable knowledge can create wealth.* We changed the value system at NCL from '*patent or perish*' to '*patent, publish and prosper*'. It paid rich dividends. It has now become a catch phrase at CSIR."

It is not the catchy phrase that is catching the imagination of knowledge developers. It is the profundity with which Mashelkar articulates, "There is a deep philosophical divide on the issue of knowledge capital that we have to deal with. The existing intellectual property rights (IPR) systems are oriented around the concept of private ownership and individual invention. They are at odds with indigenous cultures, which emphasise collective creation and ownership of knowledge. There is a concern that IPR systems encourage the appropriation of traditional knowledge for commercial use without the fair sharing of benefits, or that they violate indigenous cultural precepts by encouraging the commoditisation of such knowledge."

Mashelkar advises his colleagues to scan the patent databases before starting a research project, lest they waste time in reinventing the wheel. A few specialists have been trained to write patents in acceptable legal terminology, which reveals little so as not to allow others to easily bypass your patents. Mashelkar is spearheading the patent literacy movement with singleminded devotion, and has managed to sensitise law makers about the need to modernise the antiquated Indian Patent Rights Act. On January 15, 1999 prime minister Atal Behari Vajpayee acknowledged the success of Mashelkar's campaign. "I compliment CSIR for creating an intellectual climate supportive of the early passage of the bill to amend the Patents Act," he said.

What Mashelkar said while delivering the Sir Purshotamdas Thakurdas memorial lecture, 1999 on 'The resurgence of innovative India: The challenge and the strategy' at the Indian Institute of Bankers, Mumbai conveys the importance of Intellectual Property Rights (IPR) and its impact on our economic progress in a globalised world:

Incorporating strong systems on the generation of IPR, its capture, documentation, valuation, protection and exploitation will need a massive thrust in India now. The issue of patents, in particular, has created a national interest and debate of great dimensions. We are behind the rest of the world in patents, both quantitatively and qualitatively, partly because of our emphasis on imitative research and partly because of lack of awareness of the power of IPR in assuming a predominant position among institutions and enterprises. We need to move and move with speed. A number of patent training institutes will have to be set up. China has already set up 5000 patent training institutes.

Skills in filing, reading and exploiting patents will be most crucial in the years to come; but our ability to read or write patents is very poor. Neither can we properly protect our inventions, nor can we understand the implications of the patents granted to our competitors. Our graduates coming out of engineering and technology streams have no idea about IPR, and yet it is these young people who will have to fight these emerging wars in the knowledge markets. Judicious management of patent information will require well-structured functioning of information creating centres, information documenters and retrievers, information users, IPR specialists and information technology experts.

The industrial property systems were set up centuries ago for inanimate objects, and that too in formal systems of innovation. A great challenge is now emerging to look at the systems that will deal with animate objects (such as plants and animals) and with informal systems innovation (such as those by grassroot innovators like farmers, artisans, tribes, fishermen and so on).

The standard intellectual property system will certainly not suit innovators and their innovations. We need innovation in the intellectual property system itself. Shorter duration patents for smaller innovations, including specific improvements in traditional knowledge, need to be conceived.

> They will involve a simple registration-cum-petty patent system where the inventive threshhold would be lower but even a small improvement in material, process, product or use could be protected at much lower costs and for a shorter duration. This will give a boost to the creative capabilities or otherwise deprived innovators. We in India will have to develop our own models for this.

Mashelkar is imploring scientists and the government to take patent rights seriously lest India lose a golden opportunity to prosper in the 21st century. The patents movement is a pilgrimage into our undocumented ancient wisdom and healing sciences (some even believe that space and science technologies lie hidden in our myths). Mashelkar is truly a _patent pilgrim_ on this treasure hunt.

TURMERIC VICTORY

Mashelkar's 'patent, publish, prosper' drive and its turmeric patent victory gave CSIR a massive boost. How does Mashelkar evaluate this victory? He says, "Of course, it was a matter of great pride for us all. This was the first time that from the third world there was a challenge thrown to the United States patents and trademark office, on a patent given on the traditional knowledge of India. After all, the use of turmeric to heal wounds has been known here for centuries.

"Let me re-emphasise that it was not a victory of India over the United States. It was the victory of a system. Secondly, the importance of documenting the traditional knowledge base became very clear during this battle. I had even got some of the Sanskrit texts translated into English, and this was admitted as evidence. It broke the myth that India was quite helpless in defending its right over its traditional knowledge. People got their confidence back. In fact, we are now preparing to fight the battle on the *basmati* patent, and the experience and confidence gained in the turmeric battle has been of enormous help in preparing for it."

What was the trigger? I ask. Mashelkar replies: "I got sensitised. During my stint at NCL, I was staying in their bungalow in Pune. I, my wife, mother and son were sitting on the terrace. Suddenly a bird came and fell on the floor. He was hurt, one of his wings was cut. My mother quickly brought *haldi* (turmeric) powder and applied it to the wound. It didn't work. The bird died and we buried him. Later, when the turmeric patent issue came up, I said to myself, 'What is this? My mother knew *haldi* has healing attributes, her mother knew it and her mother before her, etc. That triggered me off."

Mashelkar continues: "I called my colleagues. We had plenty of information, we decided to collect more and collate it. I didn't know Sanskrit but we got some old texts translated into English and pulled out references from history. This kind of information is acceptable. The researchers came back with a lot of information which our patent manager examined. He said 'The evidence is convincing'. I said 'Make it clinching', and I announced, 'We are going to challenge them'. I had motivated colleagues, they were equally charged. We had to coordinate between our ministries of agriculture, environment and external affairs to launch our offensive in the US. We got our act together and approached the US patents and trademark office. We articulated our case carefully, legally and sensitively." I probe further. "What was the determining factor for your success?" Says Mashelkar: "We jampacked our claim with evidence."

Thorough preparation is the key. A case studded with data, figures and facts sequenced in logical format led to success. The devil is in the details; you cannot ignore him. Glib talk won't help, you need to present cold facts in a lucid style in the language of the receiver. Marshalling evidence is an art, it is the preserve of expert lawyers. CSIR managers seem to possess it in good enough measure.

THE VISIONARY CEO

A strong intellectual property rights culture pervades the corridors of Anusandhan Bhavan at Rafi Marg, New Delhi, where the CSIR is headquartered. Since Mashelkar took over in 1995, the 'Team CSIR' spirit has been made research and business-oriented. This _esprit de corps_ was developed by Mashelkar because he had a clear vision of what CSIR could be made to achieve.

In his first interview to _The Economic Times_, Mashelkar stated his goal: "To create CSIR Incorporated by playing the role of a chief executive officer (CEO)." Although he is a scientist, he went about it like a professional business executive, systematically putting in place the architecture of 'Vision 2001 and Strategy'. The white paper, prepared in full consultation with the entire CSIR family, set the organization goals, measurable targets and a road map to reach the vision. Mashelkar involved the 40-odd directors of the laboratories, representing their 10,000-strong scientific community, in preparing the road map for the exciting journey in the new globalised environment. Says Mashelkar, "I asked them to take the proposal to the labs, churn it in their own way and come back with the feedback. I wanted them to feel that Vision 2001 is not my brainchild. It is theirs, and they must own it." As Ratan Tata once remarked, "Dr Mashelkar's vast knowledge and standing are deceptively hidden by his great humility."

The white paper records the necessity to situate CSIR as a major player in a global setting:

> "The purpose of this white paper is to draw up an explicit agenda for realizing these aspirations of CSIR and to chart out a distinct and detailed road map for attaining the true potential of CSIR, visualized not in relation to what it used to do in the past, but in relation to what others, the world over, are likely to do in the future."

The vision statement articulates a grand but realizable dream. CSIR in 2001 would be:

- A model organization for scientific industrial research and a path-setter in the shifting paradigm of self-financing R&D;

- A global R&D platform providing competitive R&D and high quality science-based technical services the world over; and

- A vital source of science and technology (S&T) for national societal missions which combine technology with a human face.

A quantifiable task, target and deadlines have been set. What is significant is the setting of high goals for a mindset stacked with reams of research papers and bureaucratic practices. The document beautifully expresses the high aim:

"Admittedly, these goals are not a mere extrapolation of our past accomplishments but a quantum jump in our ambition."

The strategic road map aims at charting out the directional path and contours of the organizational structures and processes required to realize the vision and achieve the goals set for the year 2001. It pinpoints five main aspects of the reform process, namely:

- Re-engineering the organizational structure;

- Linking research to the market place;

- Mobilising and optimising the resources base;

- Creating an enabling infrastructure; and

- Investing in high-quality science that will be the harbinger of future technologies.

The road map then lays down the mechanisms for achievement: Reengineering the organization structures, reorienting programmes and activities, instituting an effective marketing system, stimulating an intellectual property-oriented outlook, optimising management of human capital, tackling the finance challenge, enabling infrastructure, and focusing on the role of basic research in CSIR.

The road map is only a route, the CSIR scientists have to 'walk their talk' on it:

"We recognise that the bold and daring road map drawn up is only an enabling artifact and the mechanisms and instruments suggested are necessary but not sufficient to reach our destination—the realization of our full potential. There are no shortcuts or guide maps to help us navigate through the untraversed path. The spirit of adventure and self-confidence supported by diligence and determination are the only signposts on our exciting journey. We have a long way to go, but our vision is clear and our resolve firm."

The commitment to realize the vision is firmly stated in the entire document in the language of commitment and that is very important.

Mashelkar has articulated his vision with professional excellence. It is an ideal case study for the Lalbahadur Shastri Academy of Administration at Mussoorie, the Administrative Staff College of India, Hyderabad, and in general all government, public and cooperative sector institutes throughout India. Its importance no doubt lies in the substance i.e. to give a business orientation to scientific institutes, to enhance the practical utility of huge investments, to make government's non-performing assets (NPAs) productive. Its articulation, processing and presentation are aesthetic. Not for nothing did Ratan Tata, the doyen of industrialists, say to Mashelkar in a private meeting, "It is a unique corporate-like document from a publicly funded organization, which is both bold and visionary."

Mashelkar the scientist is known. But he has become a visionary CEO, which is inspiring. We need more such visionary scientist-executives in the knowledge century. "Because the source of technology is in science, that is rooted in knowledge," says Mashelkar.

CHIEF INNOVATION OFFICER

Mashelkar's performance has received wide coverage, liberal appreciation and awards. I ask him if he has benchmarked CSIR against any similar organization in the world. He says, "In November 1997 I visited laboratories in South Africa and held a review meeting on returning back home. My observations were that organizationally they are superior to us; their use of information technology is superior to ours; they are miles ahead in management structure and electronic governance; their interface with industry is also far superior, there is in-depth interaction therefore self-financing is excellent; but in their drive for classy

187

structures, systems and fora, they have forgotten research; we have a fine balance between the two; they have mostly white staff; a major shift to involve blacks would be required to overcome racism; our labs on the other hand have interacted well with the poor and the issues of the poor; their presentations were power-point, colour-graphed, sexy-looking, and were, of course, jargonistic. Our known weaknesses were highlighted. Our re-forms process for improving industry involvement, structure, sys-tem and presentation is already under way."

I ask Mashelkar what he envisions for the future, what he con-siders his personal mission. "The CSIR of my dream will be an organization that will have all the attributes, namely innovation, compassion and passion. It will be an innovative organization, using the latest tools of science and technology in the innovation process. It will have compassion at its heart; it will make sure that it contributes to social development, worries about the downtrod-den, and tries to bring quality to their lives. Finally, it will be an organization showing an unusual passion in the way it works and delivers."

I argue: "I think we have an abundance of compassion. Would you tell me a little more about your concept of innovation?" Says Mashelkar: *"The 'I' in India should not stand for imitation and inhibi-tion, it must stand for innovation."* I probe further: "Are there any inspiring examples where we have taken on the West and proved our innovativeness?" Mashelkar points out: "In the 1980s the US denied us the Cray supercomputer, which we wanted for weather forecasting. India decided to enter this area by using the alternative route of parallel processing. India's journey from 1986 to 1999 shows the way indigenous innovation changes the control regime and *vice versa*. I remember a headline in the *Washington Post* soon after India had exported its PARAM 8000 to Germany, the UK and Russia. It said 'Angry India Does It', that is, India having been angered at the denial of supercomputers, developed its own. So this anger was the driving force for India, while Germany had none, although they had superior technical manpower to successfully complete the Suprenum project.

"The context decides the content and new innovation cycles need to be evolved as the context changes. Let us take an example of another large system innovation where India has done well, the green revolution. At one point we went to the West with a begging bowl. Then came the green revolution. It was not merely innovation by agricultural scientists. Innovative extension models, the participation of farmers in the innovation movement and so on were responsible for its success."

The third example is even more inspiring. "We have become the largest producers of milk, displacing the US to the second position. This was due to Operation Flood. How did it take place? It was not simply the innovation in animal and dairy science and breeding that brought about the white revolution. The great visionary leadership provided by Dr Verghese Kurien, a bold new model in the National Dairy Development Board (NDDB) and the novel role of cooperatives made it possible. But we have to get into a new innovation cycle again as several challenges remain. India can beat anyone when it comes to cumulative numbers. It is in our productivity—what we achieve per animal or per physical input per day—that we take a beating. So the next innovation chain will have to focus on this aspect. Our exports of milk-based value-added products are miniscule, and the next innovation cycle will have to address this."

"So *denial drives innovation*, necessity perforce becomes the mother of invention. The opening of markets will enforce innovation. Would you agree?" I ask. Mashelkar replies: "Yes. In the protected regime of the past there was no compulsion to produce innovative products, nor was there a thrust on cost reduction or quality improvement through process innovation. But now there is a new market dynamic. Only superior products, not only in terms of quality but also in terms of features, design, content, and service, will sell. Therefore, continuous innovation will have to become a part of all our endeavours. The short-term challenge for Indian industry, as I see it, is going to be quality, productivity, cost, response time and innovation. In the long term, the challenges will be scale, technology upgradation, product design and finally strategic partnerships, not only within India, but outside. Attitudinal changes will assume the greatest importance."

He explains further: "Technology buyers from India are now seen by technologically advanced nations as potential competitors in the world market. Therefore, technology sales are being conditioned with marketing territory restrictions. The age of the straightforward technology licensing agreement is also over. It is giving way to technology-cum-market, technology-cum stakeholding, technology-cum-product swaps, etc. Technology is available to an Indian buyer only if it fits in with the supplier's global scheme. The process of understanding technology involves design, process know-how, and parts fabrication and assembly. When we acquired technology in the past few decades, we concentrated on being very skilled assemblers. The real issue is mastery over process know-how and design. It is an iterative process, full of learning and creative experience."

I ask, "Is there any unique system of knowledge in Indian civilization that you have tapped?" Mashelkar answers, "Yes, there is another domain of knowledge, which has remained unacknowledged. Many societies in the developing world have nurtured and refined systems of knowledge of their own, relating to such diverse domains as geology, ecology, botany, agriculture, physiology and health. We are now seeing the emergence of terms such as 'parallel', 'indigenous' and 'civilizational' knowledge systems. Such knowledge systems are also expressions of other approaches to the acquisition and production of knowledge. They were, as yet, neglected by modern science, as the pharmaceutical industry has realized.

"There is a clear need for systematic and in-depth analysis of the parallelism of insights between indigenous and civilizational knowledge systems, on the one hand, and certain areas of modern science concerned with fundamental aspects, on the other. In particular, a strong linkage between the indigenous knowledge-holders and scientists is needed to explore the relationship between different knowledge systems. For instance, there is a tremendous scope to develop eco-technologies based upon appropriate blends of traditional wisdom and modern science. Some of the greatest opportunities are provided, especially in the Indian context, in the area of traditional medicine."

Mashelkar continues: "Examples of this new partnership between these two domains of knowledge are gradually emerging in India. Let me cite a couple of examples. The first is a medicine that is based on the active ingredient in a plant, *trichopus zeylanicus*, found in the tropical forests of south-western India and collected by the Kani tribal people. Scientists at the Tropical Botanic Garden and Research Institute (TBGRI) in Kerala learned of a traditional tonic, which is claimed to bolster the immune system and provide additional energy, while on a jungle expedition with the Kani in 1987. A few years later, they returned to collect the samples of the plant from which it is made, known locally as *arogyapacha*, and began laboratory studies of its potency. They isolated and tested the ingredient and incorporated it into a compound, which they christened *Jeevani*, giver of life. The tonic is now being manufactured by a major Ayurvedic drug company in Kerala. In November 1995, an agreement was struck for the institute and the tribal community to share a license fee and two per cent of the net profits. The process marks perhaps the first time that cash benefits have gone directly to the source of the knowledge of traditional medicines and the original innovators. In the new innovation movement in India, we need to multiply such examples by the thousands.

"CSIR is building such new innovation models by forging unusual local partnerships by reaching the unreached in the remote corners of India. A place called Athani, on the border of Maharashtra and Karnataka, is where Kolhapuri chappals come from. They were till recently made by age-old traditional techniques. Our scientists from the Central Leather Research Institute (CLRI) studied this and helped them to reduce the processing time from 30 days to 10 days through the application of some good science: The stamping process was standardised, and certain innovative changes in design, based on computer-aided techniques, were made to give more comfort to the wearer. But this was not a top down process. The oldest man in the village was consulted, he was convinced that the age-old traditions must change. Today several hundred artisans have been trained by CLRI. This has not only enhanced the family incomes of the villagers but also changed their perception of science, development and change—in short, brought about a micro social transformation. CSIR has realised that in this innovation chain, it is not techno-economics alone, but also the socio-economical and socio-cultural aspects that it needs to be conscious about."

I remark, "The role of a scientist is changing not only to that of a scientist-manager, as I thought, but even beyond." He agrees: "You are right. _The challenge before an innovator is to convert inspiration into solutions, and ideas into products._ True innovators are those who refuse to preserve the status quo, those who put in all their energy to make things happen. Their incentives are personal and emotional.

"One can clearly see the conflict between standard management practices and good innovation management practices.

193

Standard management practices are based on avoiding conflict, whereas innovators are bound to create conflict. The process of innovation brings in spontaneity and exceptionality. Standard management practice is based on how well a job has been done. Innovation leads to things that have never been done before. What kind of management do we need to have then, if that job has not been done before at all? *Innovation management is not based on turn-around strategy. It is based on turn-around thinking.* The shift is from the rigid strategy-structure-systems model to the purpose-process-people model."

"We certainly need new kinds of leaders to make our scientific institutions contribute innovatively. We do not have many such science leaders. It requires a different mindset, does it not?" I ask. Says Mashelkar, "I believe we need to create a new set of leaders who are visionaries and thinkers, who believe in discontinuities, who are capable of thinking of the impossible and inspiring people to make it happen. They say the innovator is one who sees what everyone else sees but thinks of what no one else thinks. The innovator is also one who does not know that it cannot be done. *An innovative leader sets stretched targets.* The chairman of 3M said in 1993 that 25 per cent of its sales would be based on 3M's innovation carried out during the last five years. He increased the challenge by raising the sales share to 30 per cent, and reducing the past five years to the past four years. It is clear that in innovative enterprises our Indian chief executive officers will have to assume the role of chief innovation officers!" Raghunath Mashelkar is leading by example. He has already become the CIO of CSIR.

194

MASHELKAR MADE THE DIFFERENCE

Mashelkar's key to success is his ability to communicate in the language of the audience: With children in their lingo of stories; with scientists in their type of logic, sequence and rationale; and with administrators and managers, his speech is further studded with examples of doability. It is spiced with a fair bit of nationalistic fervour, challenge and persuasion. The cocktail contains a novelty of approach, non-obviousness and utility of the idea or proposal. His search for solutions to intractable issues is ceaseless. His leadership is developed out of an innate need to excel, to prove. "At times it looks like he is overselling a bit, but look at his accomplishments in turning around CSIR," says his _guru_, Prof M M Sharma, FRS. "Change is always a product of proactive leadership and in India, where personalities matter so much, leadership is even more crucial," he adds.

Mashelkar's value creation is intentional and systematic. He strives hard to push through his ideas. He is a disciplined thinker. Despite our intellectual primacy, our value creation is poor. He feels it is because of the confusion we have in our mind about Saraswati and Laxmi—knowledge should be acquired for the sake of knowledge, and wealth is fickle, best not go after it. Now, it is slowly being realized that knowledge, and not necessarily land and capital, can create wealth. Mashelkar thinks our gallery of inspiring millionaires from the knowledge industry like Azim Premji, Shiv Nadar, or Narayana Murthy is very small. It must grow quickly to motivate thousands to get into the Indian club of billionaires.

I ask, "Mashelkar, where do you get your inspiration from?" He says: "Survival and success." What he means is survival of the intellectually fittest and success of the innovatively greatest; that's why he considers Verghese Kurien a miracle and Narayana Murthy an icon.

But entrepreneurs who support science are a rare breed (JRD Tata was one such). Since the dichotomy between Laxmi and Saraswati is getting resolved, we will have more entrepreneurs emerging from the community of scientists. Mashelkar explains why: "Technopreneurs sprung up in the US because of the Bayh-Doyle Act. This act, which allows universities to sell their know-how to entrepreneurs as well as take up things on their own, created a number of jobs and hundreds of industries. Similar examples are available in Israel. On a couple of trips to the US, I stayed with a renowned mathematician, Mr Harveblanch. A biochemical engineering company had been formed and he was one of the promoters. This was the shift that was taking place in the early 1980s, someone who wrote basic research in mathematics was becoming an entrepreneur. He triggered my thoughts on doing something entrepreneurial." The patents business came up; Mashelkar got the opportunity to apply his mind on entrepreneurial lines to become strong in patents, filing them vigorously and pursuing them relentlessly.

Whether it is the Indian Patent Rights (IPR) Act, its retail manifestation 'Patent, Publish and Prosper', the Intellectual Property Rights drive, running NCL, or corporatisation of CSIR: To achieve success Mashelkar employed multi-disciplinary skills, from polymer engineering to communications, and seamless thinking to transformational leadership. Darwin said, "It is not the strongest of the species that survives, not the most intelligent, it is the one that is most adaptable to change." Mashelkar has displayed commendable resilience to change. He will survive to lead the national innovation movement in the knowledge century.

Mashelkar's concepts are clear. Breakthroughs are taking place at the interface in interdisciplinary areas, in the borderless area between engineering and science. He thinks there is only one engineering i.e. innovation engineering. He says, "I use research as a way to relax. I believe time management is the key issue. I prefer to occupy my mind with thoughts on science. I must say I come back fully rejuvenated and charged."

Asked in an interview what were his first thoughts on learning that he was being elected to the Royal Society, Mashelkar said, "When I heard the news, I did not honestly believe that I was worthy of this honour. One of the Fellows (told me) about 10 to 12 years ago about the criteria that the Royal Society uses: 'If this person had not been born, what difference would it have made? Would science have taken a left or a right turn?' In other words, what he was trying to say was that unless your work has made a major difference in your area of science, you do not get considered for this honour. So I really feel happy that someone somewhere has felt that my scientific contributions made some difference to science."

Yes, Mashelkar did make a significant difference at NCL, CSIR and in two IPR movements—Intellectual Property Rights and Indian Patent Rights. With him they have turned in the right direction. And giving a new direction is the mark of a thought leader.

Kiran Mazumdar

"I sold my colleagues the vision of Biocon and my own personality."

The Biocon group (turnover Rs 100 crore) is India's largest producer and exporter of novel industrial enzymes; Biocon India, the first company in the group, has the distinction of being the first enzyme company in the world to achieve ISO 9001 certification. Its founder-chairperson is a successful technocrat of global standing, Kiran Mazumdar-Shaw (47), the first Indian woman to have qualified as a brewmaster from the prestigious Ballarat College, Melbourne University, Australia.

Kiran Mazumdar-Shaw was awarded the *Padmashri* in 1989 when she was 36, becoming the first woman to be honoured for pioneering work in the high-tech field of biotechnology. She founded Biocon in 1978, when she was just 25. By 1987 sales had touched Rs 10 crore, and have now reached Rs 100 crore. To give a measure of the company's excellence, consider a benchmark: Multinationals like Denmark's Novo Nordisk and Ireland's Biocon Biochemicals (Biocon India's collaborators) received ISO 9002 certification in 1991 and 1992, respectively; Biocon India, however, received the more coveted ISO 9001 in 1993 from RWTUV, Germany, becoming the first enzyme company in the world to get this much sought-after certification. Biocon's financial results and quality standards are astounding, and the story of the growth of this unique enzyme-making company is quite inspiring. Read on.

BIOTECH WIZARDRY

Biocon is the fulcrum of three main strategic activities: Enzymes, active pharmaceutical ingredients and R&D—the result of a carefully orchestrated evolution that has been underlined both by organic growth and strong strategic alliances. The group caters to a wide spectrum of industries, ranging from food and beverages to textiles and pharmaceuticals. The flagship company of the group, Biocon India, produces and markets a wide range of food and non-food industrial enzymes, hydrocolloids and food ingredients. It is an undisputed market leader in the field of industrial enzymes, particularly brewing and textiles.

Biocon India's anchor is research and development (R&D) which has resulted in a number of innovative technologies. Its clientele spans a diverse and continually growing spectrum of industry segments which include brewing, distilling, fruit and vegetable processing, starch processing, textiles, paper and pulp, baking and confectionery, dairy and pharmaceuticals.

In 1993, a 100 per cent export-oriented unit, Biochemizyme India, was established to manufacture a range of speciality enzymes, using a proprietary, state-of-the-art, solid substrate fermentation technology. This technology was an in-house development created at Biocon India's R&D laboratories. Today, Biochemizyme is a major supplier of pectinase enzymes to leading firms in the USA and Europe. Its pectinases find application in fruit juice, vegetable puree and bread manufacturing industries worldwide. A separate entity, Biocon Quest India Ltd, was set up as a joint venture between Quest International, Holland and Biocon India Ltd to scale up several new enzymes.

In 1994, Biocon India, along with a group of eminent Indian, American and Swedish scientists and investors, set up Syngene International, a contract research company. This pioneering venture is dedicated to the development of organic building blocks for combinatorial chemistry, speciality chemicals and customized molecules using r-DNA technology for the purpose of lead compound discovery and development of drugs and therapeutics. Syngene's winning edge derives from a combination of state-of-the-art facilities and cost-competitive, highly skilled and scientific manpower. The company has successfully executed biomedical research for global pharmaceutical giants and a host of smaller US biotechnology companies.

Biocon also set up Helix Biotech, a company dedicated to the manufacture of pharmaceutical products. The first products to be commercialised are statins, considered to be the most effective drugs for cholesterol control. Lovastatin is the first drug in the statin family to be successfully scaled up at Helix Biotech and is already proving to be a commercial success.

LIKE FATHER, LIKE DAUGHTER

How did Kiran get involved in this unusual business of sourcing enzymes way back in 1978 and build a high-tech group in just under 20 years? What is her background?

Kiran's father R I Mazumdar was India's first expert brewmaster and was employed with the UB group. Kiran was fascinated by her father's unusual career and resolved to follow in his footsteps. After graduating in zoology with a gold medal from Bangalore University, she completed a post-graduate degree in malting and brewing from Australia. Practical experience as a trainee brewer in Carlton and United Breweries, Melbourne, and trainee malster in Barrett Brothers & Burston, Australia, firmly established her professional credentials. Kiran thus became the first Indian woman brewer. From 1975 to 1978, she worked as a consultant in a brewery in India.

What were her father's views on her career? Kiran narrates: "My father respected career women and encouraged me to not aspire for marriage, but career as my end goal. He said 'You will eventually find the right man, but don't follow the cliched path of getting married after your studies'. It was therefore my father who was singularly responsible for qualifying me as a brewmaster, because he believed that it would give me great career opportunities. He was truly a man ahead of his times and a liberated man at that, with no gender bias. He had two sons who could have become brewmasters, but he felt I had the right background in biology. Once again, because of my father, I believe that there should be no gender differentiations when it comes to pursuing a career." What impresses is her father's professional assessment of her aptitude, enlightened views on marriage and appropriate career guidance. How else did he influence her?

She says: "My deeply ingrained sense of ethics and integrity is derived from him, as he really practiced 'Honesty is the best policy'. I therefore evolved a forthright personality. I always speak my mind even if it is offensive, but at the same time, I have the humility to accept that I can be wrong. It is, I suppose, my open and frank approach in dealing with people that has built up a strong trust level between me and my colleagues and with my business associates, including customers, et al.

"I am, however, not known for diplomacy, which can be a weakness in Indian society where I have often landed myself in serious interpersonal problems with government officials. For example, I believe that the department of biotechnology (DBT), which is key to the nation's biotechnology programme, is manned by people without vision and without any objectivity. My forthright expression of these views has earned me the wrath of many an official at the DBT, who blocked my obtaining approvals for important projects. Nevertheless, I managed to get the necessary approvals with the help of people in other ministries, as well as with the intervention of people like Dr Raghunath Mashelkar of

CSIR or Dr Prakash of CFTRI, who are the kind of visionaries this country needs."

I probe, "Kiran, have you been able to nurture these values in your organization?" Says she, "Yes, I have striven to inculcate in my entire organization the same sense of ethics and integrity through osmosis! I encourage my people not to give in to corrupt practices and urge them to preserve the integrity of our organization at all times. In reality, though, many business practices are steeped in corruption and in such cases, I suppose the agents load their contract terms with a high price. But I can honestly say that we carry out our business in as ethical a manner as possible—my father's policy, which is genetically implanted in me.

"Another important aspect was his belief in people. He always believed that every human being had strengths and it was the ability to draw and develop these strengths that differentiated a good manager from an incompetent one. My father had the reputation at United Breweries of never having had a strike and even when it did happen, it lasted only a couple of hours, as my father had a heart-to-heart talk with the unions and they trusted his word. You can get the best out of people if they trust you. He also said it is important to identify what people are best at and then allot responsibility accordingly. The right job for the right person is a winning formula. Underlying all this is my ethos that it is people who make an organization, and that HRD is the most important function of all CEOs. I do believe we have excellent people in our organization, and *we have found an effective way in which we get ordinary people to do extraordinary things, and to do ordinary things extraordinarily well*."

BONDING WITHOUT BOUNDARIES

Kiran was all set to join the UB group, like her father. She didn't, because in India's male-dominated brewing business, the best job she could get was in quality assurance, not operations where the real action is. Kiran was disillusioned and had accepted a job offer in Scotland when fate intervened to keep her in India. Les Auchincloss, the founder of Biocon Ireland, got in touch with her. Would she be interested in helping him market and manufacture industrial enzymes in India? Biocon was a big buyer of papaine, extracted from papaya which is grown in abundance in India. It also bought isinglass, a protein extracted from the swim bladders of tropical fish. She agreed; and in 1978, Biocon was formed with Rs 1 lakh seed capital as a 70:30 venture between the Irish company and Kiran. It was a low-tech operation at first, where enzymes were sourced from Ireland and formulated here. In 1984, Kiran decided this was not exciting enough. The real challenge was to be a full-scale biotech company.

Kiran says that apart from the benefits from the technical collaboration with Biocon, Ireland, Les Auchincloss as a person influenced her thinking. "What I learnt from Les Auchincloss was to create a boundary-less organization based on flexible and informal reporting and interaction. Auchincloss was also a very people-oriented person, who believed that _building personal rapport with your key people is vital to building a good team of like-minded people._ I have practiced this approach in my own organization and have succeeded in keeping petty politics and insecurities at a minimum.

205

"I have encouraged people to address me as 'Kiran' throughout the organization, right from the workshop operator to my senior colleagues. This has had a bonding effect all around. We all address each other on a first name basis. Like Auchincloss, I have encouraged myself and my people to wander into various divisions and interact with anyone and everyone. I keep myself abreast of everything in all departments by paying them unscheduled visits at regular intervals. There is no formal procedure to approach anyone directly and this holds true across the company. This free crossflow of interactions has made us a very interactive and innovative company." What comes out is that *effective bonding takes place between people in organizations without boundaries. Structural flexibility allows people free interaction, and status barriers are minimised.* Although she is a promoter, she took a very professional and liberal view, which helped to build a knowledge organization in a niche biotechnology area like enzymes. In addition to the Irish influence, Kiran had a Scottish influence and that makes it a heady brew.

THE SCOTTISH CONNECTION

Kiran's husband John Shaw is a tall and handsome Scotsman with a gentle personality. Kiran followed her father's advice—first make a career, then get married. She made her career, and then in 1998 she married John, whom she had known for eight years. John is her friend, philosopher and guide. I ask Kiran in which way John has influenced her.

Says she, "John has had a very common sense approach to solving problems. During his term as CMD of Madura Coats, he very innovatively solved a serious union issue—salary increments—by taking the union leaders on a trip to China, where he made them see for themselves that the enemy was not the management, but competition from China. This actually resulted in a very trusting relationship between my husband and the unions, who did not strike at all till the end of his term. In fact, all the union leaders sent us congratulatory telegrams when we got married. John, like me, has a very strong sense of ethics and integrity and a deep understanding of people; he has given me a great deal of strength and support in dealing with varied issues. He is also a very secure individual, who is not complexed by the fact that his wife is high-profile.

"John has basically reinforced my belief that it is common sense that is the answer to most issues and problems. Like me, he is not carried away with high-flying business jargon. His ability to explain complex business models in a simple and effective manner has made me do the same. People can relate to simple and common sense explanations far better than to confusing and elaborate jargon. This is reflected quite strongly through my presentations and talks that I give at various platforms—simple, straightforward and crisp."

John is a 30-year veteran of the Coates Viyella group. His experience as an MNC executive of different world markets like South America and South Africa comes in handy at a time when Biocon plans to move into the mass production of fermentation products.

Enzymes is currently a closed market, but Biocon has a fairly good chance of successfully opening out because it has established its brand equity.

John was posted in Amsterdam when he decided to quit Coates and return to India. He is a committed Indophile and an ardent admirer of Indian brainpower. As director in-charge of international business development at Biocon, he feels he has a challenging job. Says he, "This is an opportunity to be involved in an exciting industry where brainpower is the critical advantage. Biocon has entrepreneurship, drive and scientific talent in abundance."

ABUNDANT RESEARCH

That India has abundant brainpower is well-known. It is equally known that it is scattered and/or drained. Wherever it is pooled, it doesn't function effectively. The scene is no better in company R&D departments. Fat salaries and perks, by and large, produce adaptive research that is neither applied nor original.

At companies like Biocon, however, the atmosphere is bubbling with enthusiasm. Biocon India filed its first US patent in November 1998 for a novel bioreactor based on solid substrate technology. The US patent for the plafractor came on March 27, 2000, coincidentally on Kiran's birthday. This patent allows Biocon to licence this technology and gives it a proprietary position in pharma manufacturing at a low operational cost. It will provide the necessary impetus to Kiran's ambitious forays into pharmaceuticals. Kiran had set the objective: To invent and

208

develop innovative biological solutions that serve the dual objectives of fulfilling customer needs and preserving the environment. This was made possible by a strong R&D base, that has been instrumental in providing the impetus for the group's expansion. With an initial focus on solid substrate fermentation, the scope of Biocon's research broadened to include submerged fermentation, recombinant DNA technology and bioreactor design.

Kiran has skilfully put together as many as 180 charged-up scientists in her Hosur Road headquarters next to Bangalore's electronic city. How did she develop the focus? She says: "To start with, our R&D effort was okay, both in extraction like isinglass extracts of fish bladder or purifiers, but nothing great. I wanted to make Biocon a biotech company and I realized our R&D was rather poor. I did not want to make only two products the rest of my life. I wanted to differentiate from others and launch a blitz-krieg in research. I wanted to make R&D the very foundation of our business."

"How did you assemble so many brilliant people?" I ask. Kiran says, "I was very fortunate. A very young innovative scientist, who was a chemical engineering graduate, wanted to do his masters in bio-chemical engineering at Delhi University. His parents were based in Bangalore. He came to seek our imported samples of enzymes to formulate them. What impressed me most was that he was very passionate about it, very involved, very excited. Later, after his masters, he came to ask me for guidance as to which university he should join in the US for his Ph D programme. So I gave him honest advice. I said, 'Shri, I have taken this challenge of starting up an industry; why don't you take this challenge of starting up the R&D activity? Let us do something innovative together.' He agreed. I wanted to take up a project that was focused and do-able—result-oriented, not some kind of esoteric research. Don't look to me for money for pure research or research of the experimental kind."

She continues: "I looked to Auchincloss. He said, 'Don't worry, I'll raise the money.' I asked him, 'What is missing in your present portfolio of capabilities worldwide that we can make?' Les said 'We buy a whole lot of speciality enzymes from Japan. They follow a technology called solid substrate fermentation technology and we are unable to substitute that with enzymes that we make in the West. If you could develop that kind of technology to manufacture enzymes, that would be great.' We had to, as it were, invent the wheel. No internet, and the Japanese being Japanese, no sharing of technology, no documentation, no access. In 1984, Shri and myself with two young technologists started out with a rough idea."

KIRAN—THE HONEY BEE

Kiran narrates: "It's very interesting how people have joined me. I had absolutely no track record. Biocon's bank manager recommended his sister-in-law Jyoti Kamat. Within a few minutes of meeting her, I found her to be intelligent. She now works in our lab. Another woman, Prema Rajan, saw our van and came to meet me. She had a spark so I hired her. It was exciting. We had to improvise a lot. Because we were focused, had tremendous excitement and enthusiasm, and the will to somehow invent something, in 1988 we actually brought out an enzyme that worked. We have been creative from day one and had the guts to spend Rs 2 crore in those days. It was a huge risk."

Kiran was on the lookout for people after having decided to enlarge the research base, but she did not go on a recruitment blitz through placement agencies or ad campaigns. Kiran is like a honey bee. She was so passionately involved that she attracted research personnel to Biocon. Kiran recruits people when she sees initiative in them. She says, "It's most important in our business. I'm intuitive about people. I sincerely believe honesty is written on a person's face and in the eyes. I hate people with shifty eyes. But I like confidence in a person and creativity. Innovativeness is a very important quality too. What we aim to have is a group of like-minded people working together."

Consider the earlier meetings: Les Auchincloss, the founder of Biocon Ireland, was interested in manufacturing and marketing industrial enzymes in India. Looking at Kiran's background, which he came to know of through an Australian contact, he asked if she would be interested in helping him market and manufacture industrial enzymes. She agreed, and dropped her plan to join a company in Scotland. She formed Biocon with Rs 1 lakh seed capital, as a 70-30 venture between her and the Irish company.

Then, in 1980, Kiran came in contact with Charles Cooney, professor of chemical and biochemical engineering at MIT's department of chemical engineering, when he was visiting Bangalore as a director of the Astra Research Centre. A discussion with Cooney and his team at Astra Research led Kiran into the contract research business. Kiran's entrepreneurial mind saw a lucrative business opportunity in the increased outsourcing of bits and pieces of R&D assignments from the US. To speed up the effort of drug discovery, US firms get the requisite pre-clinical and clinical trials done in low-cost technologically-capable India. Biocon was reasonably confident of its R&D capabilities and decided to leverage them in this new venture. Gautam Das, the senior scientist at Astra Research Centre, Bangalore, joined Biocon to head Syngene International, the new contract research company.

I asked Kiran whether she had met anyone else who had helped her in business. Without hesitation, she names N Vaghul, the former chairman of ICICI. "He is my role model. The Karnataka State Finance Corporation (KSFC) had funded my first project. I had a good track record, because I had paid their dues. I thought they would back me after technical evaluation. One day, I met Vaghul at a function and he invited me to breakfast. I updated him on Biocon's progress and the need for funds for Biochemizyme. I told him I had a problem because no one at KSFC was competent to evaluate a Rs 2 crore project. Vaghul backed me spontaneously, by saying 'Done'. I was able to scale up my technology."

I asked Vaghul, what made him bet on the unknown in 1990. He had this to say: "In most cases of venture capital financing, the decision hinges on the evaluation of the entrepreneur. Kiran Mazumdar impressed me from the first day as one who had the right instincts, dedication and commitment to her discipline. I had no doubt at that time that she would be able to pull through. In fact, Kiran has grown taller with the passage of time."

The Auchincloss meeting gave birth to Biocon, the Cooney meeting to contract research; the Vaghul meeting brought in finance and the Shaw meeting tied the nuptial knot to international business development. There is an element of coincidence, and Kiran seems to have attracted the right people who helped her succeed.

Similarly, Arun Chandavarkar, the head of Biocon's technical function, was Cooney's brightest student at MIT. Since he wanted to return to India, he contacted Kiran through a common friend. Ajay Bhardwaj, head of marketing, read about Kiran, attended a meeting she was addressing, was impressed and approached her. R&D director Shrikumar Suryanarayan, the architect of the plafractor, also joined when Kiran offered the challenging assignment of setting up R&D in Biocon. Such examples are legion, proof of Kiran's claim that "_I sold my colleagues the vision of Biocon and my own personality._"

KNOWLEDGE ACCIDENT

I ask Kiran to elucidate. She says: "I and my colleagues started modestly. It's very interesting that all those who joined me had this need to create a company together, the excitement of creating a company of like minded people. The most important thing is having a close rapport. They were happily prepared to suffer, sacrifice, struggle for aspirations. They felt we are all going to work together and learn together. They believed that the company had substance. Someone said, 'I like your lab'."

What did Kiran do to retain such high-calibre research and technical personnel? She explains, "You have to be perceived as being extremely fair and open. They would never question my bona fides. My salary and my team's salary have been the same. I never took any dividends, I just ploughed it back. One thing I have always believed in: Never take any money out of the company. Earn the money not for yourself, but for the company.

"When I started my organization, I had no great urge to splurge money because I had seen the results of my father's extravagant lifestyle. He made blunders, like speculating in the stock market and supporting nephews who made a mess of our lives. Our standard of living came down two notches and I came down to earth. I had to support my younger brothers from 1975 to 1978. I learnt thrift, and that you must cut the cloth according to the coat. As for me, I concentrate on business and growth."

"Kiran, you look born to be a entrepreneur!" She denies this: "Not really. I did not plan to start an industry at all, it was pure accident that I did. The only thing I was clear about was that I was not going to be a domesticated housewife, doing nothing with my knowledge. I needed a career—a brewing job, a career in

Australia. I thought of doing academic work, but I wasn't cut out for it. I might have landed in the United States, but fate landed me here. Once I get on to any job, I must make a success of it. I started up a company and then midwifed it. I think I had a very common sense approach. I always believed that any kind of formal thought process would inhibit creativity. A challenging environment to experiment needs to be fostered." Kiran was searching for a creative outlet. It is important to note that not wanting to be a traditional housewife and not having the aptitude for academic research, she plunged into the opportunity that came her way in her domain discipline, brewing. This reveals a focused approach, a practical thinking mind and creativity right from the word go.

The inchoate need to create a company brought Kiran and her colleagues together. That is why she calls herself lucky. It is a kind of 'knowledge accident' that like-minded people— Mazumdar, Suryanarayan, Chandavarkar and Bharadwaj—came together to make a breakthrough in biotechnology. Their management of 'knowledge accidents' was explained by Partha Das, associate scientific manager (R&D): "The ultimate goal in any business is profitability and one of the key means to this end is knowledge. We at Biocon have realized that when every little bit and piece of information is put to use and applied to well-defined business goals, we realize its maximum potential. The bits and pieces of knowledge are known as 'knowledge accidents' and at Biocon, we ensure that we convert these knowledge accidents effectively into well-managed knowledge."

COMMERCIAL FOCUS

Such thinking must have led to high levels of professionalism, I assume. But as John Shaw points out, "There is a difference between a professional organization and an entrepreneurial one. Entrepreneurs own the company, they think in terms of end results, not of procedures or rules. Their world is business, while the professional's world is organization." Kiran adds, "Entrepreneurs have a commercial focus. If you have a goal that is measurable and tangible, then all our scientists are commercial. All elements are laid down in commercial terms. *All our targets are derived from the commercial price*, so if the Japanese are selling at so and so price, we have to produce at half the cost. *You cannot compromise on the quality of the end product. It's when you wonder how to arrive at it that ingenuity comes into play.*

"The mindset is important. We wanted something that would work, we wanted to get in the marketplace faster, not get lost in the science. Output cannot be publications, but a product. Today, professionalism has become ritualism. Professionals get lost in rituals. This is the syndrome of all big companies. *The organization man is a good 'ritual' expert.*"

Asked for specific suggestions on developing a commercial focus in managers, Kiran says that in Biocon:

- All R&D is derived from market needs and market-derived ideas;

- R&D targets are all based on the commercial data available;

- Manufacturing aims at competing with the competitors' estimated cost of production in the lowest cost areas, e.g. China;

- Quality assurance is also aware of the cost per analysis and the need to avoid customer returns, which would double the cost of analysis—a 'first-time-right' approach.

Basically, there is a commercial focus throughout the organization, which is based on cost competitiveness and external competition.

SPOTTING OPPORTUNITY

Biocon's commercial focus and research application have led to spotting business opportunities and making forays in new areas like contract research. I ask what specific search skills she recommends for creating or spotting business opportunities. According to her, the search skills employed in her organization are essentially of three types:

- "Those which emanate from existing skills i.e. finding an alternative use for existing in-house skills; for example, using our enzyme fermentation to produce pharmaceuticals, or using existing enzymes in other applications, like using a pectinase used for clarifying juice for de-pulping coffee, the principle being the same;

- The second way of spotting business opportunities is to do a targeted search: Ask yourself where else can you lend yourself? An example is looking for fungal-based pharmaceutical molecules and novel enzymes;

- Our third search mechanism for spotting business opportunities is basically to get feedback from customers and markets. We have developed several specialised products based on individual customer needs."

What work practices (like thorough preparation, deep study, etc) has Kiran followed that helped her to achieve success? Says she, "In terms of work practices, I believe it is a clear focused strategy which has largely enabled us to achieve success." They have focused on:

- Products with high technological barriers;

- Intellectual property rights-related products and technologies;

- FDA approval for an entry into the huge US market.

What traits of hers does she think influence people in achieving astounding results? Kiran says, "It is perhaps my effusive personality, which means I enjoy sharing in peoples' success or interesting results, that is a strong influence on people in the organization to achieve outstanding results. It is also my receptiveness to new ideas, and successfully translating these ideas to reality, that is my driving force."

NOBEL APPRECIATION

The International Women's Association (IWA) recognized Kiran's driving force and gave her the Woman of the Year (1998-99) award for her contribution to science and technology. Says Kiran, This is not a man's or a woman's world. Everybody has an equal opportunity. If you can dream, you can achieve anything with hard work and a total focusing of your energies. You must try and be a contributor to society, pursue a vocation and add value to society. Every woman must pursue life with a sense of responsibility and dedication, and search for something to do. It is a world for people who believe in themselves.

"One needs to have a very strong belief in what one wants to achieve, a sense of conviction and purpose along with a single-minded determination to succeed. Somehow, women tend to treat their own careers as secondary and less important than that of their spouse. I've also noticed that despite being good at their own jobs, women expect differential treatment, just because they happen to be women."

The legendary Nobel Prize winning scientist James Watson, who deciphered the DNA structure in 1953, is now director of the Human Genome Project, which is scheduled for completion in 2001. After attending the Indian Science Congress in Chennai, Watson went to Bangalore. There, he stopped by at Biocon India's plant and came away much impressed by the work being done by this biotech pioneer. He inscribed the following message in the visitors' book: "I am impressed with your vision and _esprit_." Kiran exults "He made my day, rather my millennium."

It is quite something to win an accolade from a Nobel laureate, not to forget receiving a _Padmashri_ at the age of 35. Kiran's creative crafting of a niche in high-tech biotechnology is impressive.

Kiran is a lady of conviction and passionate commitment, a role model par excellence. Thousands of women and men in India work in research. If they inculcate the commercial acumen of Kiran, we will have many more successful creative entrepreneurs, and undoubtedly, this country needs them in lakhs. Study Kiran, adapt her approach, and you will lead a rich life.

Narayana Murthy

"It is better to under-promise and over-deliver."

Infosys Technologies, the globally recognized Indian software major, has shown a dazzling performance in just under 20 years in an industry based on human resources (brand value Rs 5246 crore, economic value-added Rs 129 crore, market capitalisation Rs 59,338 crore, revenue Rs 921 crore, profit after tax Rs 286 crore, 270 dollar-millionaire employees). Its founder-chairman Narayana Murthy (54) is a committed wealth creator who has deservedly reached iconic status in the eyes of millions.

*I*n the course of my long career I have not met a more clear-headed manager who puts across his thoughts so cogently that little remains to be probed. The reason, of course, is that Murthy is a transparent human being who is willing to share what adds value. The secret of his long-term relationship with his colleagues, employees, family, friends, business associates and network of stakeholders is based on his sound philosophy of '*under-promising and over-delivering*'. The underlying principle: You undertake to do something you are confident you have the capability to do. You do not raise expectations with wild promises. You do not raise hopes on bravado. In the whole gamut of employee relations the key is to manage rising expectations. Therefore, to tone down expectations to manageable proportions is to lay the foundation to build a healthy relationship. Murthy has been adept at it. How did he acquire his mental make-up?

THE SCULPTING OF MURTHY

Murthy belongs to a middle class family of eight children; he is the fifth child, with two brothers and five sisters. He was born in Siddalghata in Karnataka's Kolar district, famous for its gold mines. Murthy's father was a school teacher, while his mother came from a family of *zamindars* (landowners). His father did not take an active interest in Murthy's activities and studies; nor did he give any decisive direction to his son's choice of career. But whenever he had the time, he would talk to the children about the importance of determination, discipline, good values, and a systematic timetable for studies.

Murthy topped his school examinations, passed the IIT entrance test and secured a scholarship. But his father pointed out that the scholarship would be disbursed only at the end of the academic year, and on his meagre salary of Rs 250 a month, he could ill-afford to fork out the Rs 100 needed for the monthly tuition and expenses. He challenged Murthy: "If you are really smart you can go to any college and still do something worthwhile." Murthy thus enrolled at the local engineering college in Mysore. He has no regrets. As a top-ranking graduate in electrical engineering, Murthy got another scholarship—this one paid upfront—to do an M Tech at IIT Kanpur. Murthy's personal experience of the standard of regional engineering colleges (RECs) has made him a firm believer that students from these colleges prove equal in capabilities to IIT graduates, without that elite's air of superiority. RECs therefore constitute Murthy's preferred catchment area for recruitment to Infosys.

Murthy's first job was as chief systems programmer at the Indian Institute of Management, Ahmedabad. Then came a three-year stint in Paris working on real-time cargo handling at the Charles de Gaulle airport. In France he read voraciously on a number of societal concerns and ideological issues, developing tremendous insight into the way the world works and people perform, create wealth and banish poverty. Says Murthy, "I was a strong leftist as a student, in the halcyon days of socialism, in the glory of the Soviet Union. For us Indians, the fact that America refused to build a steel plant in India, while the Soviet Union built one, glorified socialism. Also, it was in some sense an offshoot of anti-colonialism, because the colonizers were all those who had accepted capitalism *in toto*. Nehruvian socialism was the in-thing, it was entrenched in my mind. Poverty was a virtue and affluence a vice. But I realized in Paris that even the worst communists believe that you have to work hard, there's a role for the private sector, and that the only solution is to encourage more and more people to create wealth, rather than simply redistribute poverty. You have to create opportunities—wealth through legal means." Murthy says he learnt four things:

- The only way you can make the peoples' lot better is by creating opportunities, new wealth, as Mahatma Gandhi said. You cannot wipe the tears from the eyes of the poor unless you create enough wealth for everybody;

- There are only a few people who are capable of creating wealth, just as there are few good professors, few good lawyers, few good journalists, few good doctors, etc;

- These gifted people require incentives to create wealth as they are human beings. That incentive should be in terms of money, power and freedom;

- It is not the job of the government to create wealth. It has to provide a facilitating environment, a system of incentives for people to generate wealth.

But how did a leftist become a capitalist? What experience led to his disillusionment with communism? After finishing the Paris assignment, Murthy decided to make the trip home by land. He was travelling by train on the Sofia Express when one night at Nishe, a small railway station near the border of Bulgaria and the former Yugoslavia, he caught the eye of the authorities. Suspecting him of being an enemy of the state, they incarcerated him in a tiny cell-like room, its window at a height of 10 feet, where they kept him for three days. Murthy was the hapless victim of oversuspicious police, as was not uncommon at the time. Finally an officer remembered the Eastern bloc's ties of friendship with India and let him go.

Murthy reminisces, "If they could do this to a friend, what would they do to others? (I decided) If that's the system in this sort of society, I don't want it. That's when I lost my faith in communism. I learnt that rhetoric doesn't create wealth. I used the homeward journey to re-evaluate my choices and the relevance of communism. I made up my mind that I would try to create wealth. At the end of the day, you have to create wealth and not distribute poverty."

Murthy now firmly believes in the fundamentals of capitalism, and liberalism on social issues. Says he, "It is silly to assume that all are equal. Each person is talented in his own way, only incentives are needed to perform." Apart from this mindset changing experience, what other influences moulded his thought? Murthy names three famous personalities: J R D Tata, a visionary; Mahatma Gandhi, an ascetic who 'walked his talk' and demonstrated by example; and Lee Kwan Yew of Singapore, who totally changed the face of Singapore in 30 years.

Many other people too influenced Murthy, but most important was his wife Sudha, who even today drives him to the company bus stop when the driver is on holiday. An M Tech in computers, Sudha gives him intellectual company. She also supports him like a true Indian housewife, in his passion for creating money, listening to western music, and in maintaining the austere middle class values they both cherish. Despite his deep entrenchment in the Hindu value system Murthy says, "I have been by and large influenced by western thinking. The logic is simple: In the West, people are largely self-sufficient. They do most of their own housework and few keep chauffeurs. Even US senators drive themselves to work." His philosophy: One should live within one's means.

His spartan lifestyle, however, should not be ascribed to proverbial Brahmin stinginess. He truly believes man's needs are simple. He doesn't have to prove anything to the world now that he is sitting on a personal wealth of Rs 2500 crore, and his lifestyle remains remarkably modest. I did not meet him for interviews in posh 5-star hotels. I met him at his simple two-bedroom flat in the middle class locality of Santa Cruz, Mumbai. This infotech ascetic has been hewn by experiences from Kolar to Kanpur, Ahmedabad to Paris, Nishe to Mumbai, and Pune to Bangalore— with Karl Marx, Mahatma Gandhi and Lee Kwan Yew for ideological company.

INFOSYS COHORTS

When he returned from France in 1975 Murthy had an offer from Hindustan Lever, which he declined. He wanted to help society and teamed up with his mentor, Prof Krishnayya, at the System Research Institute (SRI), a non-profit organization in Pune. The infant organization applied systems theory to solve problems in the area of public systems. However, the sole customer was the government; as could be expected, the fate of SRI's reports was to gather dust. Murthy grew frustrated as he was a young man in a hurry to do something. The Pune stint, however, may have been ordained for him to meet his life partner, Sudha Kulkarni, who was working at Telco. Murthy says his courtship of the intelligent and beautiful electrical engineer in the sylvan surroundings and salubrious climate of Pune was the best period of his life, despite travails on the work front.

Murthy decided to gain some experience in the private sector before starting on his own. The environment in the late 1970s was not conducive for software development. The rules of the Reserve Bank of India (RBI) were arcane and archaic. In 1977 he joined Patni Computers (PCS) in Mumbai as head of software, and recruited the six professionals who were to later become his cohorts. In 1981, all seven pooled Rs 10,000, mostly borrowed from their wives, and shifted to Pune to start the now legendary Infosys.

Reminisces Murthy: "We brought together a mutually exclusive and collectively exhaustive set of skills. Our vision was to start India's first software company _for the professional, of the professional, and by the professional._ We wanted to prove to ourselves that we could generate wealth by leveraging sweat equity, or brains, without much finance. Software was one industry in India where professional competence could be leveraged."

PCS was the first job for Nandan Nilekani, S Gopalakrishnan and Ashok Arora (who migrated to the US in 1989). N S Raghavan joined from Union Carbide, K Dinesh from NGEF, Bangalore and S Shibulal from BEST, a PCS client. All of them came from similar middle class backgrounds and subscribed to the strong work ethic that Murthy believed in. What Murthy says about his colleagues is a rare compliment to hear: "Nandan is a very good communicator, he is probably the best articulator of ideas. Within Infosys the saying is, 'Every seventh person in the world is known to Nandan'. Raghavan is a great humanist. He is a people's man. Gopalakrishnan is a great technical person, one of the finest in technology. Dinesh and Ashok, who settled in the US in 1983, are extremely good technical project managers. Above all, they are all good human beings. There was a tremendous synergy in the value system. If I were to do it all over again, I would never ask for anyone else. They are truly remarkable men."

Murthy saw the business opportunity in offshore development, a concept that was then unknown: To create a software supplier leveraging Indian skills and targeted at overseas markets. What was India's advantage? Murthy explains, "India has a large number of trained, quality professionals to produce high quality, world-class work. The best and the brightest in India opt for software development, unlike in the US and Japan, where they head for the hardware industry. And the price factor—India is cost-competitive. Indians are smart with mathematics. They got this way by not using calculators in their youth! Also, because India missed the Industrial Revolution, the intellectuals in the country had to use pure conceptualization as an instrument to enhance their intellectual power and experience, unlike in the West, where experimentation was possible. So, Indians were left to work in areas like chemistry, physics, mathematics.

"What is good about this industry is that it produces quality jobs, disposable incomes and provides a challenging work environment and opportunity. This is one industry where India has a sustainable competitive advantage, and the government should do all it can to encourage this industry so that we can become worthwhile players."

HARD TIMES

Infosys's first decade was not spectacular. The company's sales rose from Rs 11.60 lakh in 1982 to Rs 9.46 crore in 1992, and net profit from Rs 3.80 lakh to Rs 2.25 crore. The equity, meanwhile, went up from the miniscule start-up amount of Rs 10,000 to Rs 1.80 crore. Says Murthy: "Even by our own standards, our growth between 1982 and 1992 was the Hindu rate of growth, with no clarity in the way we did business and no sense of completeness in the business strategies we conceived and executed."

It was not all their fault: doing business in the pre-liberalisation days was not easy. For example, in the control regime, obtaining a licence to import a computer took anywhere from 12 to 24 months. America's unexpected tightening of its rules on computer exports only made things worse. Consequently, Murthy had to station himself in the US for months to lobby the export services administration in Washington.

Murthy's wife backed him to the hilt. When Infosys was set up she had to quit Telco and take their children Akshata and Rohan to live in Hubli with her parents for a year. Once when a payment

229

from an overseas client was delayed, she willingly allowed Murthy to pledge the family jewellery to pay staff salaries.

I ask how the shift from Pune to Bangalore came about. "I happened to meet K S N Murthy, the chairman of the Karnataka State Industrial Investment and Development Corporation Ltd (KSIIDC), on a flight to Bangalore. I mentioned to him what I was doing, how difficult it was to get finance. ANZ Grindlays and other banks had refused us a loan to import a computer for which a time-sharing contract with MICO had been worked out. He said come to Bangalore and I will give you a licence. True to his word he gave it in two weeks. He later became Karnataka's chief secretary."

But times were hard and by 1990 the company was floundering. The team was dithering, even contemplating a sell-out. A perturbed Murthy offered to buy his partners' shares, but at the same time he persuasively argued that the light was almost in sight. He had probably sensed that the forces of globalisation and India's empty treasury would compel the government to act. The team took heart with the resolve not to give up the marathon. They continued to operate on well-tested middle class values, generating income and ploughing it back.

Timely help did arrive—the economy opened up. Murthy stretched his partners' limits of perception. He elevated the debate to macro-level issues of the direction of global market forces, the advance of a technologically wired commercial world, and the pathetic state of our economy. Murthy was certain that the structural changes set in motion were bound to liberate software, the only solution to make India rich. Here we get a glimpse of a leader's foresight in action.

INFOSYS PROVES LIBERALISATION RIGHT

The economic liberalisation in 1991-92 was a turning point. Murthy says Infosys is proof that liberalisation was the correct step. From a mere Rs 5 crore, the company's turnover shot up manifold. He identifies the measures that breathed life into the software industry:

- The government enhanced the velocity of their decision-making processes.

- Control of capital issues was abolished and obtaining equity became a viable financial operation. Restrictions on computer imports were lifted.

- Controls on foreign exchange were relaxed, making it easy to travel abroad, hire marketing consultants, and set up offices overseas.

- MNCs were allowed to establish 100 per cent subsidiaries. Motorola, TI, IBM and other MNCs arrived. Tremendous competition ensued, including for employees.

"It opened up our eyes that good people would leave unless we had a strategy in place," says Murthy. There were three ways they could have tackled this issue:

(a) They could have lobbied with the government against giving licences to high-tech foreign companies;

231

(b) They could have decided 'This is our *dharma*, we will run the marathon on our own';

(c) Or they could introspect about the reasons people might leave—because of lower salaries, an unattractive work and technology environment, or the company's brand equity.

As Murthy puts it, "We opted for running the marathon, we went public."

Pioneers in HRM

We know human resources management (HRM) has always been the key element of any business. However, in no other business has it become as critical as in the software knowledge industry. Forget land and capital; today knowledge alone holds the key.

Observe the perspective shift in Murthy's acknowledgement that "ours is an HR-based industry." Software is a knowledge business and knowledge resides in human beings. Therefore, the focus is shifted to brainware from software, from company to industry. The coinage spurs knowledge workers to think differently. Knowing the value of this human capital, Murthy says: "We decided from the outset that there would be no blurring of corporate and private resources." The following HR practices of Infosys demonstrate how Murthy and his team 'walk their talk' and how they make knowledge workers productive. Says Murthy:

- "Since we want to attract and retain high-quality professionals, we protect and enhance the respect for professionals.

232

This means making sure that the family does not play any non-merit-based role in the operations of the company.

- We publish the valuation of HR in the balance sheet.

- We provide a working environment that is more like an academic campus than a software centre.

- World-class facilities are provided: a quality day-care centre, trained teachers, an exercise centre, tennis and golf, fully staffed medicare centre, highly subsidised cafeteria, indoor games, buses to ferry to and from office and flexible working hours.

- The pathbreaking employee stock option plan (ESOP) was started in 1994. At present, there are 270 dollar millionaires. That is real distribution of wealth.

- A 24-hour work station where 'Infoscions' work with the belief that there is no tomorrow. Learnability is valued the most. *Learnability* is defined as *"the ability of an employee to derive generic knowledge from specific experiences and be able to apply it in new unstructured situations"*.

"In other words, he must have the ability to use new technology without much training. Rather than a specific set of skills, we look for attitude and evidence that a person can learn," says Raghavan, HR director.

What is pioneering in this? It is not the management of HR, it is the husbanding of HR. Murthy and his team's enlightened practices demonstrate that a knowledge worker can become wealthy through constant learning, as at Infosys. Their methods of husbanding have created an ambience which nurtures human dignity. Their middle class value-based, informal, unpretentious, busy bee leadership style has a significant impact in building a transaction-based result-producing culture.

THE VALUER FROM KOLAR

Murthy constantly talks of values, ethical behaviour, family values, the willingness to sacrifice for opportunities, the need to keep groupism at bay, value-added performance, value-added global service, or value-added tax—which he argued the IT industry is now mature enough to pay. His emphasis on transaction-oriented behaviour has this value belt underneath it. He considers a value system to be like a radar. His mind appears to be habitually evaluating performance against each value.

Valuers, whether of land or of gold, develop a critical faculty which enables them to evaluate the accurate price on yield or weight. They use their methods, systems and processes but the ultimate test lies in judgment of value. I think that Murthy's origins in the Kolar gold tract make him value everything like gold. I believe his obsession for creation of wealth originated in the same tract. Peoples' performance in the knowledge industry is as valuable as gold, if not more. And Murthy, the valuer from Kolar, is therefore constantly measuring performance against values. The bespectacled Murthy's phenomenal maths skills must come in handy in reading people like he reads balance sheets.

Says Murthy, "I really value honesty. I also place a high value on a strong commitment to society. I want to be a doer; I have tremendous respect for people who do things, rather than just talk. I am impressed by people who are honest, transaction-based, hard-working and intelligent. If a corporation wants to run a marathon, it requires a value system. A value system is what separates the men from the boys. It provides you energy and enthusiasm in moments of tribulation. We, at Infosys, have a saying: 'A good night's sleep is worth a billion dollars'. We do look to the family background, the value system, of integrity, giving value to the customer, being fair to the people, being open, etc. We assess the entrepreneurial strength. In India we have equated entrepreneurship with financial attainments and strengths. We, however, see more to mind equity—ideas, rather than financial equity. The Lev & Schwartz model was used for our human resources valuation and the generic brand-earnings multiple model was employed to value the Infosys brand."

Similarly, appraisals and an employee stock option plan are in place for evaluating performance. We know values are maps, whereas principles are the territory. When we value correct principles we get to reality, a knowledge of things as they are. By following these principles Murthy and his team ensure that values are lived and experienced.

Having talked of values, Murthy outlines a few principles that Infosys has demonstrated.

- It is possible for professionals to stay back in this country and create wealth by leveraging sweat equity.

- It is possible to conduct business honestly.

- Sharing wealth with employees only increases your own wealth.

- Investors reward you if you adhere to the best principles of corporate governance and level with them at all points of time.

- It is possible to benchmark against global standards from India.

- You create the incentive for innovation within a corporation by rendering your own innovation obsolete.

- It is possible for two fiercely competing organizations to maintain an open, harmonious and even information-sharing relationship. "Azim Premji, the chairman of Wipro, and I are good friends. We meet often. We are fierce competitors but we have a very harmonious and open relationship."

- Putting the public good ahead of your private good in every decision you make will, in fact, result in enriching the private good. This is what differentiates the developed world from the developing world.

The famous psychiatrist Victor E Frankl says, "There are three central values in life—the experiential or that which happens to us; the creative or that which we bring into existence; and the attitudinal, or our response in difficult circumstances such as terminal illness." The highest of the three values, the 'attitudinal', is of great importance to India. Murthy experienced imprisonment

in a faraway foreign land and what a transformation of attitude—
a leftist became a capitalist! He summarily banished poverty from
his mind, and instead installed the creation of ethical wealth as a
value to be nurtured.

Murthy accepts that he manages synergy well and that his people judgement skills are fairly good. He has demonstrated that
right from the start when he brought together a mutually exclusive and collectively exhaustive set of skills. The essence of
synergy is to value differences—to respect them, to build on
strengths, to compensate for weaknesses. There are psychological
and emotional differences between people. Everyone sees the
world through his lens of experience, attitudes and creative faculties.

Murthy managed differing perceptions, giving credence to each
one's stance. He went beyond either/or to win-win alternatives.
He was, it appears, able to transcend the normal conditioning
and come up with a productive formula, as proved by his astounding results. Murthy and his cohorts walked their talk. One example is sufficiently illustrative. Says Murthy, "We had already decided that we would go public after 10 years, so the mindset was
created right from the beginning," Infosys did go public in 1993.
Murthy created value. Murthy certainly evaluates, assesses, esti-
mates; that is a function of a manager. But more, he is a valuer
who apparently periodically tests Infoscions' commitment to the
core values he has instilled in them.

CREATE AN ENABLING ENVIRONMENT

"It's nice to hear about your obsession with values, but how did you develop the business mentality, the commercial skills, in your employees?" I ask. Murthy answers, "We make them understand well the mundane things, and how to derive revenue from these. The name of the game is to understand the global delivery model, to understand certain skills, so you can spend time on what leads to bringing in revenue, what to do next, etc. Reskilling and getting revenue is a value addition. A lot of entrepreneurs tend to forget that money comes from well understood concepts. Technology is not important, it's business value to the customer that's important. We train our people to:

- Increase the value use equations—make it simple;
- Increase the production;
- Reduce the cycle time; and
- Reduce the cost to the customer.

"The person has to be open minded, able to learn to work with other people and willing to forget old things, and ask at all times these questions: 'How am I bringing value to the table? How far can I take an idea that has a market? How can I put together a team and add value?' No specific degree is required," Murthy says.

I change the subject to ask what he is most proud of. Unhesitatingly he replies, "I am most proud of putting a team together, inculcating values, creating an environment of absolute professionalism, and being able to assess the person as well as the professional."

"What is the most critical skill you used in creating this enabling environment?" I ask. He says: ***"Unless you demonstrate your emotions you cannot get commitment*** because people want to relate emotionally. You have to give positive strokes, then only can you give negative feedback." I say, "Luck is a factor. The opening up of the economy in 1991 was expected by you but you did not create it, time it." Murthy says, "Luck is God's grace. Unless I make myself fertile for God's luck to smile it won't happen. We are lucky. I must make myself proactive, keep my eyes and ears open to opportunities, create an environment, be passionate.

"The entrepreneur must create an enabling environment. How can we improve the life of the customer, add value to him? You need focus. You cannot fritter away energy. You must have the staying power, the perseverance, the confidence. A lot of us don't put in even 20 per cent of effort. ***You have to relate your learning to experience.*** The key issue is how does it bring better value to the customer in your chosen profession? You have to educate the customer, add value and build business on it."

GLOBAL VISION

Looking ahead, no business is so fortunately placed in a unique synergy at the turn of the century. Murthy says, "Our vision is to be a globally respected software corporation delivering best-of-breed solutions to our customers, employing best-in-class professionals on a global scale."

It's a grand vision all right. Many other companies have similar lofty cravings. What the company has learnt over the years and wants yet to learn to realize its vision will determine whether or not it will succeed. The management of Infosys assesses the ability of an employee to derive generic knowledge from specific experiences and apply it in new unstructured situations. I was looking for the organization's performance and potential on the 'learnability' attribute.

Murthy provided it in the keynote address he delivered when he received Business India's prestigious Businessman of the year award. Said he, "There are quite a few lessons that we, at Infosys, have learnt in running this marathon for the past 18 years, though, obviously, we are still in the very early stages of this marathon and have a long way to go."

- **Strategy:** "We have realized that strategy is very important. Strategy is about being unique in the marketplace. Strategy is making sure that you are the first mover. Whether it was our global delivery model, or our reaction to the entry of MNCs into our field, or whether it was getting listed on the Nasdaq, Infosys has always demonstrated that it had a strategic bent of mind."

- **Start-up team:** "We realized way back in 1981 that putting together a start-up team of people with a mutually exclusive but collectively exhaustive set of skills, expertise and experience is extremely important in the Indian context, though it may not be so important in the American context."

- **Repeat Business:** "We believe that growth comes from re-peat business; repeat business comes from relationships, and relationships with customers are built on trust. This trust emanates from the customer's belief that the company will not short-change the customer under any circumstances."

- **Respect for Professionals:** "Since we want to attract and retain high-quality professionals, there is merit, fairness and transparency in all decisions affecting the professionals. We are transaction-based; in other words, start every transaction on a zero base so that there are no biases and no groupism in the company."

- **Trustees of the Corporation:** "Investors_want us to operate as trustees. They do not want to see any asymmetry in terms of benefits between the owner-managers and the rest of the shareholders. We have also realized that _it is better to under-promise and over-deliver_, then you are likely to have a long-term relationship."

- **Follow Every Law of the Land:** "As far as the government is concerned, we have realized that it is best to follow every law of the land. No less important for a successful corporation is maintaining harmony with the environment and relating to it. Tisco is a great example and our desire is to follow Tisco in some small way in the kind of difference that they have made to society."

It is clear that the marathon has involved substantial learning and self-introspection. Murthy had also mentioned earlier that in building Infosys he had learnt a couple of more lessons: "If you put the public good ahead of private good, it always leads to better private good. There were many occasions when we were tempted to use our corporate resources for personal gain. It is better to have a small part of a large, growing pie than a large part of a small shrinking one." What is far more appealing to hear is the desire of Infosys to learn from other corporations. Here also his reference point is Indian organizations, not foreign ones. If reference points are contextual, people are able to relate better. They make meaning. They are adaptable. Murthy lays down the agenda for learning.

"As we move forward, there is a lot that Infosys has to learn from every corporation in this country. However, I will name just a few. We have to learn from the longevity of Hindustan Lever, the compassion of Tatas, the patriotism of Bajajs, the quality standards of TVS, the dynamism of Ambanis and the customer friendliness of HDFC."

"I believe that Infosys can only achieve its vision if we are paranoid about the future; if we respect and learn from our competitors; if we show speed, imagination and excellence in execution; and, finally, if we harness the power of youth. The future is about youth, energy and enthusiasm. If we do not realize this, we will disappear like dew on a sunny morning. This is what I reiterate to my team each and every day."

FIRST AMONG EQUALS

Infosys continues to be a pioneer in adhering to global best practices in corporate governance. In 1999, it won the prestigious

242

award for 'excellence in corporate governance' instituted by the ministry of finance and sponsored by the UTI Institute of Capital Markets; and was adjudged by _The Economic Times_ as the 'most admired company'. Murthy's earlier honours include the 'distinguished alumni' award for 1998 from IIT, Kanpur, the 'JRD Tata corporate leadership' award for 1996-97, and the Ratnabhushan award from the FIE Foundation for 1997. He was chosen 'business leader of the year 1997' by _Business Barons_ and Infosys was declared 'best-managed company' by _Asiamoney_. He was voted 'IT man of the year' for 1996 by _Dataquest India_.

Infosys Technologies Ltd is the first Indian company to:

(a) Follow the GAAP system of accounting;

(b) Value human resources and publish the valuation with the statement of accounts;

(c) Value its brand and publish it with the balance sheet;

(d) Publish all required and non-required disclosures;

(e) Distribute half-yearly reports to its investors;

(f) Publish its audited balance sheet for the year 1996-97 before April 15, 1997. Incidentally for the fifth year in succession, the company received the silver shield from the Institute of Chartered Accountants of India for the 'best presented account', among the entries received from non-financial, private sector companies, for the year 1998-99;

(g) Have installed 1,400 nodes in one given location;

(h) Have 1,60,000 sqare feet of built-up software area in one location in India.

Infosys received global publicity when it listed on the Nasdaq on March 11, 1999, the first Indian-registered company to do so. Nasdaq's press release praised it as having "pioneered the concept of cross-border collaborative software development on a state-of-the-art computing and communications backbone. Benchmarked against global best practices, Infosys's quality control and methodologies in project management have helped it to achieve the industry's prestigious SEI CMM Level 4 and ISO 9001/Tick IT accreditation. By trading on our market, Infosys joins the ranks of some of the most innovative enterprises in the world, including 440 non-US companies."

Murthy stated at the time: "The Nasdaq listing helps Infosys achieve a more liquid currency for attracting the best employees and for future acquisitions. In addition, we anticipate that our presence on Nasdaq will provide potential customers all over the world a greater degree of comfort and confidence in our company." Before going on the Nasdaq, Murthy had said, "The ship is safest at the harbour, but that is not where it is supposed to be. We want to be indistinguishable from the local premium player."

When a foreign company hires an Indian software company, it is unwilling to pay the same rate it would for others. This is the central issue that Infosys tries to crack by going global. The ADR issue was a critical part of the exercise. "Infosys didn't need the money that the ADR issue brought in," said Mohandas Pai, senior vice-president, finance and administration, and chief financial officer. The issue was needed for strategic reasons. Firstly, a Nasdaq listing would increase the global profile and open more doors to scout for top level clients. Secondly, the listing allowed Infosys to create a $50 million employee stock option plan, which was the only way to attract top-level talent abroad and still keep costs down. There is a third less important reason: the money helps to set up software development centres around the world. "We will be looking at a product company that lends itself to direct marketing. If we do look at services it will be in a specialised area with a high level of uniqueness. We will not look at acquiring a me-too service. The grand idea is to improve Infosys's global brand equity so that it can get into more value-added services, like IT consulting," according to Murthy.

The global strategy is what Infoscions call the 'global delivery model', this means producing where it is most cost effective to produce and selling where it is most profitable to sell. That brings one to another plank of the Infosys strategy. In Infospeak again: _"There are four fundamental tenets of any well-run business: Predictability of revenues; sustainability of predictions; profitability of revenues; and a good de-risking model."_ If there's one thread that runs through all the tenets it is a total aversion to surprises of any kind. No single customer is allowed to account for more than 10 per cent of the company's revenues.

The investors' darling _Asiamoney_ is published from Hong Kong. Its capital market research is considered a reliable guide throughout Asia. Almost every year it picks up Asia's best managed companies by conducting a professional survey. In 1998 over 700 fund managers based in Asia, the US and Europe were polled through questionnaires, face-to-face interviews and telephone interviews.

Fund managers were asked to rank their top three choices in seven categories: access to management, forecasts, financial accounts, investor relations, strategy, small caps and newly-listed. Three points were awarded to a fund manager's first choice, two points to the second and one point to the third. Most fund managers interviewed said dependable US dollar earnings, large cash reserves and less debt are the ingredients for survival in this market. In India and the Philippines, corporates with a strong hold in their own industries were runaway favourites. Infosys was seen as poised for more growth as more business from the West comes its way because of its excellent human resources and convenient time zone. With 78 points, Infosys was the top-ranking Indian company, and stood fifth in the overall ranking (Taiwan Semi-conductors came first with 100 points). The other two Indian companies appearing in the list were HDFC Bank, (rank 21, 29 points) and NIIT (rank 43, 19 points). That Infosys is first among equals in India needs no more proof.

Murthy's phenomenal success is due to his strategic thinking. He sensed the reality that he must earn maximum revenues from dollar land (77 per cent from the US and Canada, 14 per cent from Europe). The timing was perfect, corresponding to our liberalisation. *Most importantly, making the perspective shift that Infosys's business is based on human resources, he went out to husband them (HR) pretty generously, which turned the key to unrivalled success.* It is not a formula. He did spot-buying of HR and spot-selling of software; no body shopping, only leveraging brainware. *The perspective shift is made by his designer mind.* He is building strategic assets across the globe.

THE CAPITALIST SALESMAN

The essence of Infosys's globalisation is based on the maximin principle i.e. the maximum of a set of minima: The largest of a set of minimum possible gains each of which is the outcome of a situational strategy according to the theory of games. Think local, act global. It rests on a troika of global delivery model (GDM), global development centre (GDC) and global talent resourcing (GTR), hooked to proximity development centres (PDCs).

"Operating from facilities across the globe," says Murthy, "enables us to leverage time zone differences to facilitate '24 hours a day, seven days a week' partnering with our clients. This approach, perfected over the years through our global delivery model, has not only resulted in consistently high profitability levels, but has also assured the stability and scalability of our business model. As a part of our continuing efforts at globalisation, we set up a global development centre at Toronto, Canada in January 2000. In October 1999, we established two proximity development centres (PDCs) at Fremont, California and Boston, Massachusetts. Plans are also under way to set up a PDC in the UK shortly. Further, we recently established sales offices in Australia, Belgium and Sweden."

Their business model is built to access the shoals of high-quality talent at competitive costs and use them to deliver value to targeted leading edge technology markets. Infosys's recruitment-retention record speaks for their valuable people assets, and potential worth of the capability-maturity model (CMM). Says

Murthy, "Today, Infosys has become the employer of choice in India—we had approximately 184,000 job applicants in fiscal 2000, and, from them, hired approximately 2050 new Infoscions. Intensive entry-level training, amounting to nearly 100,000 person-days in fiscal 2000, helps us equip new recruits with the skills required to mature into world-class software professionals. And with nearly 14,500 person-days of total internet-related training this year, our employees continue to be well equipped to capitalise on the opportunities thrown up by the explosive growth of the internet.

"Our stock option plan, driven by a desire to share wealth with our highly driven workforce, was and continues to be a huge success—we have around 270 dollar-equivalent millionaires in our workforce today and our attrition rate, at 9.2 per cent for fiscal 2000, is among the lowest in the industry." Plainly, Infosys has achieved 'local optima, global maxima' in leveraging Indian mathematical proclivities.

Infosys's image soars sky-high in the esteem of international investors, clients and software professionals because of its pioneering efforts to benchmark its corporate governance policies with the rest of the world. It has complied with the recommendations of the Cadbury Committee, UK and the Blue Ribbon Committee formed under the auspices of the United States Securities and Exchange Commission. The company has been rewarded for 'excellence in corporate governance' by the Stock Exchange, Mumbai, and by the UTI Institute of Capital Markets, whose panel of judges was headed by the former chief justice of India,

Justice P N Bhagwati. Infosys's annual report for 1999-2000 is a piece of management literature of the highest world quality. A company cannot be multidimensionally more transparent than this jewel from Karnataka.

Nandan Nilekani, managing director and co-founder, says, "Infosys shows that it is possible for middle class people with no family heritage of being in business to build a lot of wealth from scratch in one generation. It is creating opportunities for people who thought the only way to get ahead was to migrate to the United States." Nandan, who is in his mid-forties, is an expert sales manager and networker. In installing him as managing director, president and chief operating officer in February 1999, Murthy has ensured a successor with high competency to manage the globally wired world of software professionals.

Whether it is putting the public good before the private good, creating wealth through legal means and distributing it, harnessing the critical resource of the information age, brainware, living within the means of middle class values, influencing team members, persisting in the face of bitter disappointments, or benchmarking against the best practices in the world—Murthy has not preached from the rooftops of corporate seminars but practiced his 'doings' and shared them in humility. He wanted to become a teacher like his father; he now has the competency to become one, having earned it by dint of merit.

But I think he is more suitable to become a salesman. A teacher teaches authoritatively whereas a salesman teaches persuasively. *We need passionate salesmen of their craft.* Murthy's craft is creation

249

of wealth, surplus, abundance and hope. Murthy represents the great hope, what he calls 'compassionate capitalism'. *This public 'assetism' is built on private 'ascetism'.* The hope is pregnant with possibilities for providing fulfilling careers to millions of our young knowledge workers, creating national wealth and improved health for our teeming billions. What I am sold on is his penchant for creating wealth. Thousands of our professionals complain that we have no inspiring role models. Here is one, a real icon! Follow him in letter and in spirit; garner the courage to xerox your career.

You don't need any more proof, you need conviction. Look at what Murthy says, "If we want to sell capitalism to the people, we have to practice a lifestyle that does not seem unattainable. We want more and more people to become entrepreneurs. If the tea-stall owner in a small village can say, 'Hey, these guys can do it; so can I', and get his business into the next orbit, then our job is done." The capitalist salesman is honestly awe-inspiring.

Deepak Parekh

"We at HDFC are not just managers, but entrepreneurs and leaders as well."

In a little over two decades, the Housing Development Finance Corporation (HDFC) has come to be regarded as a model financial institution (assets Rs 15,084 crore, profit after tax Rs 401.81 crore as of March 2000). It has grown at an average of 78 per cent in the last five years. Financial wizard Deepak Parekh (56), himself a brand, is synonymous with this outstanding professional institution which has housed millions of people.

The Housing Development Finance Corporation (HDFC) was founded by the visionary H T Parekh in 1977 with the help of local financial institutions, the International Financial Corporation (IFC) and the Aga Khan Foundation. HT, as he was called, was keen to recruit his nephew Deepak Parekh, who was working with Chase

Manhattan Bank in Mumbai as assistant representative for South Asia. There was talk of a possible transfer to the Middle East, which Parekh was not interested in; but what finally decided him was his uncle's argument: "How long will you continue to go round the world? Come and settle down, this is an Indian organization." Parekh, then 34, took the plunge. He also took a drop in salary, and joined HDFC in 1978 as deputy general manager.

HDFC became a brand because of its stellar track record of creating and expanding India's home mortgage market, earning the gratitude of over one million middle class homeowners. It has become a financial supermarket, offering a range of services from banking (HDFC bank) and consumer finance (Countrywide) to infrastructure finance and leasing (IDFC and ILRFS) and now insurance. Its whopping assets of $3.25 crore and double-digit growth rates testify to its financial prowess. This is a saga of phenomenal commercial growth founded on ordinary Indians' scrupulous habit of regularly paying off their debts to fulfill their basic need of affordable housing. If HDFC is a brand, it's due to Parekh. He became HDFC's executive director five years after joining; two years later, he was managing director; and he took over as chairman in February 1993. Let's take a look at his background.

SUPREME ENTREPRENEUR

Banking and finance are in Parekh's genes. Not only is he a Gujarati, his family is one of bankers: Parekh's grandfather was the first employee of the Central Bank, and his father and uncle were also bank employees. After graduating from Mumbai's Sydenham College in 1965 with an honours degree in commerce, Parekh qualified as a chartered accountant in England. He then worked for a clutch of companies in New York (Ernst & Young) and Mumbai (Precision Fasteners, ANZ Grindlays and Chase Manhattan). Parekh gained valuable experience here and abroad in accounts, banking, finance, customer relations, commercial transactions and consultancy. Destined for a glittering international career in a foreign bank, Parekh opted to spearhead housing finance in India, and made HDFC the dominant player in the field. His game has been marked by entrepreneurship and vision.

Says Parekh, "_I have run this company as if I owned 100 per cent of the stock,_ although I didn't own even one fourth of one per cent. I have acted as an entrepreneur. I have used interpersonal relationship skills, an open policy, and flexibility. At the start of my career I worked in structured organizations, where one had to go by the rules. I don't know if I could have continued in such a structured, caged environment and influenced a change. When you start from scratch with 20 to 30 people in the organization, it's a different ball game."

Didn't he ever think of becoming an entrepreneur? I ask. Says Parekh candidly, "You are talking to the wrong person. Although I had a number of opportunities to become my own boss, I never had the courage. I am a salaried person with a job. My mindset has not changed. _I wanted to be a bank employee, and that is what I am._ I got the opportunity to promote a bank without owning it."

Parekh nurtured an institution in a socialist era of control economy. He pinpointed what I call the *'navel' of Indian society*— a *middle class* clientele in a middle of the road socialist government—with an offer of affordable housing finance. In about 15 years he translated a social need into a highly profitable business with consistent returns. *Spotting the business opportunity in the housing needs of urbanising India, and exploiting this to the hilt, is an act of supreme entrepreneurship.* Parekh focused on the middle classes before anybody else and won their loyalty by providing what they need, from housing to banking services, and from consumer finance to infrastructure development facilities. The crux lay in targeting the middle class rather than the rich.

Every phase of HDFC's growth as an organization has been imbued with the awareness that real progress begins with the first spirited move to overcome difficulties. With steadfast underpinnings of integrity, openness and accountability, HDFC earned respect. A consistent approach and a genuineness of purpose have been evident over the years. HDFC is not only the dominant player in housing finance; it also has a significant influence over the greater economy. It would not have achieved this status without Parekh's vision and durable leadership for over 17 years. What tenets of excellence did Parekh and HDFC adopt?

THE ALCHEMY OF EXCELLENCE

Excellence is not achieved in competition with someone else, although that is how it may be judged. Excellence requires one to constantly challenge self-defined standards and preconceptions about performance and behaviour. It is the pursuit of exclusivity in perpetual competition with the self, as against settling for the *chalta hai* (good enough) syndrome. You may use global benchmarking tools for product and service innovation, but the craze to do so has to be cultivated if it is not inborn. Keki Mistry, deputy managing director and an old HDFC veteran, articulates the ambition: *"We want others to benchmark with us."*

None of the five directors (Keki Mistry, Narsee Munjee, Deepak Satwalekar, R V S Rao, R S Karnad), seven general managers and 23 deputy general managers has left HDFC in a decade. This demonstrates how shrewdly Parekh uses his unique tenets to manage his corporation, people, and vision. HDFC's 861 employees are loyal to Parekh. They echo the same commitment to excellence and action across the counters in all HDFC offices throughout India.

Parekh's action agenda for change put the customer center-stage by:

- Focusing on customer service rather than eligibility criteria;

- Developing customer-friendly procedures;

- Suiting repayment methods to customer requirements;

- Simplifying the loan process—paring down paperwork to a bare minimum, speeding up approvals and computerising transactions;

- Reducing the number of times the customer needed to visit HDFC offices.

255

The alchemy of excellence lay in changing the attitudes of the staff so that the focus would be customer convenience instead of a loan target. Slogans like 'the customer is king' or 'we value the customer' are not repeated *ad nauseum* in HDFC literature. The thinking *"We need customers because they give us business and our livelihood"* was put into action through procedural changes which impacted the customers. This is quality improvement in service. Says Parekh, "We even designed our front office in such a manner that the customer could feel comfortable and discuss his loan privately. Why is all this so important for us at HDFC? We offer three very clear reasons: *Own the information, set the standards, and keep the customer."*

Today, HDFC boasts of 1.1 lakh depositors and 125,000 shareholders. Add agents and others and you get a fabulous client base of over two million, which is a measure of the trust reposed in HDFC staff and a recognition of their unimpeachable integrity.

Says Mistry: "In terms of service, we have *innovated* a lot, right across the spectrum. For instance, we set up a retail deposit network in India, which was unique at that time. We could not compete with foreign banks in terms of pricing, so we had to compete in terms of service. We laid down service criteria and rules. We set down standards, for example if a person walks into the office with a deposit receipt, then within a certain time, measured in minutes, he has to be given a deposit certificate. In the early 1990s, the concept of giving a deposit receipt across the counter did not exist."

Mistry continues: "To give another example, we set up a system of giving repayment cheques across the counter, especially to people who want to prematurely cash in their deposits. So in all our products and services, we tried to innovate, by laying down standards which are monitored by the supervisors, the internal and external auditors." HDFC was also the first to introduce a monthly income plan, with the depositor receiving the full year's interest payments in post-dated cheques at the time of deposit. Others, like the Unit Trust of India (UTI), have adopted this practice. Mistry justifiably quotes such innovations in service as benchmarks of excellence for others to strive for.

VISIONARY THINKER

Excellence stems from vision. About Parekh's vision, Keshub Mahindra, vice-chairman of HDFC and chairman of the Mahindra & Mahindra group, says, "His ability to see the big picture before anybody else, and then to systematically focus on each of its components, is as unique as it is remarkable." _Visionary thinkers often transcend economic limitations._ Parekh has not found it difficult to go beyond his domain discipline of finance to help the middle class of India realize its dream of building a house in rapidly urbanising India. His _ability to anticipate emerging patterns, spot business opportunities and prepare his corporation well in advance to launch new initiatives_ is proof of his visionary competency.

When Parekh stepped in, the housing finance sector as such did not exist; a few banks and the Life Insurance Corporation

(LIC) occasionally gave mortgage finance to their employees. Debt was associated with shame, although the average Indian wanted a home; and marketers had not yet focused on the middle class as a lucrative demographic group. And yet Parekh conceptualized the bulge and targeted it. HDFC thus pioneered housing finance, benefiting the middle class, the construction industry and the general economy. As of March 2000, its loans portfolio stood at Rs 20,000 crore.

From housing finance to consumer finance—the target again being the middle class, middle income groups in need of small ticket loans averaging Rs 10,000 to Rs 30,000. The prophets of doom felt the market was too diverse, dispersed and difficult to reach, making the proposal a non-starter. Parekh went ahead and set up Countrywide in partnership with GE Capital, the largest US consumer company. Then he launched Maruti Countrywide, a three-way equity holding between HDFC, GE and Maruti Udyog. Says Parekh, "GE, through its agents, franchisees and offices, is successfully giving small ticket loans in the US and 50 other countries like China, Mexico, Singapore and Thailand. It is lending its technology and expertise to this project. GE would like to see Countrywide grow and provide all finance and non-finance support."

Parekh's banking genes had long been prompting him to launch a bank. He had identified a number of synergies with HDFC, like trust, integrity and a huge database of customers, along with their confidence and goodwill. The gap he saw was the difference in the quality of service and facilities offered by foreign banks and nationalised banks. For example, if a foreign bank required a minimum deposit of Rs 2 lakh in a savings account, HDFC stipulated only Rs 5000. HDFC offered foreign banks' service facilities combined with the reach of nationalised banks. Today the foreign banks have started accepting savings accounts with a minimum deposit of Rs 1000, while HDFC continues with its original requirement of Rs 5000! Its confidence is built on hard-earned customer loyalty.

HDFC was among the first to approach the RBI when banking was thrown open to the private sector. HDFC Bank was co-promoted in 1994 with the London-based National Westminster Bank. NatWest took a 20 per cent equity stake and HDFC contributed 30 per cent. The bank went public in February 1995. Parekh bagged the brilliant and experienced banker Aditya Puri, former head of Citibank, Malaysia, to head the new bank. Puri got on the platter a fund of goodwill and start-up finance. Capitalising on HDFC's brand name, the bank entered into consortia with the top 100 Indian companies. Puri did his creative best to build an Indian banking institution of excellence in an otherwise squalid banking ethos.

Puri's recent coup was to amalgamate Times Bank with HDFC Bank. The benefits to HDFC Bank:

- The branch network is up from 57 to 111 outlets;
- Its geographic reach has expanded from 21 cities to 34 cities;

- Deposits have touched Rs 8428 crore;

- The balance sheet is up from Rs 4350 crore to Rs 11,656 crore; and

- The profit after tax has increased by 45.7 per cent to Rs 120 crore.

In its continued quest for excellence and market share, HDFC Bank is now launching 50 retail service centres across the country: One-stop shops offering a bundle of financial services appear to be the future. Twenty per cent of the clients are expected to generate 80 per cent of the revenue. It makes sense to cross-sell in the service centre, be it a mutual fund or insurance or car finance or home loans.

Next in the pipeline of diversification is insurance, Parekh's pet project. The government had appointed the Malhotra committee to look into the insurance industry. Parekh was a member of that committee which submitted an extensive report. Says Parekh, "Even Sri Lanka and Thailand have opened up their insurance sectors to private companies. What is essential is privatising of savings. In India, the bulk of savings is pre-empted. The Provident Fund, the single largest corpus, has to be invested in government securities. If we can sell an insurance policy to our borrower, it securitises our loan better. Also if the borrower defaults, we will have security in the form of the policy. We are not allowed to buy equity, while most of the FII investment coming in is actually from foreign provident funds. HDFC has an alliance with Britain's standard Life Assurance Company to sell life insurance in Indian cities, a market largely ignored by India's state-dominated insurance industry. The synergies are clearly formidable."

The latest offering is a mutual fund venture, HDFC AMC (asset management company). The potential for this business is substantiated at the start itself by the involvement of Standard Life. This British partner of HDFC's insurance foray has paid Rs 50 crore to HDFC as an advance towards exercise of its option to buy up to 26 per cent stake in HDFC AMC. Milind Barve, an HDFC veteran who is managing director of HDFC AMC, says, "Our schemes will be equity and income funds, and will not be sector-specific. We may include technology stocks, but we will look very carefully at the valuations." HDFC's 46,000-strong network of fixed deposit agents, its 72 branch offices and the 119-strong branch network of HDFC Bank will help to market the mutual fund schemes.

What is the guiding principle? Says Parekh, "_You must get in first._" This is a profound statement. You must know what others are thinking about in the areas of your interests and you must get there before them. This is securitisation of competitive advantage before the race begins. Parekh's diversification doctrine made him stay close to his knitting—finance and banking. He leveraged HDFC's intimate access to the middle class and national reach in his expansion drive.

To get in first requires vision, and I question Parekh on this topic. He says: "_Core values do not constitute the basis of vision. A vision provides a sense of direction on the basis of an assessment of the_ *present, the past and the likely future. Visions can be wrong, hopelessly off the mark, if they are not born from strong values, strengthened and nurtured by an analytical ability to constantly assess emerging environments and strategic alternatives. This, though, is never enough: The objective part is normally enveloped with an uncanny intuitiveness for what lies ahead. Great visionaries have had all these qualities in ample supply. When we look at great organizations, we know that there is outstanding leadership behind them born from a combination of these attributes."*

Parekh is able to see the synergy in unrelated issues; he has a propensity to see patterns, spot trends, before others do. Parekh is an infocrat; he gathers information through networking and shares it with colleagues while building a grand vision. He instills a compulsion to delight the customer—the middle class. He does not allow his focus to stray from his captive audience. He leads, so he doesn't have to compete.

A vision is like a map that guides one through a tangle of bewildering complexities. It is what one sees or feels before any systematic reasoning can be structured. Concrete features of a scheme come later. It is a telescopic view of the inchoate needs of a person which, if met with value-added products and services, yields bumper returns. Parekh's value-addition to the inherited wisdom is his craze for envisioning a sheltered (housing, saving, insurance) future for the mainstay of society, the middle class.

He is not a dreamer. He is basically a thinker and he *thinks about his visions.* Parekh's vision for HDFC is to make it a GE

Capital of India offering a veritable buffet of financial services. With an array of such services under his belt Parekh has already made HDFC a virtual organization. It is a constrained vision, but vision it is. It concentrated on the middle class, but the narrow focus paid rich dividends to society as a whole.

WALKIE-TALKIE BRAND

If we think inversely for a moment, this virtual reality, HDFC, is a map of Parekh's mind. We know the map is not the territory. The territory is the fertile brain of Parekh. The grey cells of Parekh have been functioning multifariously to make him resourceful. If it is people who make you successful, then Parekh's networking has immensely helped him. Influential financial and business leaders like Tata, Birla, Ambani, Premji, Narayana Murthy, Kurien, Bajaj, Mahindra, Goenka and Parekh wield significant influence over the industry they work in, even the greater economy. They bring about structural changes in the functioning of industry. Their track record takes them to the different boards of prestigious companies, apex industry bodies and policy-making committees. Their circle of influence widens and their contacts multiply. A rich minefield of opportunities opens up to study the interconnectedness of different complex issues, segregate the wheat from the chaff and make a meaningful contribution, help show the path to the solution.

Let's take a look at Parekh's spread of advisory responsibilities. Parekh is a director of Castrol, Hindustan Lever, ICI, Mahindra

& Mahindra and Otis. He has been a member of various committees set up by the government, including:

- A committee to investigate the possibility of setting up an apex body for housing finance institutions in India. This led to the establishment in 1987 of the National Housing Bank as a regulator for housing finance companies in India;

- A committee on reforms in the insurance sector. It made recommendations on the institutional framework and regulatory and supervisory functions when it submitted its report in 1994;

- A committee constituted by the Securities & Exchange Board of India (SEBI) to examine forward trading;

- An experts' committee appointed to study the reasons for the losses of Indian Airlines and Air India, and to suggest how they could be turned around;

- A committee to study the compensation structure of CEOs of public sector undertakings;

- An advisory committee on the financial operations of the Power Finance Corporation;

- A finance ministry committee on banking sector reforms;

- A six-member committee charged with working out a package to bail out and restructure UTI's flagship US-64 scheme.

Parekh also has a number of responsibilities entrusted to him by international organizations. He is the Indian advisor of the Commonwealth Equity Fund, set up by the Commonwealth

Secretariat to encourage private institutional equity investment in the developing Commonwealth countries. He is a member of the board of the India Liberalisation Fund set up by Alliance Capital Management, New York. This fund, which manages over $110 crore, has a primary investment objective of investing in securities related to industries dealing in infrastructure development. He is a member of the Asian advisory board of Bankers' Trust, New York, and the business advisory council of the International Finance Corporation (IFC), Washington DC. Parekh is also the Indian advisor on the board of Capital International Group, New York and a senior advisor to the Boston Consulting Group, India branch.

The crisscross connections to different industry sectors at the national and international levels with Indian and MNC organizations make him the most thickly wired Indian CEO. It's a spider's web. Such interdisciplinary connectivity has tremendous play in it. Parekh's creativity is husbanded by such rich interactions. It enables him to raise finance and get people to work for him. He is the 'walkie-talkie' brand of HDFC.

HT, his visionary uncle, psyched Parekh into one decision viz. to join HDFC; the rest he created with exemplary receptivity to the high-frequency Indian and international financial diaspora. The entrepreneur in him did not leave either the home ground of housing and finance, or his beloved middle class. The opportunity cost lay in the marriage of the two, enabling him to earn his dividends.

MILLENNIUM OF WEALTH AND WISDOM

Reflecting on HDFC's meteoric rise, Parekh says, "Till nine years ago, even I hadn't visualized our gigantic growth. The scenario metamorphosed with the implementation of Manmohan Singh's economic reform programme. Liberalisation opened up exciting new opportunities in the financial sector. After 1991 we began planning ahead, as we were reasonably certain that we would be permitted to do what we wanted to do." Parekh took advantage of the opening up of the economy by first expanding into banking, and now into insurance and mutual funds. Economic reforms have changed the standard of living of the middle class and Parekh was the right man at the right place at the right time. Having established faith and trust in the proverbially cautious middle class, he exploited the goodwill for further growth. How does he see the new millennium?

Parekh is very optimistic. "*It is going to be a millennium of 'wealth and wisdom'.* It is now abundantly clear that the days of the command economy are over. Even the staunchest leftist now realizes that you have no option but to follow the market economy. The constant worry is: Where will I find the money to pay the salaries of the government employees? The biggest worry is: Where will I find the money to pay the interest on those heavy borrowings? The public sector too has that worry. The more I borrow, how will I repay? Everyone realizes that we cannot do it to the last man because 40 per cent of our population is below the poverty line."

As an example of how the public sector is changing, Parekh says, "Creation of wealth enhancing shareholders value, return on capital employed (ROCE) is the language today's public sector managers are talking. The lingo has changed." Although the public sector executives have become more practical and are speaking in commercial terms, the obstacles are in the concubinage of politicians and their departmental bureaucrats, who don't want to give up power. "The mindset in government has not changed," Parekh rues.

In the midst of the remnants of the socialist ethos and a bankrupt government, Parekh feels the forces of globalisation, fierce competition and the internet revolution will churn up prosperity. He sees great hope in peoples' rising aspirations fuelled by the media, whose images of a better lifestyle have a profound impact on the mind of young India. The dramatic changes in consumer expectations will spur economic development. Parekh mentions three socio-political trends and their implications for business:

- Demographic changes in Indian society;
- Regionalisation of politics; and
- Urbanisation.

"Each of these in my view constitutes an important driver of the environment within which business is required to exploit opportunities. Going by the latest census, close to 60 per cent of India's population would be under the age of 30 by 2015 AD. In the information age, this demographic pattern will add momentum to India's efforts to globalise; Indian businesses will therefore have to recognize this reality in their planning. Indian politics will become increasingly state-centric and regional, rather than centralised in the national government. The regionalisation of politics will result in making state governments increasingly important business drivers.

"The census also shows that over 50 per cent of the Indian population is expected to dwell in urban and semi-urban areas in the near term. This rapid urbanisation will have significant implications for business, in terms of consumer expectations as well as in the propensity to consume. Urbanisation will drive investments and should form the backbone of India's market strength."

THINK BIG MONEY

"At the dawn of the millennium of wealth and wisdom, how do you see your future?" I ask. Parekh gives a sharp reply: "I don't think about my future. What I am totally involved in is asset management and insurance, two huge areas. We are the last to enter in asset management. How do we mobilise money when 22 organizations are there? It's a question of relationship. So one should be competent in *building relationships.*"

He continues, "It is a core competency. Trust and faith are of prime importance for creating opportunities. In the first 10 to 15 years, people came to us for loans. Our deposit schemes failed to gather momentum and mop up savings. Nobody trusted us. We raised bulk money, borrowed wholesale and lent retail. In the last eight years, however, people have started trusting us as a recognized saving institution, rather than as a lending one. With 12 lakh depositors (many of them are public charitable trusts) and

268

eight lakh borrowers, trust, safety and security have got institutionalized. Transparency, accountability and a clear conscience paved the way."

What inspires Parekh? Says he, "The satisfaction of making people happy. Twenty years ago Narayana Murthy, the Infosys chairman, took a loan of Rs 70,000 for a small flat. His wife was standing there and praying. He didn't know anybody, but without paying a bribe or using influence, he got the money. Today Narayana Murthy could buy HDFC. But he will remember his experience with us. One's home is the single biggest asset purchased by any human being in his lifetime. The happiness, the thrill, the satisfaction: It's magnificent. Seeing clients satisfied is where I derive my inspiration from. Not spirituality."

Parekh runs HDFC as if he owns it. He entrepreneured every scheme, and made his colleagues do the same. He did not allow them to work as mere employees. He gave them freedom and process ownership without interfering, and they gave him the results. As he says, "*We at HDFC are not just managers, but entrepreneurs and leaders as well.*" What are the skills required for spotting opportunities? He says, "Predicting the future will be much more important in a period of rapid change than it has been hitherto, and our skills for this are sadly lacking. **Defining core competency will be more important than ever before.** Competitive forces will ensure that we stick to what we know best. The critical skill required is to '*clinch the deal*', as they say in America: Buy, expand, acquire and consolidate. To clinch a deal, how do we make procedures simpler, with less hassles, and earn money from it? That commercial sense is ingrained in me, maybe genetically, plus my CA training, my experience in auditing and prospecting opportunities, and so on."

"What kind of leadership do we need?" I probe. Parekh elucidates, "Tomorrow's leaders will need newer skill sets, they will need to be far more aware of international trends and global information. They will also need to be aware that as tariff barriers around the world are increasingly rationalised, their corporations must be capable of sustaining such changes to effectively compete even in domestic markets. Good leadership results in sustainable brand equity. *In the long term, integrity, transparency, quality and higher levels of service do more for your brand than any advertising or communication program.* Leadership bespeaks many concepts. For my company and me, it speaks of a team of committed managers, cohesively working towards corporate excellence. This has been the spirit of HDFC since its inception and I recognize that HDFC steered its pathbreaking activities solely with the strength, dedication and integrity of its team."

"But this is incremental progress," I say. Parekh explains, "The government allowed us to start a bank. We needed Rs 100 crore. For life insurance, a capital base of Rs 200 crore is necessary. People, however, think they can achieve something with small amounts of money or small equity, like every second small-scale industrialist thinks. They feel they don't need money. We need to *'think big money'*." Echos of Napoleon Hill, author of *Think & Grow Rich*. "In that case, should we be teaching how to raise funds, which is a crucial skill, instead of management?" I ask.

"Well, both," says Parekh, "but remember that without finance you cannot get started."

Parekh muses: "I am not a very proud person. In the US, some CEOs are arrogant so and so's. This doesn't work over here. We don't have the urge to kill, either because we don't have that much fire in the belly, or because there is not that much competition around. I don't know what it is. I don't take credit for the bank. I had the idea, I got the licence, and I took good people to run it—Aditya Puri and others, whom I selected on the basis of their integrity and track record. If they had not done well, I would have lost my reputation. But I trusted them and left them alone, and they succeeded."

THE PARTY IS ON

We have a healthy tradition of inducting distinguished governors of the RBI as finance minister, like C D Deshmukh, H M Patel and Dr Manmohan Singh. Parekh's track record makes him an ideal candidate for the job. While entering the new millennium of gigantic opportunities, we need a leader with a 'think big money' mentality to fill our coffers. Parekh is a resourceful leader. His reputation as an institution builder, visionary and strategist has spread beyond the boundaries of the country. He is a networked leader.

Parekh almost always finds the time to meet those who seek him out. The visitor will leave Parekh's office armed not with feel-good statements, but practical advice. As executive director Keki Mistry puts it, "He's always approachable." Parekh is addicted to people and revels in meeting them. His is a familiar face on the social circuit—he admits to having attended up to six parties one day! Friends joke that Sunday mornings at home are the venue for 'Deepak's *darbar*'. "He's driven. Deepak crams a 48-hour schedule into a 24-hour day, seven days a week," says Deepak Satwalekar, who has worked with him since 1979. "Sometimes it gets a bit too much and I just can't manage to read all the newspapers," Parekh says ruefully.

With relentless networking, Parekh has created success for HDFC and prosperity for millions of householders, and has earned a reputation for excellence. *He put into practice the life-affirming philosophy of power networking.* Quality networking has generated a continuous flow of referrals from clients and associates.

Whether or not Parekh becomes the finance minister is a moot point. He is an inspiring role model, an exemplary thought leader; about that there are no two opinions. His networking expertise has displayed the highest form of service. It's people helping each other in a partnership desired for mutual benefits. From a strategic skill it has led to a deeply caring relationship.

Donna Fisher and Sandy Vilas in their eminent guide *Power Networking* say,

"Networking is making links from people we know to people they know, in an organized way, for a specific purpose, while remaining committed to doing our part, expecting nothing in return."

Parekh's cocktail of financial services is healthy. He relishes attending parties where he introduces himself, so people are inspired to call on him. We need him. The party is on.

Pratap Pawar

"Transform the 'aware' society into a 'commercially aware' society."

Sakal is a leading Marathi daily published from Pune, Maharashtra. In the last 14 years it has achieved substantial growth and is now the second largest Marathi newspaper, with a circulation of 5.20 lakh copies a day. This success has been achieved by its soft-spoken and amiable managing director and managing editor Pratap Pawar (56), who had no background in running a publishing house or editing a newspaper when he took over the reins in 1986.

Pratap Pawar hails from the grape-rich area of Baramati in Maharashtra. His parents were ambitious and hard-working social workers, and social issues dominated family discussions. The Pawar's home was a meeting ground for people from all walks of life: Teachers, politicians, artists and social workers. Pratap was encouraged to take part in school debates and extra-curricular activities; he was a voracious reader and an active sportsman. Pratap believes that such a socially-conscious upbringing helped him become what he is today.

FROM WINE TO PRINT

Pratap graduated in engineering from the Birla Institute of Technology and Science (BITS), Pilani in 1968. The same year, he and his brother started a company, Ajay Metachem (turnover Rs 26 crore), which manufactures speciality chemicals like eco-friendly unicote, an anti-corrosion coating, and unicare, an epoxy-curing agent. Side by side, he began his career as a social worker in Baramati Grapes Industries Ltd and Baramati Agro Ltd. The thrust of the work was to educate farmers in looking at their produce, such as grapes, milk and eggs, as a value-added product to be developed for commercial exploitation. It meant changing the mindset from that of a helpless farmer to that of a proactive producer who balances inputs in order to get the best possible yield and price. It was his elder brother's guidance and family tradition which got him involved in this work at the start of his career.

In 1976-77, Baramati Grapes, a winery started by farmers in collaboration with an Italian company, was in financial crisis with liabilities of over Rs 1.5 crore. The local shareholding farmers and Italian collaborators requested Pratap to take charge of the unit and make it viable. He accepted this challenging assignment as a social responsibility. Pratap worked with determination and dedication, neglecting his own business. In one year, he nursed the company to health, taking various measures like restructuring bank loans, erecting a winery in record time and getting employees to work in a disciplined manner. Baramati Grapes wiped off all its losses and paid back all loans. Moreover, it has been paying dividends to its investors for the last 15 years.

"How did you take up the gauntlet?" I ask. Says Pratap, "This is where my social conscience came into play. A value-added product, wine, made from their grapes, should give the farmers adequate returns. This was my predominant thoughts. They needed technical leadership. I knew nothing of winery, but being a studious person, I read 28 books on winery management, manufacturing and erection. I did all the project work and built back the winery in a record three months. A lot of engineering work was involved—fabrication, execution, etc—and I also had to personally handle suppliers and vendors on the site. The necessary coordination with banks and financial institutions too required a considerable amount of planning. Workers' attendance and idle time were issues. It was a do-or-die situation for six months, but my entrepreneurial approach and management skills helped."

How Pawar moved from the management of a winery to that of a newspaper is an interesting story. In 1970, he came in contact with the Kirloskar family, a prominent industrial house in Pune. In 1973, he was taken on the board of Kirloskar Oil Engines Ltd. It was common knowledge in Pune at the time that the newspaper *Sakal* was not doing well. The proprietors were looking for a fresh infusion of capital and had sent feelers to the late

Shantanurao Kirloskar. But he had no interest in venturing into journalism, a field far removed from his domain, engineering. He believed the Kirloskars should stay 'close to their knitting'.

Dr Banoo Koyaji, who was in charge of *Sakal* at the time, then approached Pratap's elder brother to see if he was interested in taking over. The brothers discussed the offer. On the understanding that there would be no interference and Pratap alone would run the show, they decided to invest. Accordingly, Pratap took control of the paper in 1986. "The medium is useful to educate people. I was attracted to journalism because it helps to serve the common man," he says. The driving force in taking up the challenge at Baramati Grapes was to serve the farmers. In the *Sakal* offer, he saw the opportunity to serve the lay reader. The motivating factor in both these decisions was service to the common man.

SAKAL OPENS UP

Sakal means morning in Marathi. A large number of people in Pune are addicted to starting their day reading *Sakal*. This habit has now been acquired by residents of Kolhapur, Nashik, Aurangabad and surrounding areas after *Sakal* began local editions. District readers were eager to see more focus and space given to local issues. Supplying the paper from Pune to these distant places early in the morning was becoming a nightmare due to transport bottlenecks and logistic problems. Moreover, industrialisation has brought about a change in the lifestyle of people living in these areas. Pratap took into account these trends, saw an opportunity to expand and started bringing out editions of _Sakal_ from these places. Pratap likes marketing, and the marketer in him surfaced.

What else did Pratap do after taking over _Sakal?_ "I separated the editorial from the management. I gave complete freedom to the editors and encouraged them to write independently. You know, newspapers run on advertisements. For improving the revenue, I used space gainfully by reformatting the columns, so that the proportion of pages used for news and ads changed. Annual income increased by around Rs 20 lakh. _Wealth was created through space._ I used my commercial acumen by saving on newsprint, so costs came down. A three per cent reduction in use of newsprint translated into savings of Rs 3.6 crore. I took up the issues of ink utilisation and recycling wastes; talked to workers, trusted them and we got good results. Such economical resourcing and implementation of efficiency measures in the press helped me increase the turnover from Rs 3 crore in 1986 to the current Rs 78 crore. Yes, I am a creator of wealth. But wealth is incremental in character. _If you do the work you like, money will follow._"

You have to admit, Pratap is extremely resourceful. He took up the challenge of building a winery and rebuilt a newspaper without first-hand knowledge of either of these industries. He did not belong to them professionally, neither were they his domain disciplines. I ask, "Pratap, you used your leadership skills in both situations, but how did you get the finance?" The prompt reply:

"Through contacts and my credibility. My reputation with the banks and financial institutions as managing director of Ajay Metachem, or in earlier dealings on behalf of Baramati Grapes, was quite good. I had a record of honouring commitments on due dates. I was quite transparent since the beginning; and don't forget, banks want reliable customers. Your credibility, painstakingly built over the years, increases their trust. Your reputation walks ahead of you. Your competence to handle a situation is also taken into account. I believe banks take calculated risks. If you have a record of performance, they bet on you, apart from the merit of the business proposal."

NETWORKING THROUGH SOCIAL ACTIVITIES

Pratap's leadership, managerial skills and contacts have made him the public figure that he is. At present he is president of the Mahratta Chamber of Commerce, Industries and Agriculture, Pune; and vice-president of the Indian Newspaper Society, New Delhi. He is also a director of various companies in India and abroad, such as Finolex Cables Ltd, Kirloskar Oil Engines Ltd, Pune, Pan Gulf Group Ltd, UK, and Baramati Grape Industries Ltd.

Pratap is a trustee of a number of socio-educational institutions in Pune and takes active part in the development of these organizations and trusts: the Poona School and Home for the Blind; Balgram-SOS Children's Village, Yeravada; Students Welfare Association, Pune; India Foundation; Pune Balkalyan

Sanstha; Pariwar Mangal Society; and the Kirloskar Foundation. The point to be noted is that Pratap began working for these welfare institutions from almost the start of his career, and not after acquiring a certain status, as many people do.

How did he build the network? Pratap reminisces, "One thing led to another. My family was active in social work, and therefore known to the trustees and political leaders who managed different bodies working in areas for the blind, students' welfare, etc. Leading political figures like the late S K Patil and Bidesh Kulkarni asked me if I would be interested in working for the Poona School for the Blind. This is one of the biggest schools for the blind in the country. It is the only one to have a nursery school for children below the age of six as well as a workshop for blind girls. I accepted, and I have been their managing trustee since 1970. Yamutai, the wife of Shantanurao Kirloskar (popularly known as SLK), was also actively associated with this blind school. That's how I came in contact with them and SLK offered me a seat on the board."

"Pratap, just knowing an industrialist doesn't help. What prompted him to offer you a place on the board of his respected company, Kirloskar Oil Engines?" I ask. He says: "My devotion to work impressed SLK and Yamutai. SLK used to ask very searching questions. I was transparent and never shirked any work or responsibility. I think my sincerity, concern for the blind, style of working, comprehension of situations and results must have impressed him."

"You were not a student activist. How did you get into the students' welfare association?" I ask. Pratap narrates, "My father-in-law had introduced me to the renowned civil servant, the late Narayan Dandekar, who was the chairman of that body. Please don't forget that these people at the top are always looking for good people to work for such institutions. Dandekar inducted me. He observed the quality of my work, my preparedness to spend time, eye for detail and eagerness to learn from him. This performance appears to have impressed him. Later, he selected me to succeed him as chairman. Both Dandekar and Kirloskar observed that *I implement and practice what I say.*"

THE INFLUENCE OF GREAT MINDS

Pratap's thinking was influenced by that of Kirloskar and Dandekar. He felt they were logical and practical men. He liked to move in the company of such people. He was conscious of the beneficial acculturation wrought by such contact. From where did Pratap gather this awareness? He readily identifies the source: "My mother was responsible for planting this seed. She used to say, 'Cultivate friends from the Brahmin community (Pratap is a Maratha), your language will become refined and your conversational ability will improve. You will imbibe their fine attributes and the cultural influence will be beneficial. Our own family and community values, fermented with theirs, will make you a fine person'."

Some Brahmin ladies used to be constant visitors to Pratap's house and were like family members. Pratap's uneducated mother had the innate wisdom to understand that what was good in the knowledge community needs to be learnt through interaction. Such insight doesn't necessarily come from books or degrees. It comes more through personal contact with people of different communities who have superior knowledge or skills in certain areas. _There is a science in this affiliative nurturance—great minds influence powerfully._

OVERCOMING ENVIRONMENTAL CONDITIONING

Since Pratap is so deeply involved in socio-economic work, I venture to obtain his views on some critical issues. "Pratap, is environmental conditioning a limitation for the economic progress of deprived communities and if so, what is the answer?" I ask. He answers: "Progress is taking place through education, but it's a slow process. It must be the responsibility of political leaders and social workers to educate the deprived in many innovative ways. Numerous experiments are under way and the urge to reform has to be inculcated."

I ask, "Instead of fighting for jobs or for political control, do you think these communities will see the writing on the wall, and decide to acquire commercial skills and computer education?" Pratap reflects, "Well, if they take such an approach, it will be laudable, but I don't think they will. Where the ambition level is at best to become a driver, to cultivate a business mindset is difficult at this stage. It would be a great leap, a difficult transition. Maybe in a few decades they will have that advantage. For the foreseeable future, however, they will seek government power, not market power. A tiny minority belonging to each such community may read the future accurately, but will not give up hard-earned security in favour of risky business opportunities."

ALCHEMIZE THE AWARE SOCIETY

"How do we go about attacking the issue of mindset change when there are structural obstacles like caste identity and religious beliefs?" Says Pratap, "I think we need to segment society into three categories—what I call *aware society, semi-aware society* and *unaware society*. The aware society is of knowledge workers. This segment consists of people who are aware of socio-economic problems, the restructuring of government-market relationships, impact of technological advances, globalisation, competition and e-commerce. They are proud of their knowledge. But they do not come out of their cocoons. *This aware society needs to be mobilised into action. You need to transform the 'aware' society into a 'commercially-aware' society. They are the levers of change.* They need a road map and guidance in how to usher in the new reality.

"The 'semi-aware' segment is aware of problems, but has not grasped the nature of the future. Their exposure to world happenings as well as understanding of structural societal changes is sketchy. They have little readiness to change. They would need much more information on events and facts to know how ground-level realities are changing all over the world.

"The unaware society is operating at the existence level. They see change all around, but it passes them by. They are so immersed in their day-to-day activities that they are not even aware of the issues which threaten their very existence. Ignorance, they say, is bliss."

What Pratap is saying, in other words, is _"Illuminate the strong, alchemize the aware."_ It is the same principle followed by enlightened managements to develop the strengths of managers after assessing their performance. It means that the mindset of the aware society—the knowledge society—has to be jolted into seeing the dangers of global market forces and resultant fierce competition. It has to be quickened to action lest it continue to languish in the torpor of knowledge. It is a transition from awareness to action. India has a critical mass which is now making its presence felt on the world platform; therefore, there is a realistic hope that complacency will not engulf us.

The semi-aware society has to be animated to free itself from the job mentality. This is going to be a battle of epic, Mahabharat-like proportions. It is the resurrection of work from the abyss of democratically legislated laziness. It is necessary to awaken this mass from the slumber of its illusion—that the government provides jobs and you are owed a living. This is a journey from information to knowledge and action. The unaware society needs basic education and emancipation of women. These and other related issues require massive funding. This is a long journey.

Television is a third parent. It is likely to play a vital role in the uplift of this segment.

CRITICAL BALANCING

It is clear that Pratap belongs to the aware society. He is a creator of wealth. What is he going to do to create more wealth, reach a Rs 250 crore turnover, for example? He says, "I am going to leave it to my son Abhijit to do that. I would like to devote more time to my family and relatives." So, is Pratap tapering off? He would certainly devote time to social work; but why is he slowing down on creation of wealth? He says, "That is our mould. Our priority is not material wealth, but family, and one would not like to trade off one for the other. Another factor is that we need to repay society's debt. I am going to intensify my involvement in social work."

This is the dilemma of Indian society in general and wealth creators in particular: Balancing the need to create wealth and the needs of the family. There cannot be any dispute on the philosophy stated by Pratap. But the aware society is in a minority. If they don't devote more time to creating wealth, who will? And who has the competence? Energizing the wealth creators is fundamental to the alleviation of poverty; I appreciate that it is easier said than done, nonetheless, it will have to be done.

However, Pratap's achievements are creditable and worthy of study. More so, the thought process is educative. Apart from the virtues of hard work, initiative and learning, Pratap stresses: "Be prepared to add value, make yourself unavoidably likeable, sell your competence, show skills in application. Please remember that if you are a vacant personality, you cannot influence others. Your willingness to do a thing must be visible on your face. Don't be afraid. Once you know the purpose, the skill will follow, wealth is waiting to follow you. Just try it."

Prakash Ratnaparkhi

"I believe help rushes in where strong desire exists."

The Electronica Group of Companies, Pune (turnover Rs 100 crore, seven manufacturing plants and 1200 employees) is a pioneer in developing spark erosion machines in the Indian market, and the first company to manufacture electric discharge machines (EDMs). At the helm is a triumvirate of three engineers—two brothers, Prakash and Ravi Ratnaparkhi, and their uncle Shrikant Pophale. The bearded Prakash (54), a forthright person of firm convictions, spent two years trying as many as 67 different ideas and products to develop a spark erosion machine before his persistence paid off.

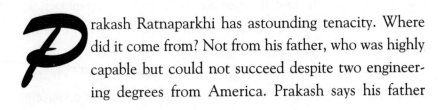

rakash Ratnaparkhi has astounding tenacity. Where did it come from? Not from his father, who was highly capable but could not succeed despite two engineering degrees from America. Prakash says his father "lacked social skills" and that he learnt tenacity from his mother, brother, sister and teacher.

THE AMBITIOUS STRUGGLER

Prakash's mother managed the household so capably that for some years he was not even aware that they were poor. Prakash recollects: "We may not have gone for trips because of financial difficulties but the house was full of joy, always filled with guests. My mother, brother and sister were full of encouragement for everything I achieved like getting a scholarship or prizes in games, or coming first in an elocution contest. My mother was methodical, whether in writing her accounts or ironing the clothes and keeping them neatly in the cupboard. My brother and sister were role models for me. My sister completed her education on a scholarship."

Prakash's mother, instead of complaining about her husband's none too successful career or financial problems, created joy in the house. It was not a mere discharge of duty. It was inherently *competency-strengthening behaviour*; she was always ready to give a pat on the back and a reassuring smile.

The greatest influence came from his teacher, Mr Kavthekar. During vacation classes, he used to teach how to repair radios, cars, transistors—how to connect and create. He went beyond his syllabus to teach the boys 'what leads to what' or '*what makes things happen*'—the very foundation of creativity. In such a learning ambience, Prakash became methodical, committed, strong and intense. Joy and creativity, the quintessence of nurturance, led Prakash to become the ambitious struggler that he is.

SECOND MOTHER

After he completed school in 1962, a friend pointed out an ad in a Marathi newspaper inviting applications for going to the United States under the International Student Exchange Programme. He applied, got a call, studied systematically, and was selected. What Prakash learnt then is important. "I did not miss the bus. Because I couldn't have afforded to go by rickshaw, _I had to prepare and organize myself._"

Prakash left for America at the age of 16 to live with a family he did not know at all, the Ross family, in Bloomfield Hills near Detroit. Initially, the relationship with Mrs Ross got strained because she did not take Prakash along with the family to see Niagara Falls. In retrospect, Prakash says, she handled it extremely well by explaining: "You have not come here for sightseeing. You are here to get accustomed to our way of life, our discipline, our work ethic."

In fact, she made him wash clothes, or even wash the toilet at midnight. These actions seemed like insults, but Prakash later realized that she was disciplining him. He changed his behaviour and their relationship grew. Says Prakash, "The lady raised me like she raised her children. She was like my mother, giving positive strokes to her children, husband and me. The decor, demeanor, decency, discipline, were all like at home in Pune; it

291

was an extension of my mother's environment. I realized I was 20 years ahead of my friends back home. I returned as a very confident person after a year's stay."

DESTINY CALLS

I ask Prakash, "Tell me, how did you grow from a garage workshop to seven manufacturing establishments and so many offices throughout India? Is there any thread to all this?" Prakash is forthright: "There is no such thread in my life. It is all vision, commitment, environment and drive. I think destiny was guiding us; I believe in coincidence. For instance: I knew Mr Bhatt, the mercurial promotor-director of Automatic Electrics, Mumbai. Once I happened to meet his assistant, one Kulkarni, to whom I mentioned that we were trying to make a spark erosion machine. Kulkarni in turn told me about the work going on at IIT, Powai on spark erosion. I knew Apte and some other people over at IIT. I found they were doing different things like generators, etc. Putting together some information, I made contact with IIT and got some inputs for our endeavour."

Prakash narrates another instance where coincidence played a part. "Once a friend of mine who'd just been to Japan said that some Japanese who made woodworking machines were looking for a collaboration to sell other products. Shrikant, my uncle, suggested we try this out. To sell your own product, you can first sell other peoples' products to get an entry. We felt such possibilities might exist elsewhere in the world. We went to Mumbai, collected information on relevant companies, obtained addresses

292

and sent enquiries. We were an unknown entity, with a turnover of only Rs 30 lakh. To our surprise, one day we received a cable from Switzerland from one of the topmost companies of the world to 'come and discuss'. We collected money from everywhere, went to Switzerland and signed an agreement in two visits."

Prakash goes on to tell of help received from an India-lover. "There was a very senior executive in this Swiss company who had earlier worked at Ambernath near Mumbai. He used to do yoga and had great respect for India. He had a collaboration offer from Hindustan Machine Tools (HMT), Bangalore, but did not want to get 'swallowed' in a big organization, so to say. Like us, he too had started in a garage. He trusted us to build a machine with hard work and sincerity, while giving him due credit and respect for his contribution. He had no interest in earning money, the amounts involved were chicken feed for him. He gave us machinery worth Rs 35 lakh. That helped us to double, triple, quadruple our turnover. Electronica became 10 times bigger.

"Such were the enabling developments, one leading to another; that's how destiny unfolded. But mind you, it enhanced our drive to take initiatives, leave no stone unturned for collecting exhaustive information, explore what's in store and remain doggedly entrenched until we get what we want."

MASTER OF TECHNOLOGY

This very drive led Prakash to forge a marketing strategy to sell spark erosion machines, then an unknown product in India.

Electronica developed hundreds of entrepreneurs by demonstrating what the machine does and how it is to be operated. Prakash says, "We tell the guy, you are an engineer, go back, secure a loan, start job-work without a machine and see what you earn— that motivates him to learn and succeed." R&D was a major focus right from the beginning for Prakash and Electronica, resulting in a slew of technical achievements, including:

- The manufacture of EDMs for the first time ever in India in 1973;

- The launch of an indigenously-developed digital readout system (DRO) in 1980;

- The launch of a CNC retrofit for the first time in India at IMTEX '82;

- The launch of the first 100 per cent indigenously-developed CNC wirecut EDM in 1985;

- The launch of the first CNC lathe in 1988;

- A technology transfer to Japan for EDM and CNC wirecut EDM in 1990.

Prakash's proclivity to take up challenges and commit whole-heartedly to achieving what he undertakes to do is unarguably his most appealing characteristic. Let me give one example: The CNC wirecutting machine came to the world market in the 1970s; at the IMTEX '79, Electronica imported the first Japanese wirecut machine and displayed it in India. Seeing the market potential, Prakash decided to develop this machine totally indigenously. As this was a very new product, it was impossible to get any technical cooperation from any leading manufacturer. After six years of R&D, the first 4-axis CNC wirecut EDM was developed and offered to the Indian market by Electronica at IMTEX '86. In order to programme the job on this machine, a special software had to be developed using the APT language. Prakash's in-house software group handled the job.

Their wirecut machines were a success. Till date, they have supplied over 350 machines in India and exported over 200 around the world to countries like Australia, Belgium, Egypt, Malaysia, Poland, South Africa, Germany and the UK.

The long list of awards that Prakash and his company have won includes the prestigious Parkhe memorial prize and the FIE foundation award. Prakash has been mainly responsible for new products and technology tie-ups with foreign companies; his achievements testify to his performance. In the growth of Electronica, his uncle Shrikant became a financial wizard and his brother Ravi capably fathered the expansion of the manufacturing base to seven units. I had to draw out Prakash to speak about himself, because he insists that it is the three of them, along with others in the company, who have worked as a team to capture success.

WHY CAN'T WE DO IT?

"Prakash, you earlier told me that the unique selling proposition of your spark erosion machine was its drilling capability, irrespective of the hardness, that it was a USP of technology, not of the machine *per se*. Similarly, for breaking the hard mental barriers to growth, what incisive psychological inputs did you secure for working on yourself and your team?" I ask. Says Prakash: "We were *never shy of seeking outside help*. We engaged many consultants for training, organization development, marketing and you name it. We ourselves attended many training courses, conferences and exhibitions, in fact a disproportionately high number compared to our requirements. We spent a lot of money on collecting information and literature that helped growth."

I comment: "You look like an R&D entrepreneur-turned-businessman. For your open mind, therefore, data gathering and learning come easily, don't they?" Prakash retorts: "I don't like catchy phrases to package reality, so I wouldn't call myself an 'R&D entrepreneur'. We hadn't gone abroad nor did we have the urge to go to the US. That made us think, how do we progress, what do we do next? I am not saying that we were mesmerized by nationalistic ideology. The only question we always asked ourselves was, '*Why can't we do it?*' In other words, when the Americans, Germans or Japanese can do it, why can't we?" Prakash's tone, his manner, his body language and the way he thumps the table while raising this query, 'why can't we do it?' to himself and to his colleagues, all of this demonstrates how his whole being throbs with creative dissatisfaction, the unwillingness to accept a *fait accompli* or defeat. He is constantly seeking impulses to jump from 'Why can't we do it?' to '*How can we do it?*' It is this obsession to make a technical breakthrough, or penetrate a market, or morph competent teams, that led Prakash to source more and more information, learn and relearn, until he was able to evolve a unique product.

SUCCESS HUMBLES

I ask Prakash: "You saw the hand of destiny in your growth. How did you interpret it, what meaning did it convey to you?" He answers: "The primary motive I saw was that if we have been blessed with so much early success, we are destined to become great. _Through vigorous efforts, we must enable destiny to allow further growth._ When we got the Dahanukar award for entrepreneurship in 1977, we took a conscious decision to make Electronica one of the largest companies in India in our field. _We had no backing, no background and yet our astounding success gave us a positive kick to leap forward._ So instead of plateauing, we decided to undertake more ambitious expansion plans. We got the feeling we were born to do something big, because we were getting more than we deserved. _Success humbled us._"

It is significant that when lady luck was smiling, the triumvirate did not indulge in merely enjoying the fruits of their labour, but rather they did some basic thinking. They decided to not get swollen heads or become complacent, but instead to intensify their efforts so that destiny would continue to favour their fertile terrain.

I probe: "What is the source of this thinking?" He says: "We felt that if we continue doing constructive things, what we want to happen will happen. This fundamental belief was developed in

297

childhood, that there was nothing material which we could give except 'doing' i.e. working and sharing." Sharing what, if there was nothing to give, I probe further. Prakash replies: "*Sharing humour, clever moves, little achievements, intelligent thoughts. You would share the best in you in informal chats with friends and relatives.* Later, since harnessing technology was my domain skill, I always said to myself let's create and show, and the intermission of satisfaction will throw us into higher spirals of growth."

Look at the rich tapestry of thought: Some are humbled but overawed with success and this sows the seeds of obsolescence. To make meaning out of turning points like unexpected success, what's required is creative application of mind to events in the unfolding drama. Prakash is often engaged in meaningful dialogue with himself in understanding the mystery of destiny. The renewed commitment to enriching the work ethic through more experiments on product development comes from his scientist-engineer mind. His philosophical thought forays provide profound meaning to these thought processes.

ORGANIZATION MENOPAUSE

I decide to provoke Prakash and ask him: "I am impressed by your incisive thinking, rare to find in an engineer. However, a Rs 100 crore turnover in 26 years is okay, but it's nothing great. Is the organization going through some kind of menopause?" Prakash answers honestly: "Well, you're right. *Growth is arithmetical but not geometrical because we are short on thinking manpower.* This question haunts us too. We are taking an unduly long time to respond to the opening up of the economy. The quality of people is not adequate for our tasks. There is a quantum jump in technological upgradation and quality improvement since 1992 due to globalisation, and we are falling woefully short. I must admit we lack strategic focus. The excellent people are not prepared to rub shoulders and train their juniors. We know the malaise. Loss of dependability leads to more and more dispensability and who wants to become vulnerable?"

What is the prescription, then? "We need to make the organization entrepreneurial by inculcating a culture of risk-taking and experimentation; secondly, by hiring people with an entrepreneurial drive. We need to give more attention to this than we do at the moment."

Here is an example of a dynamic company passing through a phase of loss of focus. The triumvirate is aware of it, but somehow immobilized. They will find a way out, however, given their innate brilliance and proven track record of struggle. Such out-of-focus periods do occur in the lives of organizations and individuals. It's a question of personal alchemy and renewal. If you start looking for opportunities you do find them. What is applicable to spotting business opportunities is relevant for organization and self-renewal as well.

JUST DO IT

How did they spot opportunities at the beginning or during their growth period? Says Prakash: "You just have to start 'doing'. I started working on ideas and products in the garage, relentlessly followed it up for two years, and the spark erosion machine was born. *Start doing what you feel like doing, what you understand.* Just as writers must overcome 'writer's block', you must overcome the 'doer's block', the initial resistance, hesitation to start. A certain cycle of events evolves. Speak to a few people. Take feedback, make corrections. If your antenna is sensitive, you'll spot the opportunity. *Your sensing ability is the key.* Increase interaction with yourself, and have a 24-hour involvement as I had while working on the spark erosion machine or the first electric discharge machine (EDM).

"Reading, thinking and talking about the problem doesn't help. The only thing that helps is 'doing', jumping in the water and swimming, so to say. Don't procrastinate. Get out of the house. Take your instruments in hand—whether you are making a chair, a screw set, an electric drive, a design board for designing a circuit-breaker, or whatever. Even if you have a great idea for making a TV commercial, pick up a pencil, brushes and colour and start working. Draw fishbowl diagrams if you like. Go out, meet people, and remember, *opportunities are also waiting to be born.* The 'doing' will put you in touch with them. Work with your hands. Do things when you are at college, attend conferences and visit exhibitions by spending your own money; they provide great learning opportunities. When you are young, your risk-taking abilities are higher. When you are on your own, you have greater freedom to 'do'. When you are on a job the freedom is less because you are paid a salary for the days logged in. The meter is running."

"Prakash, there may be some initial hesitation due to lack of skills to start. How does a person who is just setting out overcome that?" I ask. Prakash is clear: "Do apprenticeship. None of us three is a management graduate, and yet we are managing an organization of 1200 people. The moment you begin working you realize you have the skill. If you realize you are not able to do it, ask. Go ahead and acquire it if you don't have it, the skill, the wherewithal; period. That you are not able to do a certain thing is at least known to you—then, my dear friend, go and ask, request, plead, implore, _show intense willingness to learn_ at the convenience of the other, be polite, pleasing; you will acquire the skill."

What kind of 'bullet thought' is required for such involved 'doing', I wonder. Says Prakash: "The commitment to succeed. No genetic coding is required to make, for example, a wooden table for a lakh of rupees. _If you start doing, you get five years' experience in five months. The roadblocks will be crossed with deep-seated commitment._" What happens if you fail? "_Try again._" Obviously Prakash believes that the _'doing' must lead to 'finding'._

Prakash speaks of the ingredients of self-esteem and commitment. "As I told you, we have reached a roadblock within the organization, managers are unwilling to turn entrepreneurs, but we are doing something about it. Investigation skills are coming with commitment. Changing the structured mindset is very difficult but it has to be done. Self-esteem is needed for commitment. If it's not there to begin with, build it, develop it. Low self-esteem and lack of performance give birth to political vandals. _I burn the midnight oil to do what I promised to do_, what is missing is self-pride.

Performance is an extension of personality. What I say, I do, I certainly do. *What I commit to, I discharge. That is how it has to be.*"

TRAVELLING ONE'S WAY TO SUCCESS

Prakash speaks of how travel and exposure have benefited him and his team immensely. "*Extensive travel worldwide can be factored as 80 per cent of our success formula. We obtained many ideas by attending conferences, seminars and exhibitions.* We could study differences; read foreign magazines; take the initiative to know people who were ahead of us. You may get a setback, meet difficult people, but you may also forge a contact. It was hard-core learning and exhaustive travel that provided this kind of opportunities. It requires infinite patience and intense will to chase and get what you must feel inside, deep within yourself, that you want and deserve. *I believe help rushes in where strong desire exists. I consider work as my meditation and I honestly feel life is very simple.* We didn't do anything extraordinarily great. We simply toiled a lot. *Intelligence walks through when you work hard;* we only kept our eyes and ears open."

WHAT I MUST DO

What does Prakash think they must do from now on? What are the new imperatives? He is very clear about this: "Four things: *R&D, HRD, reliability and quality.* You can hire people for finance, marketing, manufacturing, accounts, where results are measurable and you get people who sell their abilities for a price. But R&D, HRD, reliability and quality are paid the least in organizations and stand low in the hierarchy. These disciplines require an incredible amount of reading, thinking, concentration and reflection. R&D is crucial and must feel needed. People don't practice HRD, it is very important that they do so. The thoughts of the top man have to be understood, digested. Those who are in contact with him will change, and might even get transformed. It is like a _guru_'s touch. Reliability means commitment. If I say I will do something, it means I will, and no follow-up is required. Quality means excellence.

"These activities form the four pillars of an organization's edifice. The quest for knowledge and experimentation are its attributes. Organizations get pilloried for non-performance if they fail in this. We are proud that we could build a machine that HMT could not. We are known for honouring our commitments in letter and in spirit. Of late, we are seeing a remarkable change in the thinking and personality of the organization, mainly springing from an awareness of the input of globalisation. The refocus process is under way."

LACK OF RESOURCES NO BAR

I ask Prakash, "You may have decided what must be done, but how should others with different backgrounds and patterns of upbringing go about it?" Prakash's advice is simple: "If you keep a goal in front of you and immerse yourself in the activities you

303

undertake to reach that goal, you are bound to attain it. Many people like Dhirubhai Ambani, Narayana Murthy or Raghunath Mashelkar started with nothing. They are simple people and have attained something extraordinarily high. *You don't need a special kind of DNA, any particular genetic coding.* You can succeed even without it. If you have some facilitative factors like the right up-bringing, the right environment or an appropriate education, to that extent you have some bank balance to start with. If you don't have a starting balance, you need to struggle that much harder, '*work smart*', and pull success your way."

Prakash believes that "You can succeed independently if your awareness is high about the presence and absence of background factors and lineage. *Irrespective of caste, community, religion and all such variables, you can definitely succeed if you have unwavering commitment and a passion for success.* Whether or not you have resources, success will come if you aim high and are prepared to put in the best of efforts. If a person from a deprived background reads, submerges himself in his desires and goals, and moves forward, he can succeed even at the age of 80. Apply the formula, you are sure to succeed."

Prakash lists three necessary ingredients which trigger static energy to become dynamic:

- The intelligence to understand what you have and what you don't have;

- A liking for sweat equity—making relentless efforts with an improvised approach, ever-new methods of work and renewed enthusiasm; and

- The capacity to tactfully handle success and failure.

Says Prakash, "_Static energy at various levels has to be triggered to make it dynamic._ Instead of cribbing about whether or not you have a particular mindset or upbringing, you should proceed to learn and inculcate what is missing. The earlier I acquire what is lacking, the faster I'll succeed. _A person gets what he deserves, not what he desires. For desires to becoming deserving endeavours, you have to work. If you don't get dreams of success then read, learn, study, internalise the techniques, you will get them._" Prakash proceeds to quote Rohinton Aga, the late chief of Thermax, who said, "Constraints are internal, not external."

I ask Prakash, "What exactly are the triggering techniques, the catalysing elements in making energy dynamic?" Prakash is not sure. "I do not consider myself very successful in triggering people to achieve higher goals. I need to learn more techniques. The problem is that people do not yet understand that things can be better. _Roti, kapda, makan_ (food, clothes and shelter) are not man's basic needs. Get a job and you are done. The basic needs are food, sleep and sex. They can be satisfied and are being satisfied with impunity, hence the population explosion! There is no benchmarking, you have to move ahead of someone. You should have the intellect to see dreams. Instead of just sitting idle in the factory during breaks, or in the office during lean work periods, read a few books, at any cost. You will have inspiring stories to tell your children and grandchildren."

Prakash is forthright in the expression of his views. His convictions do not tolerate ambiguity couched in grey zone talk. He can immediately spot if the other person is trying to wriggle out of a commitment, or is insincere about a commitment about to be given. In Prakash I find a true thought leader, throbbing with effort, intelligent thought processes and creative focus; a formidable formula for success.

Ronnie Screwvala

"You must love what you are doing."

A bubbly, smiling and amiable man, Ronnie Screwvala (44) is an instant hit with anybody who meets him. Owner of the Rs 175 crore entertainment and media group Unilazer, Ronnie's animated speech and expressive eyes exude a charm that is irresistible. He lives on Mumbai's posh Carmichael Road but his apartment reflects a simple lifestyle. An ace television talk-show host, his manner is unassuming and his dress informal.

Ronnie Screwvala's Unilazer group, of which UTV is the flagship, is a conglomerate of companies predominantly in the fields of infotainment and audiovisual communications. Its strength stems from the diversity of its operations in related fields and the strong cross-functional synergy amongst its various constituent companies. UTV has a strong presence in the Far East as well.

It is perhaps India's most comprehensive communications group, with activities that include tele-shopping, production of commercials, corporate videos, in-flight programming, dubbing of animation classics and theatrical films, television programming, news and current affairs, and acquisition and sale of channel media time.

Unilazer's hectic recruitment spree attests the vast employment potential of this service industry. Ronnie already has 300 animators and plans to add another 120, or a whopping 40 per cent. He has picked up $14 lakh worth of orders from Hollywood studios on the strength of the great salesmanship that he has exhibited within a year of entering the animation market. His motto is: '*You are in business so long as you are able to sell yourself*'.

THE ENTREPRENEURIAL BUG

Ronnie's Parsi upbringing provided him with a good grounding in ethical values, simple living and an understanding of the value of money. His parents wanted him to take up chartered accountancy, but he wasn't the studious type. In school and later at college, he was more drawn to extra-curricular activities, including the theatre. With a view to earning some money from activities they enjoyed, he and his friends began organizing annual events such as dances, plays, cultural events and New Year's eve parties. Apart from gaining organizational experience, Ronnie was thus introduced to the financial see-saw of a business venture.

Ronnie soon wanted to go beyond the confines of theatre as the media was his first love. Although he was doing programmes for Doordarshan, it was not enough to satisfy his entrepreneurial inclination. So along with a few partners, he started providing cable TV connections in Mumbai's Colaba area in 1981. This was the very birth of the cable industry, and Ronnie was in on it from day one. Although theirs was a small enterprise, it involved all the facets of setting up a business—persuasion, soliciting support, publicity, setbacks. After a year-and-a-half, their efforts bore fruit and the concept was sold. This was the first time the Indian viewer was getting a choice outside of Doordarshan (DD). Ronnie set up the network and also provided the software.

FIRST BRUSH WITH BUSINESS

Ronnie's ambitious mind set him on his path soon after he graduated from college. His first foray into business was a manufacturing enterprise, rather than a media-based one. He decided to go ahead with manufacturing in a nanosecond—he spotted an opportunity, worked out the commercial calculations and made a mental jump that transformed an ordinary event into paying business.

It so happened that while travelling in London with a friend, Ronnie chanced upon some tufting machines that were being scrapped. His quick mind seized the opportunity and came to the conclusion that the machines (used to make toothbrushes) didn't look second-hand, they were only three years old and had a good

35 years of life left in them. He returned to Mumbai, opened a letter of credit and bought the machines. He has always maintained that to build a balance sheet, one needs a manufacturing unit. This ability to take such entrepreneurial leaps explains how his company has reached its present position. That first snap-of-the-finger decision has resulted in an annual turnover of Rs 25 crore: Unilazer is India's largest toothbrush manufacturer, supplying major corporate giants such as Hindustan Lever, Colgate and Balsara.

KEEP SMILING

Ronnie attributes his amazing success to a four-pronged approach—patience and resilience, followed by professional management and quality production. This success formula, amply supplemented by his special immunity to frustration, is failsafe. His immunity to frustration, he says, is born out of his strong conviction that *any problem, no matter how tough, has its solution*. The only thing left is to "seek it and get it". He admits to feeling momentary frustration over things done wrongly or badly, but he has no place for sustained frustration that cripples action.

"What about interpersonal conflicts?" I ask. Ronnie says firmly, "*Not getting along is a bad word in the organization*. It does not work. All hell will break loose if interpersonal issues are not resolved. So there is pressure to resolve these issues. I am not going to sit in arbitration. More time has to be spent in building belongingness and commitment."

Ronnie's immunity to frustration comes in handy when delays beset new ventures and nothing seems to work. For instance, when UTV was started in 1991 to provide software to DD, only 13 episodes were approved at a time and there was an interminable wait for the next approval. Instead of losing motivation, Ronnie started thinking about how to use the free time and the services of the creative production team between approvals. Thus was born the idea of approaching airlines for upgrading their in-flight programming to suit passengers better. The 'sell and sail' philosophy translated into two years of hard-core selling. The fact that today his company does programming for 14 Indian and foreign airlines amply demonstrates Ronnie's indomitable spirit and his *ability to spearhead a profitable business by gainfully utilising spare time and making intelligent lateral moves.*

'DUE DILIGENCE' EXPERT

Ronnie soon realized that in order to consolidate activities they needed to raise funds. Established industries have hard collateral like mills or machinery of various kinds. UTV had to convince nervous banks of the value of "our collateral of 4000 programmes." Ronnie has put in tremendous effort and managed to woo nine foreign investors to invest in his venture. They have invested around Rs 99.50 crore in the group's various companies—UTV, USL, Vijay TV, UTV Singapore, UTV Malaysia and UTV Interactive. Hong Kong-based equity fund E M Warburg Pincus has invested about Rs 20 crore in USL, the post-production arm of UTV. IL&FS has invested about Rs 15 crore in Vijay TV. For Warburg Pincus, this was their first media investment in India; they became interested in UTV because they were impressed by Ronnie's vision, determination and abilities. It will be another feather in his cap when his group gets listed on the Nasdaq, as he plans. The nine hard-core international investors have done 18 rounds of 'due diligence' so far, which is an incredible amount of auditing. As the group has 11 joint venture partners, Ronnie has become an expert in due diligence management!

Ronnie had the advantage of his Parsi upbringing; the attention to detail and legal savvy required of an entrepreneur are characteristic of the community. Thus Ronnie has carried his inherent ethics and a homegrown value system to the citadels of the high-tech media industry. He was among the first people from this industry to raise private equity. Raising finance for ventures in new, unknown fields is a daunting task, but he accomplished it. His credibility and transparency played a major role in this.

His USP is simple—no tall claims, no name-dropping and no partying; Ronnie's selling technique reflects this transparency and sincerity. He now feels he ought to have done more networking; but even without that, he has managed to create the right background and move in for the kill with the twin tools of performance and integrity in relationships. When it comes to the crunch, *focusing on product reliability works best* and Ronnie says he has always placed a high premium on this aspect.

GROWING THE INDUSTRY

Media is a fairly new entrant in the Indian service industry. As it gets corporatised, UTV will be one of the pioneers to have laid down the ground rules. Very few company chiefs take serious interest in the progress of the industry that has sustained them. Fewer still have the time or the inclination to do the donkey work required for it. A higher level of entrepreneurship is called for to make an impact on and mould industry structure. Ronnie has taken it upon himself to upgrade the media awareness of government bodies. He is helping shape the Indian Broadcasting Society and his group is also engaged in foundational work. He has sold the concept of creating a media wing to the Federation of Indian Chambers of Commerce and Industry (FICCI) and to the Confederation of Indian Industry (CII). A presentation has been made to the finance minister and the group will soon be on the export council. As much as 25 per cent of the company time is devoted to industry work and interacting with people. "We spend a lot of money on research and data collection. We do not have any readymade data," Ronnie tells me. It is heartening to see his expanding vision strengthening the lobbying power and the foundation of the industry.

GLOBAL VISION

Ronnie has a strong vision statement—to be an Asian media powerhouse in diversified media fields by 2003, and establish a global presence by 2007. The first part of this statement is well on

313

its way to being fulfilled, with the group already making its presence felt in three Asian countries and in seven languages. The group forayed into the South-East Asian market in 1998. UTV Singapore and UTV Malaysia are in air-time sales, news and current affairs. The core strength of these channels lies in building shows in multiple Asian languages such as Tamil, Mandarin, Bahasa, etc. Today, UTV Singapore provides content for TV channels in Singapore such as TCS, TV12, Star and SCV.

"What made you set your sights beyond our shores, Ronnie?" I ask. He says that *"reading, watching, observing and discriminating"* are behind the evolution of his global vision. The amount of reading must be vast: He subscribes to 19 business magazines from around the world! The autobiographies of personalities like Sam Walton give him a direction in his quest to advance in media, tele-shopping, infotainment and audio-visual communication. *Observing the progress of benchmarked organizations and the people in those businesses also serves to influence his thinking.*

In visualizing a global future, Ronnie does not subscribe to a structured approach. He has no systematic year-by-year mark. Yet, the organization has grown systematically from what was started with a paid-up capital of Rs 37,000 to a Rs 175 crore group. His financial benchmark is to be a $1 crore company and one of the top 200 companies in the world. Instead of a structured approach, he has a philosophy: *"You must love what you are doing."* Coupled with this is his belief that the ability to build an organization and create wealth is the critical determinant in this achievement. Definite echos of Marsha Sinetar's classic, *Do what you love; the money will follow.*

ADRENALINE SURGE

Ronnie must have incessantly envisioned, at times unconsciously, the build-up of his media conglomerate into what it is today. How else would he have reached where he is, instead of remaining a local cable operator? It speaks of a relentless drive and vigour to bring his dreams to reality. His process of self-renewal is to put himself through the grind, as if he were on a treadmill, continuously taking that next step forward. He does not find solace in stilling the mind with yoga or meditation because there's a marathon to be run, and he and his colleagues need the _adrenaline surge_.

What are the criteria he applies in selecting people to run in this marathon? "I look for ambitious, ambidextrous people who are updated in skills and conversant with the economy, people with _a fire in the belly_, passion and commitment." He believes that people should break out of the 'parental' mode, or job-mindedness, to explore the work world and not hit a career plateau. He believes in the beneficial role played by exposure, fresh air, travel, meeting different people and doing the unusual. If one has to reach somewhere one cannot be confined to a balanced life. For Ronnie, renewal comes from reaching out.

"How do you motivate your people?" I enquire. Ronnie explains, "In this business, we have designations like producer, director. You can't be called a super producer. Can Spielberg become a 'super director' in designation? No, he remains a director, no matter how many blockbusters he produces. _For highly creative people, scope for creation is the only motivation._"

315

Spectacular success can be the only driver, and recognition the only impetus. If everyone is involved in generating wealth for the company, they will get some share of the profit. The cool shade of a secure corporate brand under which they can grow and prosper is not available in the media industry. But the awareness that they are creating the industry is motivation in itself. It is a 'being to becoming' journey.

THE ALCHEMY OF PASSION

In an industry largely seen as disorganized, unprofessional, extremely high-risk, somewhat nebulous, believed to be governed by the stars, Venus and Neptune, and therefore peopled by deceptive characters, how does Ronnie maintain his equilibrium? "In the media business there has to be passion, *75 per cent of the business is passion* and the balance 25 per cent is corporate. The challenge is to maintain this ratio and remain creative, yet corporate and professional as well."

The passion with which Ronnie conveys his commitment provides clues to his process of thinking. *Commitment in the first place begins with the language of commitment. Language creates the context.* The talk-show host's rhetoric mobilises action at Unilazer. Ronnie's passion is infectious and his commitment provides an impetus to the entire team.

Hats off to a disarmingly simple yet very ambitious media icon visualizing greater glory for India in the process of doing what he loves.

316

Sartaj Singh

"The more I network, the more I learn."

FMC, a diversified $5 lakh company based in Chicago and Philadelphia, USA, is one of the leading producers of chemicals and machinery for industry, agriculture and the government. The company participates on a worldwide basis in three broad markets—performance chemicals, industrial chemicals, and machinery and equipment. At the helm as country manager is the affable and soft-spoken Sartaj Singh (43).

Sartaj Singh has three roles to play. He is the managing director of the newly incorporated joint venture FMC-Rallis India Ltd, which manufactures FMC's range of agrochemicals; as FMC's country manager, he has to oversee FMC's food, technology, biopolymers and machinery businesses which already operate in India, with a mandate to scout new opportunities for other businesses of FMC; and as regional director, he oversees FMC's agricultural products group in South-West Asia covering Myanmar, Bangladesh, Sri Lanka and India.

Sartaj's first job was with the renowned British multinational Imperial Chemical Industry (ICI), where he worked for 16 years. He made a significant contribution to the rubber chemicals and speciality chemicals business, becoming its youngest director before he left. What powered this performance? "I believe I have excellent people management skills. I am very exacting, but I know how to handle and motivate people. I have always been humble, acknowledging team efforts in every achievement. ICI must have taken all this into account. *These companies groom you to govern.*"

LEADING BY EXAMPLE

Sartaj then joined Cargill Seeds India Ltd. The company had spun off its original line, industrial chemicals, into a separate venture and acquired a large number of seed companies worldwide to emerge as the largest seed company in the world. As he was new to the seeds industry, Sartaj had a lot to learn. He is quick to acknowledge the contribution and support of his team. They provided him with information inputs so that he could clue himself in on the industry.

As CEO of Cargill, he realized that heading a separate legal entity was a different ball game. "It was essential that I lead by example. *Absentee leadership doesn't work.* I have to be there, on the job, demonstrating what I mean, putting my money where my mouth is, so to speak." As he points out, new thought processes had to be driven home; for instance, teaching people to 'own' the economy drive that was undertaken. Every employee had to feel that he or she had a stake in going all out.

"I had to drive home the point that you won't earn salaries as a matter of right, you simply have to work for it. Every decision has to be costed out. This is my biggest contribution to my team, to train them in thinking 'value for money'. In the process, I too have learnt so much. The *scope for wastage is immense in all the things that we omit to do.* I pinpointed the following areas: Not negotiating hard enough, making quick payments but not expecting prompt payments, not checking and auditing. The commercial aspect of doing business must go hand in hand with the technology. It is not enough at the end of the day to say 'I did my bit'. Your performance has to be part of the big picture. You must ask yourself 'Have I got what I asked for? Did I look for viable alternatives? Did I do my costing'?"

After he'd been with Cargill for two years, it was taken over by Monsanto. Sartaj became the managing director and CEO of Monsanto Technologies India Ltd (the erstwhile Cargill Seeds India Ltd) and director, marketing and business strategy, for Monsanto's integrated chemicals, seeds and biotech businesses in India. He successfully integrated the seed businesses into Monsanto's traditional and mainline agrochemical business, and restructured the company to operate the combined business, providing the Monsanto organization with an understanding and appreciation of the complexities of the seed business. He then joined FMC in January 2000.

A COMPLEX SYNERGY

"With all these skills, Sartaj, didn't you ever feel the urge to be an entrepreneur?" I ask. No, he says, he recognizes the fact that his career prospects lie with a good organization. "I couldn't have been an entrepreneur; I can't put money into the stock market. I manage my business commercially, but genetically I am not cut out for becoming an entrepreneur." His strengths are his ability to spot opportunities and his gut feeling for marketing. He says he relies a lot on his hunches and instincts, which have usually proved correct.

Cargill's merger with Monsanto enhanced his career prospects, according to Sartaj. He had to play a multiple role since he was made responsible for the chemicals, seeds and biotech businesses as director of marketing and business strategy. During his short stint of about a year in the merged business, he had to zero in his management skills on to what was required—'change management'. Maximum synergy was to be achieved through cultural amalgamation of the Monsanto and Cargill staff.

It is a complex synergy, and yet Sartaj makes it sound so simple. What does he attribute this to? "Discipline and respect, inculcated at the very outset by my father, who was an army colonel.

People in the army respect hierarchy and are normally excellent at teamwork. After that, my school, and my nine postings in ICI."

HUMBLING INFLUENCE

In 1987 Sartaj and his wife Sarina had a baby girl, Chandani. The happy event turned tragic when they realized that, as he puts it, "God chose us" to be the parents of a mentally retarded child. When Chandani was diagnosed with Down's syndrome, Sartaj was awash in grief. For some time he even kept the fact hidden from his wife. As he came to terms with his daughter's condition, he underwent a shift in consciousness. Sartaj says: "I have learnt so much from this; my entire perspective changed; my demands on life became modulated; you become less greedy, less ambitious. You realize that there is something bigger, a larger destiny to be fulfilled. You have to give priority to something else. You become very humble."

However, in spite of consciously cutting back ambition, Sartaj remains motivated, dynamic and result-oriented. It is a fine balance that he has found. He continues to "achieve while having fun". This is a quality that endears him to his people. He is able to focus on their energies. He makes himself available to them. He sees several steps ahead. Meticulous planning, an eye for detail, motivation and leadership are, he considers, his contributions. Added to this is his alchemy in making managers and staff 'own' their part of the 'process' journey. Sartaj has learnt the knack of ownership transference, which is clearly evident in the way he operates.

321

TEACHER, NOT PREACHER

Sartaj says: "A leader is a teacher but I make sure that I don't become a preacher. That is an art. I pass on as much as I can through examples, stories. I don't directly 'tell' people what to do. I share and cite from my personal repertoire of experiences. I don't simply provide all the solutions. I try to make people arrive at alternatives. I allow them to make mistakes. I don't spoon-feed people. *I don't provide the 'how'*. I leave them to handle 'how' to do it."

"Here again you have achieved a fine balance, Sartaj," I say. "How do you manage?" He agrees that it is very difficult to refrain from giving the solution, especially when people seem stuck. "I tell people 'I won't do your dirty work; manage relationships at your level'. The guidance I give is only to indicate that people should not use positional power." They should manage with their personality, charisma, aura, and straightforward dealings, he says. "I guide the person to see my way and hunt for solutions. Again I make him own his search process."

If people appear helpless and ask for specific help, if it seems to Sartaj that they are not applying themselves, he simply says: "Leave it to me, I will do it." This usually works—encouraging, sometimes forcing people to chalk out their own path. In his characteristic jovial fashion he quips: "My other objective is that I should do the least possible amount of work!"

Sartaj is not shy in admitting that he is a role model. "People like me," he states. "They treat me like the head of the family. I am genuinely interested in people. Talking to them, I learn more. I do a fair amount of networking. *The more I network, the more I learn.*" He is greatly aided by his honesty, fairness, helping nature and eye for detail, and by the true mentor's *ability to guide and not interfere.*

AVOID OVER-PROGRAMMING

Sartaj says, "Today, youngsters want everything programmed, they suffer from overstructuring. Some amount of programming is okay, but why not leave the space for some things to just happen? Do not have too many milestones in mind. Just work hard. Develop many contacts, establish your own identity early in the game, and work in leading organizations. Focus on leading ideas. Stick to personal values."

He points out that people are over-programming every aspect of their lives, even relaxation. "I don't necessarily want to go on a trek or do something special for rejuvenation. In fact I don't want to think too much or too seriously. I think I am focusing well. I don't make too much effort to 'improve myself' in any predetermined way, such as meditation and so forth. In fact, I don't continuously concentrate. I can relax by simply doing errands, watching movies, spending time with my family, and that's it." He feels that people with programmed ambitions and set milestones lose their natural charm and style.

A LIVING INDIVIDUALIZED CORPORATION

Sartaj is clear about this: "You can have a more relaxed style, while remaining fully focused on your purpose, process and people." Sartaj may not have entrepreneurial risk-taking proclivities, but he demonstrates what Sumantra Ghosal and Christopher Bartlett highlight as the three common characteristics of the institutionalized entrepreneurial practices of 3M, in their bestseller *The Individualized Corporation*:

- Inspiring individual initiative requires that individuals feel a sense of ownership in what they do; this is easier to achieve in small organizational units.

- The complement is a strong sense of self-discipline, a performance standard that comes from within each individual. Unlike control, it is not imposed from above.

- Management needs to reflect its respect for the individual in a supportive culture that is open to questioning from below and tolerant of failure.

Sartaj's career and thoughts reveal that, without having read the book, he was in fact functioning along those very lines. In essence, Sartaj himself personifies a living individualized corporation.

Ashok Soota

"Knowledge is the only resource that doesn't diminish."

Ashok Soota (58), chairman and chief executive officer of MindTree Consulting Private Ltd, a Rs 40 crore e-commerce and telecom software company launched in 1999, is the man who earlier built IT giant Wipro Infotech from scratch. Although the company belonged not to him, but to Azim Premji, Ashok went about the task as if he were an entrepreneur. The story of how a series of fruitful coincidences first took him to Wipro and later brought MindTree into being demonstrates his ability to seize opportunities and shape his destiny.

MindTree is a textbook entrepreneurial formation which brought together a group of experienced professionals with a longing to strike out on their own: Ashok Soota, Subroto Bagchi and seven others, culled from Wipro, Cambridge Technologies and Lucent. Bagchi, MindTree's vice-chairman, had earlier worked with

Soota at Wipro. Later, while he was a director at Lucent Technologies (India), he had spoken of his dream of a new start-up with Som Dutt of Walden, a venture capital fund that specialises in high-tech deals. Bagchi and his colleagues were looking for a leader, a chairman to head their venture. *Serendipity* was manifest when Ashok too spoke to Som about his own plans. He, too, wanted to quit his job and venture out on his own in the high-tech field…

A BRILLIANT BUSINESS GUESS

The *Business World* records how Ashok made a brilliant guess on who else had an identical dream of a unique start-up. Som tells Bagchi that he received a call from Ashok Soota; Bagchi narrates: "Ashok wanted to know whether Som would be interested in funding his venture. Som asked Ashok about his business model and was amazed at the synergy in his proposed model and our own. As a venture capitalist, Som could not tell Ashok much. Instead, he told Ashok that some senior and former Wipro employees were planning a similar venture. Ashok said: 'Let me guess—you are talking about Subroto Bagchi.' Som asked if Ashok would be open to a merger of his dream with ours, and whether Som could take me into confidence. Ashok did not hesitate. He said, 'Go ahead'."

Speaking about his felicitous meeting with Bagchi, Ashok says: "Some external force brought us together. Personally, I am delighted it happened." Bagchi was overjoyed at finding Ashok (he terms it as 'unbelievable'). Without demonstrable achievements, affable leadership, respect and trust, nobody is sought-after like this. This itself speaks volumes about Ashok's charisma and standing among top-notch professionals in this high-tech business. His professional insight helped him to 'read the signs' hidden in chance meetings and coincidences. This manager-cum-entrepreneur admits to being superstitious.

COINCIDENCES ARE SIGNIFICANT

Ashok cites an earlier, similarly fortuitous encounter. He had taken a break from his first job with the Shriram group and gone on a sabbatical to the US. While there, he met an old college friend from Roorkee who was in the consultancy business. This same friend met Wipro's Azim Premji a year later. Premji was at that time scouting for someone to start a computer company for him; the person didn't have to be from the IT industry. Ashok's friend spoke about him to Premji, who liked his profile. Out of the blue, Ashok received a call from Premji which led to his switchover to Wipro—something he had never planned. Ashok took up the new assignment in 1984 after several months debating the move.

It was a difficult decision because Shriram Refrigeration was a Rs 35 crore company and was doing well. But Ashok realized there were inherent limits on progress for Shriram Refrigeration. Moreover, he could see the huge potential in the IT industry and expected IT companies to operate in a very professional environ-ment. So he took a gamble, which turned out to be a good one.

The various events have elements of coincidence—Premji looking for someone to start an IT company; his readiness to con-sider a non-IT professional with a proven track record; Ashok meeting his college friend in the consultancy business in America; Ashok then meeting Premji a year later and deciding to leave a secure job where he had standing. Serendipity is also evident in Ashok telling Som Dutt about his dream when Dutt was already involved with Bagchi's; their dreams dovetailed.

When Ashok spoke to me about the contribution of coinci-dence in a professional's achievements, he was not talking about the 'do-nothing fatalism' that is an affliction of so many Indians. For him, coincidences are significant turning points. Your aware-ness of such occurrences provides vital clues and pointers on the road map to success. I met Ashok over dinner at the Marine Plaza hotel on Mumbai's Marine Drive on March 7, 1999, when he was still at Wipro. I asked him: "How do you look at your career from now on?" He was not quite sure where his future anchor would be, saying only, "I would be continuously active, that's for sure." I got the feeling that Ashok was unconsciously searching for an opportunity to give fuller expression to his being. My hunch turned out to be correct; Ashok left for MindTree within a few months. I quote *Business World* again:

"You can never predict when the entrepreneurial bug will bite a man. It bit Ashok Soota at the age of 56. Till the beginning of 1999, the dapper bachelor had never exhibited any signs of start-up fever. If anything, Soota was the quintessential company man, changing jobs just once in the past 35 years.

"The electrical engineering graduate from Roorkee Engineering College, who holds a business management degree from the Asian Institute of Management in the Philippines, started his career with the Shriram group in 1965. There he remained before resigning in 1984, when he was already the CEO of Shriram Refrigeration. He joined the fledgling Wipro Infotech as its president and spent the next 15 years building it up into an IT powerhouse and becoming the vice-chairman of Wipro.

"And then, one fine day, Soota rocked the industry with his announcement. He was quitting Wipro to set up a software start-up. But why? And why now? 'Well, for the last one year there has been a growing internal urge to seek self-expression. With the boom in internet and electronic commerce, there are so many opportunities for entrepreneurs today. I want to be part of it,' says Soota."

FORMATIVE INFLUENCES

Let's take a look at Ashok's background. His father, an army doctor, had over the years earned the enormous goodwill of the families of the rank and file; his 'caring' genes have found their way into Ashok's psyche. Ashok learnt 'sharing' in the company of five brothers and sisters. The regular postings that went with his father's job, and the subsequent relocations, taught Ashok how to _adapt to change_. Ashok feels these basal ingredients moulded

329

him into the person he is. In addition, he developed a western outlook on life from his English-medium schools. The years he spent studying at the Roorkee Engineering College exposed him to Indian culture. This amalgam has helped him identify intimately with Indian values, and yet maintain a global worldview.

THE IMPORTANCE OF PRESENTATION

While he was working at Shriram Refrigeration, Ashok was seconded to Usha, Sri Lanka. It was a multi-functional responsibility, which he was given in the third year of his career. After working for eight years, he decided to take a sabbatical and went to Manila to do a masters in business management at the Asian Institute of Management. This rigorous input provided a conceptual framework to his practical experience. It brought about an external orientation, an exposure to different people and cultures. It was during this time that Ashok developed a desire for continuous learning. The institute emphasised the value of expression in management—*not only should you know your work well, but you should also be able to communicate well.*

The courses he took on communications increased his verbal and presentation skills exponentially. They made a significant impact on his creative accomplishments later in life. Acquiring these skills and sharpening them gave him tremendous confidence. Addressing large audiences, using his speeches as a catalyst for self-learning, has consistently provided him with stimulating experiences, he says.

SIGNIFICANT MENTORS

Ashok was very fortunate in meeting two mentors early in his career: Dr Charat Ram, the legendary industrialist from Delhi, and Bishan Sahai, his company secretary. Both these bosses demanded results. Charat Ram was a great developer of young employees; he rotated them throughout the company on different assignments. Bishan Sahai was a good role model for thoroughness in work. Charat Ram discussed work, Bishan talked about career choices. Watching them, Ashok learnt that opposite styles and approaches can deliver results. Ashok also speaks of Tarun Das of the Confederation of Indian Industry (CII) who influenced the formation of his professional identity. "Tarun got me interested (in the CII). Taking on responsibilities at the state and regional levels gave me a wider canvas. Also CII involvement gave Wipro significant visibility even before the company became so visible in its own right," Ashok says.

THE IDEAS MAN

Ashok candidly admits that he was born into a privileged network of the right parents, a nurturing family, inspiring mentors and challenging work opportunities; and all this at the right age. However, his reputation as an innovative manager has been hard-earned. See his record at the Shriram group between 1978 and 1984: within one year Ashok turned round Shriram Refrigeration, which had been making losses for five consecutive years; he went on to increase profits year after year and introduced many new products and technologies.

Later at Wipro Infotech he introduced the Wipro PC, which became the best Indian brand. On the premise that larger volumes must come from fewer lines, Wipro gave up the Apple line, defence surveillance and hardware for exports. The center of gravity of the company changed. Wipro Infotech has been voted as the most admired and respected Indian IT company for several years by different magazines. Personally Ashok was recognized as 'IT Man of the Year' on three occasions by *Elcina, Dataquest* and *Computer World.* Says he, "My innovative moves are based on international best practices, learning from the competition, travelling and seeing things, and discussions with all levels of staff. *Anyone with a viable idea can become an entrepreneur.*"

I ask Ashok to give me an example. "Look at Sabeer Bhatia's hotmail success story. You make the mail free and get the advertisements. That means you have sold the space and at somebody's cost you are sending the mail free. It is not the idea alone but it is also *the conviction.* I am sure there are hundreds of such ideas and venture capitalists are looking for ideas and people."

The major pitfalls the financiers watch out for are lack of domain skills, poor communication, the inability to say 'no' and poor project management. However, cross-cultural training and other training programmes will make good these deficiencies over a period of time. Understanding the market and industry is important. Solutions can only be found with in-built knowledge of the nature of the industry and its problems.

Says Ashok: "IT is impregnating traditional industry and changing the very structure of its operation by devices like the internet. It will happen over here, the internet will take off. Cultural change will come. For example it will be a virtual community of professionals echoing identical cultures seeking each other out, and people tuned to real time in life. Personalities interconnected through the internet would therefore undergo change."

A global community of thinkers is morphing, loyalties are getting transferred to one's profession from one's organization. Ideas come to Ashok in what he calls a very 'unconnected' way. He gets ideas while taking a walk, reading, conducting group discussions, in conversation with colleagues, or while relaxing. Frequently, he jots down an idea immediately, lists a few points, and then takes it up later to develop it further. He is able to spot a gap while playing facilitator. Ashok's driver is technology. The whole idea of brainstorming fascinates him. This process of a team putting its heads together leads to identifying opportunities.

THE TRUST FACTOR

Ashok speaks with some amount of pride about building Wipro Infotech under Azim Premji and turning round Shriram Refrigeration. He attributes these successes to earning the confidence of bosses, peers, in fact the whole team. What were the skills that he used in gaining this trust? "They didn't feel that I would use information or data, provided by them, against them. I would give them their due and show that it added to the value chain. I would assure them that I would get back to them in six months with whatever issues there were."

Analytical ability, strategizing, selecting and nurturing the right people, working in a team and leading from the front are Ashok's abilities. His asset base is identifying and recognizing trends, not mere visual patterns. The return on assets is creation of goodwill and trust. The domain skill he uses is mathematics coupled with his commercial acumen. His proficiency in learning from the behaviour of advanced markets has proved to be of invaluable use in the high-velocity IT industry.

HANDLING PEER RIVALRY

"Have you encountered peer rivalry or had your leadership questioned?" I ask Ashok. He replies: "I have been lucky. I encountered only very little rivalry at Shriram Refrigeration early in my career. I learnt not to adopt a confrontational approach early in life. My father had enormous capabilities, but I feel his confrontational approach with his superiors in the defence services prevented him from reaching much higher levels at work than he did. At the same time, I saw and picked up the way he built bonds with his people in the large field units he looked after." On the basis of these observations, Ashok chose to become proactive in handling peer resentment. He has been able to generate trust by setting an example, and thereby increase his 'circle of influence', to use Stephen Covey's term.

How Ashok learnt from his father's faulty approach is a lesson in key _behaviour change_. Ashok has amply proved that _empathy and persuasion, rather than confrontation_, give better results. Many careers go wayward due to an offensive approach, behaviour that spells effrontery, aggressive body language and postures. Occasionally, confrontation may be desirable as a tactic for leading an issue to a solution. However, as an overall approach or style of functioning, it is counterproductive and an impediment to smooth team functioning. Whether you work in a large or small organization, or on your own in a network, team performance is a crucial determinant of success.

TIE WORK TO PERSONAL VALUES

Ashok recommends that youngsters play, study and work in as many group activities as possible. He thinks they should establish an early identity, develop many social contacts, specialise early in life and focus on a leading idea. "Youngsters must learn to tie work to personal values," is a golden rule that he keeps reiterating. There cannot be a dichotomy between the two, he strongly feels. Like software engineer Dinesh Vijapurkar (38) of Tecumesh Products India Ltd, Hyderabad, many who have worked with Ashok feel that they would like to be like him—making him a true role model. "Boys and girls coming from good schools and excellent family backgrounds have many vocational choices. _The key to effectivity is acquisition of communication skills, presentation skills, articulation skills_," Ashok says. He talks admiringly about young people's knowledge and intuitive skills, and believes that

335

they should build their careers on these foundation stones. *"Knowledge is the only resource that doesn't diminish,"* he says.

Fertile Mental Terrain

Ashok himself became a full-fledged entrepreneur only last year. Ashok's mental terrain is fertile, where the tree of electronic commerce has taken root and is flourishing. His ability to spot opportunities is paying rich dividends.

Ashok renews himself with regular exercise, diet control and value clarification. Through reading, planning and empathy with his colleagues, he achieves social synergy, which is a part of his renewal process. How would Ashok like to be remembered? "As a fair and thoughtful person who created enormous goodwill with people. Beyond a point, success in terms of money doesn't carry any weight in my mind; the satisfaction of a job well done and the introduction of a new product, those are what matter at the end of the day." An inspiring example indeed, of an achiever who is half a century young.

Vikram Tannan

"Work is the greatest 'high' for me."

Banner Pharmacaps (India) Private Ltd (turnover Rs 100 crore, 1000 employees) is a joint venture between Vikram Tannan, a pioneer in the field of soft gelatin capsules in India, and Banner Pharmacaps BV, a wholly-owned subsidiary of Sobel NV, Holland. Tall and polished, Vikram (55) heads the JV as its managing director.

A few decades ago, for reasons of health, I used to take the pearl-like Seven Seas cod liver soft gelatin capsules, called softgels by the industry. I was intrigued to know how they were made; I was grateful to the manufacturer because the softgels were a monumental improvement over the smelly oil I detested taking in childhood. So when Vikram Tannan's name was forcefully recommended by a common friend, I jumped at the opportunity to meet him, and what a fine person I met.

PEARL-LIKE SOFTGELS

Vikram's company manufactures soft elastic gelatin capsules to exacting specifications and under stringent controls. Banner Pharmacaps established its identity in India by expanding and modernising an already existing plant at Sarigam, Gujarat, where it has created a capacity of one billion capsules per annum. The plant has received good manufacturing practices (GMP) certification from the World Health Organization (WHO). Characterised by innovation and quality, Banner Pharmacaps is known for producing innovative drug delivery systems for their clients. The company encapsulates products for major players in the pharmaceutical industry, mostly multinationals.

Encouraged by this success and to cater to the growing domestic and international markets, a second plant was set up at Bangalore with a capacity of two billion capsules per annum, which can be augmented to four billion. This Rs 45 crore project has sophisticated, state-of-the-art, high-speed machinery from the Banner stable. The plant has been designed to meet the stringent US FDA, Australian TGA and UK MCA requirements and is the only world-class facility of its kind in the Asia Pacific region. Set up on an eight-acre plot, the plant incorporates the cutting edge of technological advances in manufacturing.

TAKING UP A CHALLENGE

Vikram's father B R Tannan, a chartered accountant, was a doyen of the profession, well-known and respected in corporate

338

circles. He was on the board of leading multinationals such as Rallis India, Colour Chem, BASF, Hoechst and Boehringer Knoll. Vikram feels that a secure family background and the in-culcation of the right values during his formative years have been the greatest assets in helping him conduct his business in an ethi-cal manner. A loving but strict upbringing also taught him the merit of hard work and perseverance.

Being a close-knit family, the Tannans spent a lot of time in family activities. The years he spent at boarding school gave him the opportunity to make a number of friends, and a taste for sports and outdoor activities. "A close-knit and happy home life has been a springboard for greater effectiveness in the work place. Also, cooperation and wise counsel by the family have contrib-uted a great deal to my success," Vikram says.

In 1963 his father founded a company, Capsulation Services, at Deonar in Mumbai. Vikram, who had studied accountancy like his father, joined the firm in 1969. The death of Tannan senior in 1974 served as a challenge for Vikram to ensure that the good work started by his father continued and prospered. Fortuitously, says Vikram, "At around the same time, I had made enquiries with the world famous 'Seven Seas', and a call from them resulted in a golden opportunity to bring them to India. After protracted negotiations, I became the first licensee of this traditional British company, which was at the time a wholly-owned subsidiary of Imperial Tobacco."

"What drove your interest, Vikram?" I ask. He says, "My inter-est was stimulated in more than one way, that is to manufacture and encapsulate a quality product which would conform to strict international standards, keep our encapsulation capacities busy, and re-introduce an age-old product into India." Several opportunities ensued, with various tie-ups with leading multinationals. Vikram is in such a niche area, how is it he is never featured in the media? He says that he is simply "shy of getting into the limelight".

VOYAGE OF SEVEN SEAS

How did the Seven Seas voyage start? After contacting Seven Seas in England Vikram received a call from them, which he had not really been expecting. It was a great opportunity. "How did you spot this opportunity?" I ask.

Vikram narrates, "On a casual visit to Crawford Market for sundry purchases, I saw a soft gelatin capsule. *I was curious* to find out who was behind it. The manufacturers turned out to be in Hull in the UK. I approached them. They invited me to meet them. I made a presentation and came back to India. We made a trial batch but it failed. Their engineer visited us, we took another trial and finally succeeded in making it to their specifications. When first I had made the presentation, there was general distrust of Indians on quality, cleanliness and maintenance standards. But I commissioned a market survey and they also saw us in action. We got the agency."

Vikram does not come from a family of entrepreneurs. His father was an outright professional. His connection with pharmaceutical companies probably gave him the idea to set up a small unit so he would have something to do after retiring as a CA. Vikram too trained as an accountant. "So where did your interest in entrepreneurship come from?" I ask. He says, "From a certain degree of perception, I guess. *I rolled up my sleeves and got in*, hands on. I read a lot and digested knowledge from the people around me. *I turned potential circumstances into commercial opportunities*. I made a decision and followed it through."

What was the driving force? "*The motivation to make money along with the ambition-to-completion axis were my anchors*. The niche market was there. The soft capsules business I had inherited was archaic. I had to make a lot of innovations. All machines are built here, there is an on-going technological modernisation. It was a big challenge and I don't like to let go of challenges, my nature is to pursue and follow things through. *Work is the greatest 'high' for me*. Despite occasional setbacks, my persistence paid off. One thing led to another." Vikram's voyage of discovery across the seven seas to explore opportunities for making money had begun.

THINK BIG—THE DUTCH INFLUENCE

Did Vikram have any mentors? The answer is a firm "no". However, he admits having learnt a lot from his Dutch collaborator, Sobel. Says Vikram: "I was my own master, but I was in my shell, and not growing. Van Droon, the Sobel chairman, said 'Think big'. The association with the Dutch and Van Droon's personal influence changed my mindset. I was exposed to a greater world. The 'bigness' was there to see, observe and feel. I signed my first joint venture in 1990. It opened up my eyes to greater opportunities. Then came Banner Pharmacaps, Sobel's US subsidiary. Americans really think big. My entire horizon changed. *One has to be focused, otherwise somebody else will take the opportunity."*

This sounds like Jack Welch's profound advice given to General Electric employees: *"Control your destiny or someone else will."* The meaning is simple: *Take responsibility.* Vikram did. Otherwise he would have been required to accept a fate that may not have been to his liking. 'Thinking big' doesn't mean building castles in the air. The plan, strategy, risk, execution, details and reliability on quality and deliverables have all to follow in synergistic sequence.

Vikram's methodical approach did just that. The results speak for themselves. When he joined in 1969 the turnover was Rs 10 lakh; today it is Rs 100 crore. Starting from a small unit in a Mumbai suburb, to become a member of a world-renowned big organization like Banner Pharmacaps BV, meeting their exacting standards in technology, quality and good manufacturing practices (GMP), is really becoming big. Vikram not only thought big, but also worked assiduously to become big.

THE INNOVATIVE LEAP

What led to the innovative leap? Vikram says, "My greatest opportunity was relative to the specialised aspects of the manufacture of soft gelatin capsules. We were operating an outfit with insignificant progress on the technological front. We were somewhat at a standstill. When a foreign collaboration came our way with a demand for a 51 per cent equity stake, I was compelled to change my mindset before I agreed. By acknowledging our deficiencies and going ahead with a positive approach, we have been able to score points with a sharp improvement in the bottom line, as well as a technological leap forward."

What was the business scenario like, at the time? Vikram says: "The business of soft capsules was in very low focus, with poor visibility in the Indian market. Our JV propelled us and this is evidenced by the rapid growth of products presented in this dosage form. Our own marketing company has had many 'firsts' as well, by introducing innovative products in this dosage form. All these new products have been developed by in-house R&D. _I look to challenges when I sense an opportunity._ Several of these have been based on hunches, most of which have paid off."

TECHNICAL EXCELLENCE

Entrepreneurship _per se_ does not work. It requires process improvement. I was curious about how the technical process works in the case of Vikram's company. Vikram explains, "Innovation has always been our greatest motivator. So we consistently strive for creative development within our company while pursuing productive relationships with our partners in the industry. Sometimes, partnerships simply add new life to an aging process, or evolve from an R&D breakthrough that pushes the possibilities beyond the current horizon to create a new solution. An excellent example is our patented softlet technology, which gives pharmaceutical and nutritional products in tablet form all the benefits of gelatin coating. In the softlet process, tablets are enrobed in gelatin and hermetically sealed, offering security, swallowability, and a full range of colours for brand identification. In addition they are visually elegant, and softlets can also be used to mask an unpleasant taste."

PATERNALISTIC MANAGEMENT

India was nowhere on the world softgel map before Vikram's incisive thinking, drive and managerial ability gave us a toe-hold in softgel production. He can now export to anywhere in the world. The state-of-the-art plants at Savigram and Bangalore have world standard affiliation. Although it is a relatively unknown family organization, Banner Pharmacaps (India) has made recognizable progress by creating wealth. In the beginning Vikram dealt only with MNCs because of their clean payment terms and an opportunity to learn, and that has paid off sumptuously.

His lack of a public figure did not pose too much of a problem to Vikram in recruiting professionals: He poached the best professionals from his MNC clientele. Vikram follows a paternalistic style of personnel management. "A personal touch, constant interaction, acknowledgement of personal problems and an open door policy give me a great deal of value-addition," feels Vikram.

He nurtured a performance-oriented entrepreneurial climate in his company. His industrial relations have been trouble free. Growth has been substantial. We can therefore say that his _paternalistic style of management seems to have worked._ Multinationals are not able to generate this kind of warmth despite sky-high salaries, perks and facilities. There are a number of lessons the net entrepreneurs and promoters of JVs can learn from a quiet organization like Vikram's.

"What would you identify as the unique factors that enabled you to show such astounding results?" I ask. Vikram says: "Ability, coupled with smart work, integrity, honesty of purpose, evaluation of purpose, dedication to the product, and focus; but don't forget, _luck is a part of that package._ Although I got certain things on a platter, I had to work sincerely. The question to ask is, '_Am I earning my salary? Am I doing justice to what I am paid for_'?"

GO AND GET SOMETHING

What does he believe that freshers straight out of college should do? Vikram answers unhesitatingly: "Decide on a vocation. Set targets. You may not have money but you have the mental faculty. '_Go and get something_' should be the maxim. You have to have or cultivate a basic conviction, find out what you are cut out to be." Did Vikram himself have this? "Yes. I was restless to achieve and get going. I felt I was naturally suited to make a breakthrough and achieve something on my own if I could spot something. The drive to excel propelled me further and further;

to excel in the softgel market, technology and growth. I was always looking at the top of the goal, there was no sacrificing that global horizon. Remember, *you have to aim higher, not at the middle, otherwise you'll slip to the bottom.*"

PREPARATION MAKES THE DIFFERENCE

Vikram has some more advice. "I would urge youngsters to please eschew mediocre, *chalta hai* tendencies. Develop the skills of 'spotting'." I ask how they should do that. He gives the formula: "A cocktail of reading, exposure, who you hobnob with provides the kick. The exact nexus cannot be proved. Read about achievers and learn about networking, commercial management and general knowledge. Develop the ability to convince others that what you are doing is correct, the ability to consciously sell yourself. You have to keep the audience interested; you must know the subject well; you must represent your company well. For that *you require subject mastery and the ability to communicate in techno-commercial language.*"

"What is the crux ,Vikram?" I ask. He stresses, "Prepare yourself. Jot down your points for discussion. Anticipate the questions; *trial-run the meeting.* Overcome the initial obstacles, learn on the way. **Persistence pays. You have got to have the resilience to learn, the preparedness to show, and the enthusiasm to convince.**" *Doggedness and dedication alone do not make a difference; preparation does,* and Vikram Tannan is an excellent example of that.

346

Sudheer Tilloo

"I need everyone; nobody needs me."

The Japanese giant Hitachi Metals has complete faith in their Indian collaborator, Sudheer Tilloo (53), group chief executive, DGP Hinoday Industries Ltd and DGP Windsor Ltd. Hinoday now has a turnover of Rs 123 crore and 1200 employees compared to Rs 1.6 crore and 140 employees in 1980, when Sudheer joined the company, then known as Morris Electronics Ltd. This confidence-inspiring wizard is a picture of innocence and pleasantness in a slight frame.

It was Sudheer Tilloo's struggle with himself to excel as a manager that led him to spot opportunities. His father's exhortation "Polish shoes, but ensure that they shine well", in other words, "Do whatever, but do your best" sowed the seeds of his search for growth and excellence. His father, a self-made man, had established himself as the best lawyer in Mandleshwar district, Madhya Pradesh. Sudheer's father passed on to his son his respect for value-based learning and his drive to be the best; while his mother's loving care and fortitude in looking after Sudheer's mentally retarded brother taught him to handle adversity with calm and patience.

Having decided to do something different instead of following in his father's footsteps, Sudheer took his first step in that direction by graduating from BITS, Pilani in 1963. He went on to do his masters from the University of Wisconsin and then worked in a couple of American companies for a year. He came home and joined Siemens India as a project engineer, moving on to become an export sales engineer two years later. Sudheer kept learning: He subscribed to the *Harvard Business Review*, which provided him with major inputs on general management approaches and strategies. After spending six years in exports, he felt the need for some managerial exposure; so he joined Automatic Electric in Mumbai, a small company making industrial panel instruments, as a manager. His one-year stint there brought him in close contact with the mercurial engineer-proprietor M G Bhat, from whom he "learnt to learn" and get results.

THE LEARNING VOYAGE

Sudheer's big break came in 1980 when he joined the Piramal Group as project manager for diversifications. That year group chairman Dilip Piramal bought over the then Morris Electronics Ltd, Pune, from the pioneering American scientist who had started it in 1963. Sudheer moved to Pune and assumed office as executive assistant to the chairman.

The impact of a world-class organization and the opportunity to practice general management on the Morris Electronics turf opened up a challenging career path for Sudheer. He instinctively knew that technology induction had to be his first anchor for building Morris Electronics. The learning and practicing voyage had begun.

In his search for appropriate technology, Sudheer turned to big corporations in specific domains of expertise. He activated earlier contacts that had been forged when he was with Siemens, which led him to the offices of Hitachi Metals in Tokyo. During his first visit to Japan he met general manager Mr Kanayama. The first task was to gain his confidence. Sudheer informed him: "India has enormous iron oxide stocks. If you were to convert it into quality oxide, you would earn good money and we would get quality oxide for ferrites." There was silence. Sudheer sensed that the Japanese had a problem: How to trust an Indian whom he was meeting for the first time? Conceptually Sudheer knew what was in it for them. He said: "The Indian market will grow. With your support we will become number one." Sudheer invited Hitachi Metals to visit India to do a feasibility study, and offered to pick up the tab. The proposition was a confidence-building measure. It laid the foundation of a commercially viable relationship that turned out to be durable.

JAPANESE *GURUS* AND INDIAN *SHISHYA*

Sudheer won the trust and friendship of Mr Kanayama. He treated the Hitachi Metals chairman, Mr Matsumo, with appropriate reverence. In his first meeting, he took on the role of a *shishya* in front of a *guru* learning the secrets of becoming a manager. He reports the conversation verbatim:

Sudheer: What is your working schedule?

Matsumo: I get up at 6 o'clock in the morning and sleep at 11 at night. History and music are my hobbies.

Sudheer: What is the best way to develop managers?

Matsumo: On the job.

Sudheer: What are India's strengths and weaknesses?

Matsumo: Population size and people are its strength as well as weakness.

Sudheer: What is your goal for Hitachi Metals?

Matsumo: To make it a global organization.

Sudheer: How would you do it?

Matsumo: By catching growth where it happens. Let local people manage.

Such encounters are culturally welcomed and traditionally respected by the Japanese. The process helped Sudheer sell himself first, rather than sell his company or make appeals for selling the technology. In fact, as he puts it, "*I developed the craze to become the product of what I was doing.* You can become as good as your *guru.* If you take a second-rate teacher, you become second-rate; whereas if you take an excellent one, you are bound to become superb. I created a few such *guru-shishya* relationships between me and a few of Hitachi's executives over the years. In other words, I created my own *gurukul* and thereby learnt a lot." In the process, Sudheer developed a formidable reputation in the course of the 50 visits he made to Japan from 1982 onwards.

DGP Hinoday Industries Ltd is a joint venture between Hitachi Metals and Dilip Piramal's Rs 800 crore DGP group, of which the VIP brand of luggage is the flagship. Sudheer explains: "Since Hitachi was not allowed to lend its name to joint ventures, we chose 'Hinoday' from the Japanese word 'Hinode', which means sunrise. With the connotation of 'suryoday', it also sounds suitably Indian." Morris Electronics was thus rechristened Hinoday in 1996.

OPTIMIZING RESOURCES

Reveals Sudheer: "At my first discussion with Hitachi, I saw that Japanese technology was based on big investments in technology, using cheap funds and a few expensive people. Our resource mix was the opposite—expensive hardware, high taxes and interest rates, but inexpensive brainware. We had to use Hitachi Metals' know-why and our know-how to optimize the Indian resource mix. Morris became the most indigenized, lowest cost plant with the best foreign technology in the ferrite industry." Sudheer has proved to be an expert importer of 'know-why' technology, which took Hinoday's turnover to Rs 123 crore in 20 years, with ceramic magnets accounting for 48 per cent, ferrite cores 33 per cent and automotive castings 19 per cent. Sudheer believes that "We need technology knowledge, 'know-why'. That is the source. Let them pass it on to my executives. The 'know-how', however, has to suit local conditions."

Sudheer reflects that the Japanese were attracted to him because he was earnest and always prepared to learn. Developing personal contacts and building a relationship of trust is the first step in preparing potential collaborators to listen to your proposal. Sudheer's hunger for learning and his capacity to absorb knowledge were noticed: He gained the reputation of being 'a sponge'.

Sudheer religiously followed a basic motto: "Do your best to acquire the best technology. Ask yourself the question: Why should the customer come to you and not go to the competitors? Why should the shareholders invest in your company and not in another? For defining opportunities, forget the fact that you are already in business. Don't become complacent."

MASTER OF 'SHOW AND TELL'

Recounting the run-up to the successful collaboration, Sudheer recounts how the Maruti car makers, Suzuki, brought Hitachi Metals to India. Hitachi Metals was Suzuki's main automotive castings supplier and they proposed to extend their relationship to this country. Hitachi Metals therefore sent a team to study 19 foundries in India. Two of their technocrats arrived in Pune and

Sudheer invited them to visit his plant. They were impressed by the way it was being run. The Japanese feel comfortable when they see a clean environment, a defect-free production process, well-laid out improvement standards and innate customer orientation. Says Sudheer with satisfaction: "The technocrats went back to Japan and told the management that Hitachi Metals should put up the foundry only with Morris." In this exploration of opportunity, Sudheer used his favourite technique of 'show and tell'.

Morris, the market leader in ferrites for cars and television sets, thus diversified. Sudheer brought a casting from Hitachi Metals to India and showed it to customers. They approved, but the price was an issue. Sudheer says: "My objective was to fill up the plant. I invited the team to do a market survey for us at our cost in four months. They agreed. I did not know the business. My team and I studied it. The question was, can we make profits? We checked and rechecked the parameters. I told them, 'We will do it cheaper. Give us the 'know-why' and our engineers will do it.' Hitachi Metals agreed to send an experienced man to design our facility with the best of Indian resources." Sudheer adds: "_You have to get interested in them and get them interested in you._"

BEST PRACTICES

Sudheer's approach reveals the best practices he followed:

- He starts with a hypothesis, tests it and then checks it with customers. Actual calculations are checked by outside experts.

353

- He is open. He doesn't like people betting on him—in that case he doesn't believe them. He wants them to bet on the demonstrated idea.

- He involves innovative customers, collaborators, suppliers and his own people to test every idea and plan. He exhorts his executives, 'If you can't win an argument in a discussion group, how can you guarantee you can win it elsewhere?'

- The skill he used in the entire operation was *trial runs, one step at a time.* "Cumulatively the muscle becomes strong by sprinting," says Sudheer. Does he use any special computational skills? "Back-of-envelope skills and rational thinking" is his reply.

Sudheer's ability to take a holistic view is far better than that of most people, and he knows it. So he positions himself correctly with collaborators. It is important because you are able to understand them well. With his penchant for quoting great management thinkers, Sudheer adds, "I genuinely believe you need a couple of people to test your holistic view. *The trinity of 'thinking', 'doing' and 'feeling' is required,* as Drucker says, and I believe it."

GUIDING HABITS

In sensing growth opportunities, Sudheer was guided by his habit of looking at the performance of better companies and better managers. He cultivated the habit of spotting gaps in product efficiency, market demands and customer needs by comparing these factors with world standards. He studied competitors' strengths and weaknesses. What resources did he harness to take advantage of opportunities? He says: "I gathered good partners who would want to win together, executives eager to achieve something." He was able to influence their performance by working out a credible vision, a step by step path. His innovation is based upon the desire to grow professionally and personally.

Sudheer confesses that he was not a good listener until a few years ago. But today, a major transformation has taken place in his working style. He has become a far better listener. He empathises gainfully. He is more collaborative; forges better team work. As a part of that building process, his consultation techniques have seen significant improvement. The 'mine is right' assertion has virtually disappeared. Stephen Covey's 'seven habits' influenced him to change over to the 'interdependence' mode. Sudheer's self-observation and development process deepened from the time globalisation was unveiled in India in 1991 in the form of liberalisation. However, from 1984, Sudheer had already begun 'thinking global and acting local' in all he did.

FOCUS-REFOCUS

Sudheer took serious note of minor ill health signals and began yoga and *Vipassana* training. His conceptual canvas widened as he mulled over the great thinkers' thought processes. In attempting to implement their concepts, his leadership style too changed. Such self-improvement measures helped Sudheer overcome his greatest obstacle, the fear of failure. Sudheer is candid in his self-appraisal. He is passionate about results, performance and value addition.

The fundamental question he asks in relation to superiors, customers and employees is 'who needs whom?' It has led him to focus and refocus on his goals and follow-up action. His actions are grounded in the firm belief, "*I need everyone; nobody needs me.*"

Sudheer says his company is very rigid on maintaining quality, and that on-time delivery keeps its customers happy. With at least 96 per cent of all deliveries being effected within two days of the promised date, DGP Hinoday has a high customer satisfaction index. "The key thing distinguishing us is that just 25 customers give us 75 per cent of our business." Sudheer points out.

Sudhir's advice to youngsters in search of a rewarding career is to first take an aptitude test. "In addition, think seriously about what you enjoy doing and how you can contribute. Work in that field in any organization, big or small. Acquire some functional skills in manufacturing, customer service, finance. Be vigilant about opportunities. Ensure that the ladder is on the right wall." *Stick to what you like to do* and improvise as you do it, he advises. He refers to Covey's dictum: When your search improves and you come to the stage of identifying what you would like doing almost permanently, 'sharpen the saw'. I question Sudheer about the pitfalls that may be encountered while dealing with others, such as cunning people. Simple, says Sudheer, "Have a straightforward approach, take small steps, feel your way. There is nothing wrong if the other person is cunning, the question is can he be trusted? The world is not a place of honest people. You need to know if the other person will play straight with you." Sudheer adds: "_Since the world is going to belong to the owners of 'work' and not of 'jobs', take the entrepreneurial route._" Entrepreneurship has more options. Opportunities abound. Find out where your strengths lie. Use the PC, go to the library, attend conferences, listen to tapes, read newspapers, magazines, books, and a hundred ideas will come to you every day.

SUDHEER'S NEW _MANTRA_ OF RESULTS

Sudheer is on the ball all the time. His eyes shine with enthusiasm. In his new challenging assignment to turn round Windsor, the plastic manufacturing major in Dilip Piramal's stable, he is making the Windsor team practice his new mantra:

- _Quarterly Results;_
- _Monthly Progress;_
- _Weekly Movement;_
- _Daily Action._

In the new millennium, Sudheer could take this one step further; he just may add a fifth pair of words: 'Hourly Score'!

Sudheer Tilloo is a model manager-cum-entrepreneur. An avid reader of management literature, he goes all out to put into practice what he digests. His search skills for spotting business opportunities and inducting technology are derived from deep study of the best practices adopted by the leaders of major corporations all over the world. Sudheer is not a socialite. He takes time to trust people. He cultivates essential contacts with constant follow-up. Sudheer's absorption of best practices and acquisition of influencing skills make a potent combination indeed.

Manoj Tirodkar

"I can be a billionaire only if my colleagues become millionaires."

Started less than 20 years ago, Global Enterprise has blazed its way through Indian business skies like a comet, backed by a revenue of Rs 800 crore in 1999-2000. The dynamic and young Manoj Tirodkar (36), its founder and CEO, was selected as the India Young Business Achiever as well as the World Young Business Achiever for 2000. He is the executive vice-chairman of Global Tele-Systems Ltd, the group's flagship, and chairman of International Global Tele-Systems Ltd, its wholly-owned Mauritius-based subsidiary.

Manoj Tirodkar comes from a traditional middle class Maharashtrian family. He lived in a chawl and studied up to the twelfth standard in Chikitsak, a Marathi-medium school in Girgaum, Mumbai. Without losing pride in his cultural identity, Manoj recognized that his Maharashtrian upbringing also meant that he had a legacy of non-communicative, non-selling and insular attitudes. How he consciously and deliberately extricated himself from that narrow, service-oriented mindset is a saga of unbelievable drive, innovation and entrepreneurship, that too in the high end of the technology business.

This is an inspiring biography of a young man who turned his liabilities into assets in just under 20 years. His creative strides in realizing his ambitions form *an ideal syllabus for mindset change*, which we need so badly for the 21st century. Let's take a look at his mind-boggling performance.

AWE-INSPIRING ACHIEVEMENT

The Global Enterprise, set up in 1981, today consists of two companies and seven subsidiaries spanning engineering, software, virtual private networks (VPN), managed network services (MNS), data centers, transaction processing and B2B e-commerce. It has offices at 26 locations in India and 11 locations in other countries; over 40,000 shareholders; around 300,000 customers including 45 Fortune 500 companies and 300 MNCs, 120,000 end subscribers and 40,000 software licensees. The Global Enterprise last year collected Rs 130 crore from exports and contributed Rs 80 crore to the exchequer by way of direct and indirect taxes.

The group's flagship, Global Tele-Systems (a joint stock company that was started from scratch), is currently among the top 20 companies in India, with a market capitalisation in excess of

$2.5 crore at one point of time. It is the fifth largest traded scrip. Well known brokerages and financial institutions such as DSP Merrill Lynch, Jardine Fleming Securities India, Casenove & Co, ABN Amro Securities and Morgan Stanley have extensively researched the company before investing large sums of money in it. Global granted stock options to 750 employees when ESOPs (employee stock options) was a new idea. This has led to wealth creation of Rs 136 crore amongst the employees of the group.

The Global organization has passed through the phases of inception, growth, and consolidation. The inception and growth phases saw the company selling subscriber end-equipment, and venturing into network and telecom infrastructure. In the consolidation phase it ventured into the software business, with a model that was different from the one followed by everyone else, Data Network Unified Messaging. At the same time they ventured into application services, recognizing it as a trend. Now Global is in an innovation phase with a repayment gateway, procurement ERP online and call centres. As on April 24, 2000 the company had achieved near zero-debt status without further fund-raising; it had approximately Rs 300 crore of surplus cash, with positive cash flows ($70 lakh) and profits ($40 lakh) on its books.

Young Manoj began 'thinking global' in 1981, 10 years before India embraced globalisation in 1991 by initiating steps to liberalise the economy. Manoj is a self-made man, a first-generation entrepreneur. He has conceived, built, nurtured and grown the

Global Enterprise, making it a force to reckon with. He has shown entrepreneurs how to create new wealth. How did he do it?

THE MAKING OF MANOJ

Manoj's father, Gajanan Tirodkar, worked in Shaw Wallace until 1978. Then he went into the shipping business in partnership with some friends. I ask, "Manoj, why didn't you too go into the shipping business?" Manoj says, "Well, actually I did. When I was in the eighth standard, I started going to my father's office on my own during the summer holidays. I used to sit in front of the marketing officer and watch him. Once I even did a cargo ship loading by myself; my father was amazed. By listening to him on the phone, hearing him, reading books, I absorbed everything they were doing."

This process had begun rather early, hadn't it? "Yes." He continues, "Before the office was furnished, meetings used to take place at home, which was in a chawl. I could interact with business visitors. My father's partners were rich and well-travelled. I used to watch them. I used to take telex messages home. I learnt typing and how to operate the telex because ship brokers used to negotiate ships, cargo and that kind of business by telex. You had to learn how to send and receive telexes. I learnt how to do things by myself." The shipping business has clearly left its mark on Manoj. His small office in Janmabhoomi Chambers at Ballard Pier in Mumbai reminded me of a ship's cabin, with Manoj's portly frame filling up most of the space!

Traditionally, trading communities like the Marwaris and the Gujaratis take their children to their shops. Knowledge and its practical applications are there to see, absorb and apply. Just as customer goodwill has to be cultivated, these communities cultivate 'skill-will' by observing and imitating. That is how skills are passed on from generation to generation. They create wealth by 'doing'. However, that is not the Maharashtrian way, with a few exceptions. It was not Manoj's father's idea to take him to his office. So how did young Manoj get interested in the business?

Manoj is pensive. "I'm not sure. The desire was probably inherent, the genes may have a role to play. I had no friends in school who could guide me. I used to watch people and I still continue to do that. If I found something important, I made the effort to get it. I was extremely good at science and mathematics. I was an athlete and I represented the school in table tennis. I was active and passionate in whatever I did. After completing the twelfth standard, I went to Europe to do a course in shipping. Then the question was whether to go for further studies to the US. I decided to break that Maharashtrian credo and return to India to join my father's business."

Manoj thus broke the value code of the typical Marathi 'higher education-service-H1B visa' mindset. The desire to follow his father emanates from his curiosity to find 'what is out there?' He picked up the impulse to know when he saw business visitors coming and going. The next step was to get to know what people were doing—what is that fellow sitting there (the marketing chap) doing, what is a telex, what is he saying on the phone?

The atmosphere in his father's shipping firm increased Manoj's curiosity, creativity and questioning ability. After a two-year stint in Europe, observing things and people, the desire to learn on the spot brought him back home. He asked himself the question: Why do I have to go in for higher education? Rather than studying further, as might have been expected, he made a choice of critical importance. That was a turning point in his life.

FROM SHIPPING TO TELE-SYSTEMS

Manoj started working in his father's shipping company. His long-time friend Fritz D'Silva, a graduate in biotechnology, also joined. They started thinking of diversifying. They looked at various possibilities like computers, fax machines and telecommunications. They obtained distributorships for Apple computers and desktops.

Manoj convinced his father that shipping had no future: Information technology (IT) was the future and they should concentrate on it. He was persuasive; by 1990 they were out of shipping. How did he come to the conclusion that IT was the future? Says he, "By general reading. I studied telecommunication sales and after-sales service literature. A new telecom policy was announced in 1989. Rajiv Gandhi gave a thrust to computers. Fritz and I were knowledge-conscious and market-savvy. We felt IT was a major area of opportunity."

THE IMPORTANCE OF READING

Where did he get the will to make it big? Manoj explains, "It begins with self-motivation and a tremendous drive to succeed." About the factors that played a role, he says, "I have been travelling extensively since I was 14 or so, I have travelled more than accomplished pilots. Besides, I have acquired the bulk of my knowledge by reading a lot; *Time, Newsweek*, magazine sections on technology, telecommunications, the internet. I pick up well written books on successful people; read, chew, absorb. At first I was interested in running and owning ships—I was a little flamboyant in that! Then I decided that I wanted to achieve things at the higher end of technology, not like businessmen who just want to make a quick buck. I wanted to go for long-term goals, take risks, do something very big. *This idea of something big came from reading.*"

BUSINESS ICONS MOTIVATE

I ask Manoj who influenced him. He tells me: "I don't think the influence came from my family. The driving factor was not my father, but more successful people. Very early in school I had read about the legendary Maharashtrian industrialist Shantanurao Kirloskar. I was impressed by the Kirloskar companies, but felt they were not growing fast enough. I follow benchmarks like Narayana Murthy. I have global standards like Bill Gates. I am definitely motivated by success stories, market capitalisation, shareholder value, huge factories. I was driven by Dhirubhai

Ambani, JRD Tata. I was so crazy, I used to keep paper cuttings on all such individuals in a file called 'five years later'. In that file are also kept my own assessments of who would succeed five years later. I started doing this in the 1980s after I returned from the UK.

"Take Dhirubhai Ambani or Amitabh Bachchan. I am not fascinated by their fields; I am fascinated by their success in their chosen field of activity, whatever that may be. To me, Ambani for metavision, Narayana Murthy for tough decisions, Azim Premji from edible oil to IT."

GETTING OVER AN INFERIORITY COMPLEX

Because his father's partner (who impressed the young Manoj) had had training in Denmark, Manoj decided to stay for two years in Germany. "I too must have such training somewhere similar," he thought. The experience was productive in that he got over an inferiority complex (something he demurs at). "A very successful German man was my boss. I used to observe him, study the how and why of his doing, his style of dress, table manners and responses. These were critical factors for moving into higher circles. Now I don't worry much about such things because only performance matters.

"I was very keen to present myself well because I came from a typical Maharashtrian background. I didn't have an inferiority complex, nonetheless I wanted to overcome even that occasional feeling. Because of this preparation, when I went for parties I was comfortable talking on all subjects—business, economy, telecommunications, movies, anything. I was not an expert, but I could dominate the conversation because I had command over the language. I developed all these essential prerequisites."

SPAWNING ENTREPRENEURS

However, Manoj is still not satisfied because Global is not, as yet, a benchmark. His colleagues share his thinking, his vision, his feelings. He wants to go down in the history books as a person who created a lot of wealth, which means over a thousand millionaire employees. Employees with a service mindset cannot become millionaires, whereas with entrepreneurial thinking they can. This calls for Manoj to turn his employees into entrepreneurs. As he says, "_I can be a billionaire only if my colleagues become millionaires._" Global is engaged in charity work in the areas of rural education, cancer, the blind, terminally ill children and thalassaemics. The craze to do more is there, corresponding to the obsession to create more wealth. For fulfilling such sky-high ambitions he needs competent people who are committed to providing excellent customer service.

In his grand scheme of things, does Manoj see any problems? Manoj realistically assesses, "Survival is the problem because of competition and global economic churning. Very often changes or developments in other businesses, even if they're not connected to your industry, might hit you hard. Growth and opportunity do not depend upon how clever you are, how intelligent you are, how technology-savvy you are, but *how market dynamics could change the future frame of mind.* To manage it you require a great deal of learning. You are not going to be a great original scientist. You cannot predict accurately. So *you have to become an organization that manages change effectively.* All companies have ups and downs. IBM went through that due to the arrival of microchips. We are not the only ones being swept by change—everyone is. We must realize that our ability to change must increase exponentially. Are we emotionally involved? Managers fail to see change."

Manoj has a fire-fighting theory. He feels the world is advancing at such supersonic speed—with new products and new services, and all this in a globally wired economy—that we will always be fighting hard for survival. He says, "There is no invention here. We are all adapters, followers. The dilemma is how to manage transformation, because so much time goes in managing finance. Except for a few colleagues, and this number I am increasing, others are five years away from my thinking. You are moving at mega speed. They may not want to go at that speed. I have no problems with democracy, they may have a view, strong likes and dislikes. But I am going to do surgery every two years."

He has no hesitation in sacking people with the wrong attitude. In a rapidly changing world, managing people is a transforming game. There are brilliant business managers but they don't take the linear jump. Creating a learning organization, a think tank for the future, is Manoj's task. He is not an engineer or a telecom technologist, he is an entrepreneur committed to creating entrepreneurs. For that, how is he going to make his organization entrepreneurial?

I Ask What I Want

Manoj's biggest asset is his tongue. Straightforward, simple talk; how to make it simple, not complex, is the crux. For him, driving passion in employees means not talking about electronics, e-commerce or telecom, but talking about the end result he is looking for, international benchmarks, and how his enterprise could marry the two. He feels that an organization striving to learn this will reach there; skills are related to the ability to learn and motivate. _Presentation skills are crucial._

"I am able to get down to their family concerns, personal issues, business, politics or financial problems, in other words, to relate to what is important to them. I can be rough or rude, but not hurtful. By and large, if I have spoken to somebody, I will get things done. I am a need-based man. I drive ethics. I can tell you, in your room, in the bulk of time at our disposal, what I want. I attribute it to what I call the 'I ask what I want' capability. People have the passion within them to give, it's up to me to appeal to their right chord, to that passion. It's amazing, the number of times I am able to get things done this way," says Manoj with satisfaction.

I ask him to elucidate. "It's a combination of business and emotional talk. Ask in a simple way. Convince the other person that if you do it this way, you will help me. You appeal to the conscience of the person. *I need everybody, nobody needs me. I can go to any level of persuasion.* What I am asking is genuine, I have a right to have it, it belongs to me and I am only imploring you to grant me what is mine. If you do that for me, if you grant me that which is mine, you will help me, and I suppose you want to help me. Don't you? What you will do is reasonable and just." These are compelling arguments.

OTHERS HAVE A VIEWPOINT

If his tongue is Manoj's biggest asset, he uses it relentlessly, making him the restless talker that he is. Manoj confesses that he would get extremely rough at one moment, only to cool down the next. He has mellowed over the years, realizing that that kind of outburst doesn't help to get work done. Manoj says, "*I was not so good at listening.* In the last two to three years I have taught myself to calm down. I will not hurt anyone. At the end of the day, I am prepared to help, just as I seek help. Of late I have started to listen a lot."

"What brought about this change of heart, Manoj?" I ask. He says: "I have great insight. I have learnt to understand that others have a viewpoint, and that my ability to manage it is critical." In Indian culture, ears are trained not to hear such passionate conviction, and the mind is conditioned to write off the first part of his statement as a display of self-assertiveness; but I found Manoj's affirmation tremendously invigorating. We need such an elixir. The lingo must first change to transform the mindset. A 20-year track record gives Manoj sound grounds to back his claim. Cynics and fatalists may take heart: Success, like life, is transient anyway.

What was the actual spur for this change in thinking? Says he, "To have qualified people and to retain them is a job. The response time is the issue. I wanted something and I got it after painful, frustrating follow-up and if others do the same thing with me, I accept that. It's partly selfishness, partly a sense of priorities, and partly a lurking need that me motivates to go ahead. _Even at the cost of being humiliated, I go back to get things done._ I am influenced by Fritz and, to an extent, my wife in this change in thinking."

I ask Manoj if he was required to make a lot of adjustments. He elaborates, "Since I am good at managing external change, I suppose I am good at doing it within myself. At one time I wanted to do everything, but over the years, I say 'let's wait'. I have become cautious; I have become conservative. My frustration is within myself and not with other people. My ability to manage frustration has improved. My people are my drivers. I tell them you must come back with a solution and if you don't have it, come back and say so. Then you motivate me and you show your confidence in my ability to resolve the problem. It will keep me on my toes and motivated. I am a great fighter. I am a firm believer that out of extremely difficult situations, when I feel I am completely gone, so to say finished, I resurrect myself."

TRANSFORMATION WITHIN

Manoj was at his best while explaining the transformation he is undergoing. He has started listening, understanding that others have a viewpoint. He is fighting his frustrations. Manoj is in a business that changes at the speed of thought. Says he, "*If change is the only constant, then learning and listening are the other constants.*" Even on seeking advice, for which he feels there is a need, what he says is profound: "Unfortunately, given the position that I am in, very few people can advise me, or feel free to advise me, or are in a position to advise me. I may not be open to receiving the advice of a lot of people. But I have to seek the advice of a few people. That process of internal change is happening now. The end result of a transaction also carries advice."

"How does that work?" I ask. Manoj says, "I realize that otherwise I am mulling over some things. The advice has to come in fulfillment of the goal. The threat to the realization of your goals forces you to seek advice. There's no choice. If I want to get anything done in a meeting, there are 90 per cent chances of success if I handle it well, which means *listening and compromising*; the motive is selfish."

This kind of transmutation was usually witnessed in people in their fifties or sixties, in the stable era of average 3.5 per cent annual growth from 1950 to 1990. That an ambitious man like

Manoj is undergoing such a metamorphosis while he is only in his thirties is a sign of what cataclysmic technological advances are demanding, and how the new super-achievers are trying to master illimitable change. Manoj represents the evolution of a new humankind, the kind of breed India needs in millions to meet the challenges of the new millennium. For initiating a transforming process of that kind, the leaders have to clearly communicate their expectations to managers. How does Manoj stimulate such thinking in Global?

COMMUNICATE EXPECTATIONS

Manoj confesses, "The problem of current management is that the bulk of time is spent on activity, rather than on the end result. That problem is with them and to an extent with us. We have certain expectations of our people, but we have not written these down as such. They can tell me what problems they face. They can communicate with me how they should or should not be working. There is constant communication on that. Everybody wanted to be Reliance five years back. Now everybody wants to be Infosys—but why and how? That 'how' is a cultivation of a culture or character that requires years of planning and commitment, and that is not a permanent model."

"What is a permanent model, Manoj?" I query. He says, "There is _no lasting model_ as such. Reliance was not successful 15 years ago, Infosys may not remain at the forefront 15 years hence. So there are cycles of technology, cycles of management, cycles of delivery. The issue is that my people can tell me whether or not a certain thing is working. I sometimes wonder if I fail to communicate my expectations in specific clear terms. The current system of communication is not consistent enough. Lack of focus at the moment is responsible for our current impasse."

I say, "What people think, preach and practice are different things. Habits don't change overnight, do they?" Manoj responds, "It is a cultural issue. People only change if that makes a difference to their livelihood, for betterment. If you haven't specified your expectations, you have no feedback. Feedback comes in numbers in quarterly reviews, not on strategic designs. We must look to leadership that shapes culture. I am not successful at building a reliable model." Manoj is in search of such leadership and models. That's why he turns to successful companies.

FOLLOW SUCCESS

Global took a conscious decision to shift from a product to solution to service-centric position. This shift is based on knowledge gathered from what is happening in the world, a study of global and Indian benchmark companies. The exercise revealed that the company was remaining behind in terms of shareholder value; it had to move to solutions and to services because successful companies were doing so. 'Can we follow the world trend?' was the question, and Manoj had the hunch that they could. Well, they did, and they achieved success. How did he get that hunch?

Manoj reveals, "We don't invent, we follow the inventor's process. You try to own the process and give it a brand name. It is far too late to go back to inventing. *You want to perfect the process of delivery.* It's not merely distribution, it's software services, e-commerce. In 1990-92 we took the shift following world trends. It's a global influence, how companies are created, values are created. This process goes on the basis of sharing information with colleagues. Things are dynamic, it is an on-going process. Events are in constant stream, one following the other. If you see me next month, you will see me thinking in a completely different manner. These are drivers; e-commerce is an event, Yahoo is a pointer. You apply your core competencies through these drivers. My entrepreneurship is driven by information phenomena, by the fact that you are not an Archimedes or Galileo; you *follow, observe, learn.* I try to benchmark on success stories. I copy successful companies. General Electric does that. When you go astray you try to evaluate what went wrong with someone who has done it better, that is the benchmark."

How does he convert his convictions to help move his organization forward? It is information management plus learning from other people. Any kind of value creation or value addition, whether shareholder value, employee value, product value or delivery value—it's like a value chain—must be based on the basic drive in people, on that live value chain assembly. Everyone in this chain must have a fire in the belly to excel.

Manoj and Fritz applied trend analysis to get into the e-commerce field. They had done the same thing while learning the shipping business. Shipping was not a bad sector to be in, but they wanted to do something better and different. They studied what was the 'in-thing' in terms of markets and technology, and made a logical shift. As Manoj says, "It was purely a necessity of the times, not a virtue of invention."

To Manoj, an event is a trend frozen at a moment in history, a benchmark, especially in economic matters. The next question he asks is, "Have I the competency to follow the trend? The internet is a trend, an event. Can I and my people put our fingers in it?" Such searching questions show the path. Global is dropping fax machines because they have now advanced to the high-end of the value chain. Such tailing off of products is required for business progress.

I remind Manoj. "You earlier said you were influenced by icons like Dhirubhai Ambani, Narayana Murthy, Jack Welch." Manoj stops me, "Yes, a particular person may influence me for a particular period. It's not about personalities, it's not hero worship. What influences me are the attitudes, capabilities, creation of wealth, creation of a company. I must be able to apply the idea of their creation in my business. I am fascinated by what these people go through and where they have reached. But I am not going to bet any money on their future, because I might court failure." Manoj tries to discern between failure and success, but even more between success and success. He tries to gauge the durability factor in that success.

He even says: "I am a paranoid guy on the brink of collapse. I *do* need guidance." I reassure Manoj, "Don't worry, you're in good

company. The success of Andrew Grove (chairman of Intel Corporation, USA, famous for *Only The Paranoid Survive*) is partly
due to his *insistence on analysing failure.*"

SEARCH ALIGNED TO GOALS

What kind of guidance does he need? What is he searching for?
Manoj says, "My search is aligned to my goals. I look to attributes,
ethics, the way they handled events, the value they derived. You
have to know your goal. Their defining achievements open up
new avenues, stimulate my learning aptitude. A vision is where
you want to go, but the next step comes from keen observation."

But luck is a factor, isn't it? "All successful persons are not
merely lucky. They take the right step, the right direction, and
luck jumps on their bandwagon. If you don't have the basics, then
you would be a follower like 90 per cent of people are. That is
okay so long as you know it, and you strive to become a leader. I
don't think circumstances are the only drivers. You have to have
the drivers. There are rags to riches stories. What counts is your
ability to push yourself towards your goal. Then you cannot complain. You have to have a goal—that's critical—and then take
one step at a time. In the bargain, you need to improvise on your
goal and develop a 'never say die' kind of thinking. It is within
you. You are both self-centric and poly-centric. *The difference between a leader and a follower is the intense desire to pursue a goal.*"

What values would Manoj want to transmit to his children,
and to all young people in general? He says, "Creation of wealth,

377

economies of growth, people management, mind-boggling achievement, and untiring learning." These values are badly needed to enrich our young nation, of which Manoj, as a young business leader, is a shining example. And that sums up the story of a young, restless and highly successful Indian.

Part II

THE SOURCE CODE

Introduction To Part II

My conviction from the start of this exercise has been that by studying the thought processes of outstanding business leaders, managers and entrepreneurs, I would be able to discover patterns, paradigm shifts and commonalities in upbringing, traits and other features of their successful areas. I did find all that.

I had also decided that I would be open-minded about taking a leap into the unknown to find out the source code of the *gestalt* that works, the *alchemy* that produces impressive results. My methodical search led me to detect the code. Cracking the value code was difficult, but deep personal reflection abetted the process of inquiry. The end result was the emergence of a **thought leader**.

Most importantly, I do not think these managers were destined to become exceptional from the start. Their parent-mentor programming, clubbed with critical events, was helpful. It was, however, not a singularly decisive combination which made them exceptional. Circumstances were not synchronous in each one's case, and yet, they proceeded to make a difference. Their personalities flowered as they took charge of their careers. They astutely traded their assets on fate's stock market. These non-ordinary people did not give up in the face of initial setbacks or subsequent difficulties. They persisted. Once these people knew what they had made, what was their creation, what had worked, they relentlessly refined their combinatorial skills and value-addition equations.

For me, everything in the studious journey and the destination is new. I stake no claims to originality in methodology, process or the outcome. I have narrated the story as it happened.

Chapter 1

The Nurturance Syndrome

D r Raghunath Mashelkar rose from abject poverty to become a fellow of the Royal Society, UK, and today heads the giant science and research government monolith CSIR, whereas Manoj Tirodkar, an undergraduate, has built from scratch a Rs 800 crore global enterprise in the high-end of information technology. Yet both these exceptional men are thought leaders alongside the technologically qualified middle class Narayana Murthy and blue blooded Verghese Kurien.

We therefore need to know the significant elements of our thought leaders' nurturance which prepared them to tread their paths and produce impressive results. Only then will we understand what is missing in our making, and how to make up for the loss.

The canvas is wide, made colourful by resourceful personalities with diverse backgrounds (as seen in the annexure). The personality of each one is shaped by his unique nurturance syndrome. They were not hatched full-grown as role models. Their rise to that status is evolutionary. The syndrome has three interacting elements—*characteristic upbringing, mentors' influence* and *turning points*. Its chemistry reveals certain distinguishing features.

CHARACTERISTIC UPBRINGING

Although 16 of the participants are over 50, their psychological age is 40. All of them are bubbling with glorious visions of India unlimited and are working with full vigour, despite health problems, major or minor.

There is no communo-linguistic barrier to becoming a role model. Humayun Dhanrajgir, born to Raja Dhanrajgir, an orthodox Hindu, who headed a *mutt* in Hyderabad, and Zubeida, the beautiful Muslim actress of the first silent movie *Alam Ara*, became managing director of the Indian subsidiaries of two world-renowned MNCs, first Glaxo and now Kodak. Verghese Kurien, an aristocratic Syrian Christian, led the 'white revolution' of India by creating a farmers' cooperative dairy structure. Their admirers, followers and *shishyas* are spread across the length and breadth of India. Their appeal bridges divides of language, community and region.

The Indian family is by far the strongest root structure in the family constructs of any of the world's communities. Its rock-solid base, protective sheath and parental fostering had the most significant impact in building the steel frames of our role models. The process of upbringing may differ slightly but what is patently visible is the configuration of values of honesty, integrity, education, learning, hard work, self-confidence, discipline and commitment.

There is a conscious development of curiosity, openness, idea generation, choice making, and independence. Chaudhari's search for making Praj a benchmark in the global market is based on the belief that curiosity is at the heart of the global market. Says he, "My father encouraged me to take an independent jump; he used to say, be curious." Mashelkar's uneducated mother pushed him to strive for higher education despite the monumental odds she was facing. Says he, "The hunger for education was planted by her." Mazumdar says her father "encouraged me to not aspire for marriage, but career as my end goal. He made me independent."

Reading, writing, debating and arithmetic skills were purposefully cultivated. Says Aga, "I picked up my love of reading from my father. He encouraged me to be independent and to take up higher studies." Bakhle's mother encouraged him to read English and Marathi literature: "Her example, coupled with such reading, developed my cognitive and conversational skills. My exposure to literature on spiritual topics provided answers to some of my philosophical queries." Ratnaparkhi said, "My mother, brother and sister were full of encouragement for everything I achieved like getting a scholarship or prizes in games, or coming first in an elocution contest."

Novelty was encouraged. The novelty of approach which Jain displayed in taking sleepy Jalgaon on to the world map was planted in him by his uneducated mother. Jain reminisces, "She told me to start my own business as it would offer a greater challenge. She said I could always try something new." Risk-taking is also moderately supported.

Dhanrajgir swears that he owes his success to his value-based upbringing. The values of frugality, integrity, truthfulness, respect for elders and empathy were inculcated in him by his parents from an early age. "My mother used to say, you must know how to separate the wheat from the chaff. She managed to develop the power of concentration and methodicity in me and planted the seeds of achievement," says Dhanrajgir.

'*Self-Made Impact Making Entrepreneurs*' published by the Entre-preneurship Development Institute of India profiles 26 successful entrepreneurs. The study reveals three important drives: "*The urge to implement new ideas and take challenges; the need for independence or autonomy, and to improve the quality of life.* All these three factors are consistent with the concept of achievement motivation."

Our study confirms that the seeds of achievement motivation were planted by parents in the kind of value-set they nurtured in their families. The uncommon gestalt of these attributes appears to have solidified these leaders' resolve to excel while they were growing up. To what extent nurturance was traditional and/or contributed by parents/situational factors is a moot point. But it appears that it was mostly parents who were the drivers. Managers who possess these entrepreneurial competencies become 'entrepreneur managers'. The rest remain bureaucrats with fancy managerial designations. Entrepreneurs *per se* or entrepreneur-managers don't take the beaten path. They want to make a difference, as our role models did.

Most of our subjects have gone into business connected with their domain disciplines; e.g. Ravi Khanna, an electrical engineering graduate, manufactures controls and switchgears. This confirms that education plays a very important role in the choice of business. Five out of the 22, however, are in lines of business totally unconnected from their basic disciplines; e.g. commerce graduate Vikram Tannan manufactures high-tech softgels. It may be noted that only three of the participants are MBAs (Masters in business administration)— Deepak Kanegaonkar, Sartaj Singh and Ashok Soota.

The thread visible in the success of our role models comes from family values, innovative thinking, mathematics-based engineering education, and management of relationships. Most of them sing paeans about their mentors.

MENTORS' INFLUENCE

Mentors are trusted counsellors or guides who, without apparent exertion of force or exercise of command, gently bring about beneficial changes in the thinking and behaviour of those they advise. Teachers are mentors but they operate within the authority structure of schools. Those who use more gentle methods and add value to the counselees' learnability are constantly referred to with reverence. Prakash Ratnaparkhi refers to his teacher Kavthekar who used vacation classes to teach students to repair radios, cars, etc. The demonstration had a significant impact. While learning how to repair things, the students learnt the more basic elements of creative thinking—'what leads to what' and 'what makes things work'. Prakash became methodical and committed. Getting the insight and learning the skill to connect led him to make a spark erosion machine.

In Anu Aga's case, it was her husband Rohinton who shaped her career. Accurately assessing Anu's potential, Rohinton enticed her to grow as a person and as a competent executive. He exposed her to transactional analysis. He evoked her response on the emotional plane by expressing his need for a professional companion. Rohinton used the medium of seminars for providing conceptual inputs and exposure to practical work for gaining valuable experience. Both enhanced her skills and self-confidence. On the founda-

387

tion of her degree in social work Anu built HR competency and grew as a person. Rohinton made an enduring value addition. Husbanding incorporates mentoring, not invoking the authority of a husband. Professionals need to learn this skill because their equally qualified working wives will look for guidance in personal growth rather than only family growth.

Verghese Kurien had Tribhuvandas, from whom he learnt the skills of networking and managing political bigwigs. It was the most difficult skill to learn. As one cannot wish away political systems, one needs to develop the patience to learn social skills from political bosses.

Humayun Dhanrajgir had his roommate Narayanan, former managing director of Ponds, who gave him the *mantra*, 'No free lunches', meaning no shortcuts. Narayanan taught him the methodology of studying, and the importance of precision and speed on the drawing board.

Kiran Mazumdar's father was ahead of his time: He had no gender bias. He encouraged Kiran to give priority to her career over marriage. This is a lesson for fathers—to shed conservatism, become mentors and meet the crying need of not only sons but also daughters for guidance on careers. You need to become a 'value-adding' father. Kiran met another mentor in the Irishman Les Auchincloss of Biocon Ireland. From him she learnt how to build a boundary-less and flexible organization.

Many participants spoke of the benefits they derived from skillful mentoring. I asked what motivated them to listen. *Self-interest, growth, value addition in concepts and skills* was the essence of their replies. The mentors mentioned in this book have by and large shown unique sensitivity to their counselees' needs. They were gentle in approach, persuasive in style, had a perspective to share, and the skill to demonstrate with convincing examples. They appear to be competent in providing the needed conceptual and skills input.

The need for mentors is a continuing need. Social philosopher Charles Handy has profiled 29 original individuals, such as the Britisher Richard Branson of Virgin Airlines or the Indian Jayesh Manek, an investment management expert, in _The New Alchemists_ (Hutchinson 1999). Handy found that mentors and role models were important for almost everyone. Our 22 visionary managers themselves needed mentors through at least two-thirds of their careers. Success must not blind managers, more so those whose desire to excel has not diminished. Our _guru-shishya parmpara_ (teacher-disciple tradition) is the perfect model for the mechanism of guidance and learning. As much as the disciple is in search of a _guru_, the guru also is in search of the right _shishya_, a disciple whose 'learnability' (attitude towards learning) is high. The mentoring process requires a certain chemistry to work between the two.

TURNING POINTS

Critical events often become a turning point in life as a result of a shift in awareness. These critical events bring out the best in some of us, while others go under. It is instructive to see what meaning our participants made out of such events in their lives.

Ravi Khanna dreamt of building a factory of his own, a dream sparked by the Partition and the creativity of the refugees. Completely dispossessed, they were doing whatever they could to better their lot, making whatever they could—torches, batteries, chemicals, soaps, whatever. They were not educated, but they worked very hard and they were innovative. Necessity was the mother of invention, and Ravi watched it in action. The environment was full of 'doing', creating, setting up small workshops, and producing goods and services of all kinds. This external ethos coupled with the home influence of an entrepreneurial uncle infused Ravi with the dream of building a factory of his own. He elected to see the creative side of deprivation, the fact that the refugees were creating something out of nothing. He resolved to build a factory even if he had no capital, and he did.

Sartaj Singh's wife Sarina delivered a baby girl, Chandani. Sartaj, then 30, was climbing the career ladder at the renowned MNC Imperial Chemical Industries (ICI). When Chandani was diagnosed with Down's syndrome, Sartaj and Sarina were bewildered, sad beyond description. They struggled to make meaning out of the trauma of looking after a mentally retarded child, and concluded 'God has elected us to be her parents. We believe we were chosen to look after her.' Asked how much this affected his career, Sartaj says, "In fact, I have learnt so much from this; my entire perspective changed; my demands on life became modulated; you become less greedy, less ambitious. You realize that there is something bigger, a larger destiny to be fulfilled. You have to give priority to something else. You become very humble." See the perspective shift on career, the change in priorities. Despite the voluntary dilution of ambition Sartaj remains motivated and has progressed in his career, as his profile shows; a devout Sikh, he is still fun-loving.

Deepak Kanegaonkar had to face a horrible partnership fight while running a sugar factory in Sholapur at the start of his career.

His partner duped him. Recently married, Deepak had to leave his wife Sulekha behind and shift to Mumbai in search of opportunities. He had only Rs 150 in his pocket. Despite the pleas of his father and father-in-law, his resolve was to not do a job, but to start a business of his own, and he did. Says Deepak, "I was lucky to meet good people, nice people. They trusted me, my word, the convictions I voiced. But I did not trust anyone, especially in money matters. In 1977, when we started the sugar factory, I had no capital, no experience and I trusted everybody. In 1982, I had no capital, five years' experience, and I did not trust anybody." Observe the shift in thinking, 'trust to distrust', the effect of cheating. But aren't business relationships built on trust? Deepak's reply is that he has not lost faith in humanity. Deepak became practical in money matters but did not settle for a job, as most Maharashtrians would have.

Narayana Murthy was a staunch leftist as a student in the heyday of socialism. The critical event that led to Murthy's disillusionment was his incarceration in Nishe, a small railway station near the border of Bulgaria and the former Yugoslavia. He was locked up by overcautious police who suspected him to be an enemy of the state. Says Murthy, "If they could do this to a friend, what would they do to others? What kind of a system is that? I didn't want to be a part of it. I lost faith in communism. Glib talk doesn't create wealth; intelligent, focused work does. Freedom helps." It was the feeling of entrapment that led him to re-evaluate his ideology. Murthy felt insulted. That trigger caused a perspective shift, producing a capitalist Murthy. That was a sharp U-turn. The new *avatar* (incarnation) led to creation of wealth.

Dhananjay Bakhle, while in his second year of MBBS at Grant Medical College in Mumbai, happened to see the movie *Poseidon*

Adventure. Watching the passengers trapped in the sinking ship, he empathised with the experience of entrapment and suffocation. That set him pondering over the dance of life and death, life after death; he was haunted by the faces of helpless patients fighting to survive incurable diseases. The powerful movie sucked Dhananjay into the vortex of death and survival, demanding a perspective shift: Instead of only treating the patients or operating on them, why not search for more fundamental cures through drug discovery? The turning point changed Dhananjay's career track—from medicine to sustainable research, although this was not so popular with medical students in the 1980s. He changed not only his career choice, but also his life goal.

Anu Aga is a fun-loving person. She was fully enjoying her dual roles of housewife and professional companion to her creative husband Rohinton while working with him at Thermax. Then came a terrible personal tragedy: Rohinton died of a heart attack in February 1996. The death of a spouse is a life-changing event. Within 14 months she suffered another enervating loss, the death of her son Kurush in a car accident, and she also lost her mother-in-law and pet dog. This is like serial bomb blasts in real life, or serial murders in a horror movie. From the peak of bliss, Anu was plunged to the depths of despair. The meaning she salvaged from her psychological wreckage is profound.

Says Anu: "Death is a great leveller and God is partial to no one. More than death, not getting on with people when they are alive and not investing in a relationship is a tragedy, and it is a disaster when we stop growing, emotionally and spiritually, by not rethinking our old ways. Self-pity and sadness can be very seductive but one must not lose the opportunity to revalidate goals." Anu read extensively on death after Rohinton passed away. Two days after he died she had to take charge of Thermax as chairperson and managing director. She bravely managed transition, and the ambitions of colleagues. The group did not split or splinter. She kept it together affectionately.

Notice the perspective shift, the desire to grow out of a trauma. Her grounding in transactional analysis (TA) came in handy. She took the help of books. She did not shirk responsibility. Valor is gender-neutral and Anu is compassion incarnate. She started looking still more deeply for the positive aspects of a person, rather than being judgmental in the negative sense. The thread between the happening, the unfolding of the theme, the meaning, and the action is visible. Anu, the sensitive thinker in tragic transition, is herself the thread which made the difference. She scooped profound meaning from the critical shift in her consciousness.

All turning points provide a shared meaning:

(a) The trigger, the event, the happening leads you to look to the deeper currents of your life.

(b) The feeling of entrapment, suffocation, dead-end and the visual impact of the critical incident become a strategic inflection point in your mental evolution.

(c) You revisit life goals, career objectives, role responsibility to your calling, quality of your ambitions, and what you would like to do next.

(d) It results in a critical shift in consciousness and consequent deliberate action.

None of these people disbelieved in fate, good or bad luck, but they made the difference with their unique perceptive thinking. They did not take the event lightly. They treated it seriously to change their careers. We can make a difference to our lives if we want to. This is what this teaches us.

Some had neither a congenial upbringing nor significant mentoring. But they did not complain or waste time in blaming parents, schools or others. They made up for the lacuna with extra efforts to overcome the odds. Some did not face any critical situations, but as events unfolded, they appear to have made perceptive shifts naturally. Whether or not the leaders had similar nurturance, in the end, they ended up with a set of common traits which made them what they are. These are examined in the next chapter.

Chapter 2

Common Traits Emerge

E ach of our participants has a unique story. And the stories are unfinished. Each of them is in the making, none has arrived. They have not stopped growing, not even Kurien at the tender age of 79. Although the die is cast in childhood, if the attributes are malleable a person matures with different proclivities. As I had hoped I found some common traits. These are: *commitment, persistence, difference, curiosity, persuasiveness, risk-taking, focus, values, high energy, learning, humility,* and *non-listening.* I have broad-banded the traits with shared meaning under a lead word. These words have been alternatively used to convey the same meaning.

COMMITMENT

Commitment, or drive, dedication, passion, obsession, zeal. By commitment, these leaders mean carrying into action what they deliberately undertake to do. It is a pledge they want to honour. Their dedication is to the cause like Verghese Kurien's in building farmers' cooperatives, Bhavarlal Jain's in progressive farming through farmers' education, or Raghunath Mashelkar's to two IPR movements—Indian Patent Rights and Intellectual Property Rights. Kurien and Jain built businesses on a social mission while Mashelkar is exploiting science for India's commercial benefit.

Anu Aga and Pramod Chaudhari are passionate about improving the customer service process. Anu considers acknowledging a customer within 24 hours to be a religious endeavour in her energy and environment business, while Pramod thinks that his customers worldwide must prosper as a result of using his solutions in the alcohol and brewery plants that he supplies to them. They are passionately involved in refining the organizational processes to lead to prompt service and tangible gains to the customer.

Creating wealth has become an obsession with communist-turned capitalist Narayana Murthy. He realized that rhetoric doesn't create wealth, dedicated intelligent IT work does. He has created 270 dollar millionaires and his company, Infosys, has a market capitalisation of Rs 59,338 crore. Young Turk Manoj Tirodkar's obsession is to become a billionaire by making his colleagues millionaires. His craze has so far led to wealth creation of Rs 136 crore among 750 employees. Deepak Kanegaonkar smelt money in the speciality chemicals business. With gumption and drive, his defining characteristics, he has built a business of Rs 52 crore in just under 20 years with the help of his 150-strong staff. United Television's Ronnie Screwvala is doing what he loves to do. Starting with producing plays and entertainment shows, he went on to build a Rs 175 crore media entertainment group with missionary zeal in just a few years.

For most of our leaders, at the start of their careers, money was as much a necessity as a measure of success. As they earned enough money other motivating factors like prestige, power and enlight-ened interests in social causes grew in importance. Almost none had the ambition to become fabulously wealthy for the sake of wealth alone. In fact, the commitment to do public good through creating wealth, surplus and profits has remained a central theme of their stories.

PERSISTENCE

Persistence, or doggedness, determination, hard work, insistence, tenacity. Commitment generates energy because the self merges in action, and action leads to friction, and friction to energy. You need to persist until you accomplish what you want. You are exhausted, when the supply of energy takes a pause for self-renewal; after the intermission, it returns in response to your tenacity. Hard work is neither fun, nor worship, nor duty. It is purely and simply experi-encing the self. Doggedness determines the quality of the experi-ence.

When I asked Bhau Jain, "When do you go on vacation?" He shot back, "What is a vacation?" His unwavering determination took Jalgaon, an unknown town in Maharashtra, onto the world map be-cause he made his Jain group (turnover Rs 400 crore) world leaders in custom-made irrigation systems. Bhau Kelkar's long years of hard work in creating original fragrances and reaching them to customers in record time led to his admission to the exclusive Paris club of 'Creative Perfumers.' The Kelkar group (turnover Rs 150 crore) has made India proud.

All our leaders have laboured long hours, particularly in the early stages of their start-ups. Now, in the wired world, mobile telephony means constant connection with work. In fact, work travels with them. Yet most of them claim that they and their spouses are happy with the balance that they have achieved between work and family, despite this 'balance' being skewed towards work. Screwvala of United Television says today's high-tech business demands that you 'stretch', which undoubtedly creates some stress; he is opposed to stress reduction techniques since restoring the balance could also lead to a degeneration in performance.

Involvement of your total being in your creation absorbs all your time. Rajabhau Chitale's insistence on maintaining high standards of quality *mithai* (sweets) at all costs has tied him to his Rs 125 crore business 24 hours a day. Similarly, Kiran Mazumdar's passion in nurturing her start-up Biocon India (turnover Rs 100 crore) has led to the distinction of its being the first enzyme company in the world to achieve ISO 9001 certification. Her passion has become an obsession, as it has for the others.

Obsession leads to doggedness, the capacity to keep going when the going gets tough, like when Jain failed in his diversification, or Chitale's *mithai* shop was flooded, or Murthy's partners were calling it a day when Infosys was floundering for lack of orders, or Kurien's 'Operation Flood' was drying up for want of milk powder and related products.

It is strength of character that carries you through doubts and uncertainties, when things are just not working, sometimes due to omissions and commissions or even blunders. Almost all our subjects have faced failures of some kind. Brilliant ideas are not likely to work all the time. But these people treat mistakes or failures as learning experiences. Jain went on to give an ad in the newspapers, owning responsibility for his humiliating failure in diversification. Learning through three gruelling years, he has just come out of the woods. He calls it an 'eclipse cleared'. Most of our study participants display similar adroitness in weathering the storm with the unshaken belief that they will rescue their trapped ships.

DIFFERENCE

Difference or distinctiveness, differentiation, positive attitude, personality, innovativeness, talent. Managers who become leaders want to make a difference, that is the mission of their lives. If they don't have it to start with, they cultivate a desire to make a difference in their sphere of activity, their vocational calling. Most of them says they wanted to do something different.

Dhananjay Bakhle, a brilliant medical doctor, chose to do a masters in pharmacology rather than follow the beaten path of doing a masters in surgery; more significantly, he became a true master in medical informatics by learning computer applications. He crafted a special career niche and made appreciable progress in original research, medical journalism and medico-legal battles. Dhananjay made a difference to his career and to the results of his medical division. Deepak Kanegaonkar ventured into launching up-market perfumes in Paris, building a business out of his hobby.

Sudheer Tilloo, rather than become a lawyer like his father, chose to study engineering at BITS, Pilani, followed by an MS from Wisconsin, USA. From day one, he latched on to Japanese businessmen, brought in their technology, learnt the know-why and turned the unknown Morris Electronics (turnover Rs 1.6 crore) into a well-known organzation, now named Hinoday (turnover Rs 123 crore) with a dominant market share in ceramic magnets, ferrites and automotive castings. Narayana Murthy wanted to make a difference by building a software giant 'of software professionals by software professionals', and he did. Pramod Chaudhari was more interested in building an organization that would be a reference point for the industry, rather than simply achieving growth in volumes. He has succeeded in making Praj, suppliers of brewery plant equipment, into such a unique company.

CURIOSITY

Curiosity or intelligence, creativity, clarity of thought, kaleidoscope thinking, originality. Creative artists such as singers, dancers, cartoonists and musicians make a difference, as research suggests, by cultivating a niche, an edge, a talent. They disassociate from the herd mentality. Each one erects his special *shamiana*. The secret of their success lies in their uniqueness, an admixture of alchemical faculties. Commitment, persistence, innovativeness, strategic thinking, integrity, initiative, fierce independence, national pride, game-playing, risk-taking, self-confidence and self-esteem—all contribute to make a noticeable difference.

Sometimes creative people are thrown into a situation, as Verghese Kurien was. A blue blooded Syrian Christian, Kurien was consigned to god forsaken Anand in Gujarat. He was tempted to extricate himself from the fly-infested cowsheds at least a dozen times. In the farmers' cooperative setting imbued with Gandhian thought, he was a rank outsider. There were many alluring offers, but he consciously decided against them since he felt there would be little to be done in an established organization. Note the clarity in thinking: He felt he could make a difference with experimentation and drive, and he did. A metallurgy engineer with no particular love for cows soon became the world's best-known cowherd.

Whether Manoj Tirodkar, Ronnie Screwvala or any of the others, each of our leaders has a maverick hidden in him. They are also intolerant of conformity. Mashelkar is dissatisfied with the vast network of government research laboratories. The maverick in him is provoking the angst of the science bureaucracy. Kiran Mazumdar takes the biotechnology mandarins head-on to single-mindedly pursue her goal of excellence in enzymes.

PERSUASIVENESS

Persuasiveness or communications, negotiation and presentation skills, influencing, play act, play out. It is not merely a cold presentation of data with cut and dry facts. It is much more. It is persuasiveness, sharing your convictions by making meaning of data. Facts don't speak for themselves, your advocacy does.

This is a critical faculty in the age of information technology and transparency. All our participants have this ability to persuade in ample measure. Ashok Soota made special efforts to learn the art and techniques of presentation in his study course at the Asian Institute of Management, Manila. Play acting comes naturally to talk-show host Screwvala. To Ratnaparkhi, expressing his convictions comes easily because of debating skills. Anu Aga has the ability to use the most appropriate words and convey her thoughts on the emotional plane because of her immense capacity to empathise.

Kiran Mazumdar is a businesslike, no nonsense communicator whose sincerity of purpose stands out. She is accurate in her self-assessment when she says, "I sold my colleagues the vision of Biocon and my personality." Deepak Parekh's patient negotiation while working on different government committees has paved the way for liberating industry from government control; insurance is an example. Kurien is a master negotiator who outplayed Khurodi and numerous *phoren* administrators. Mashelkar takes to the public platform to popularise the patents literacy movement. Murthy is out to sell the most needed perspective and mindset change on the creation of wealth.

RISK-TAKING

Risk-taking, or entrepreneurship. Risk-taking is the quintessence of entrepreneurship—taking on responsibility and being accountable for the results, experimenting without fear of failure, learning from mistakes without thinking they are fatal, creating by trial and error. Since the world is moving toward entrepreneurship, managers cannot afford to remain static managers; they have no option but to become entrepreneur-managers, whichever the organization they work for. Forget free lunches, businesses can no longer afford even subsidised brunches. A nine to five mentality won't make you a visionary manager.

Vikram Tannan's trials in making soft capsules to the specification of Seven Seas in England is a case in point. He corrected errors, learnt a lot, made another presentation and got their agency. Pratap Pawar risked his prestige to build a brewery in record time. Ravi Khanna, the son of a High Court judge, started up from his garage to build the Control Group (turnover Rs 200 crore). He voices his belief fervently, "Lack of resources makes you resourceful." He himself became resourceful after witnessing how refugees from Pakistan became resourceful and innovative in improving their lot. Manoj Tirodkar says he has become paranoid in his pursuit of building a global enterprise at the high end of technology. Kanegaonkar risked his mother's jewellery. Murthy and his cohorts borrowed money from their wives. Chaudhari consigned his safe and prestigious career to history. Tirodkar got his father to fold up his going shipping concern. Raising capital is a calculated risk. Loss of face and prestige damages esteem, even health.

FOCUS

Focus, or centering, zeroing in, concentration, goal orientation. Focus simply means concentration. Whether or not you are concentrating on your objectives, markets focus on results, tasks, deliverables and deadlines. The need for information and transparency is increasing day by day. For example publication of quarterly results (Q1 to Q4) has become the norm, which means '_focus is under focus_'. Prakash Ratnaparkhi's monomaniacal focus for two years with 67 trials gave birth to a spark erosion machine. Today, his Electronica logs a turnover of Rs 100 crore on spark erosion and other machines.

Deepak Parekh's concentration on the need of the middle class for affordable housing in rapidly urbanising India led to the creation of HDFC (assets Rs 15,084 crore). Deepak himself has become a walkie-talkie brand of the one-stop financial shopping mall. Narayana Murthy's global focus has taken Infosys to the Nasdaq. Dhanrajgir's zeroing in on Zinetac, the premium Glaxo drug, to launch it into the Indian market via third party production was an example of sustained focus on an objective until success. Sudheer Tilloo went through *Vipassana* training to improve his health. He overcame a greater obstacle, which was fear of failure. While pondering on the fundamental question of 'who needs whom' in relation to superiors, customers and employees, he came to the conclusion: "I need everyone; nobody needs me." The clarity of thinking helped him to regain focus. Bhau Jain overestimated his ideology and underestimated his core business strengths. He lost focus and his diversification into unrelated areas proved expensive. Bhau learnt from his mistake and has regained focus. Without focus, you lose direction, miss targets and diffuse objectives; with focus, you reach the set destination and mature in leadership.

VALUES

Values, or honesty, integrity, honouring commitments, keeping one's word, truthfulness, independence. In adhering to a set of values, a person values his self. Values are like maps. Respecting elders is a cherished value in Indian culture. It is an expression of your core belief system. You are shamed if you do not honour your word. You weaken the fabric of your personality. You fall in your own eyes, whereas maintaining values of honesty and integrity enhances your self-esteem; you feel you are a cultured being. Our leaders in this book cherish their values over everything else. It is one thing they are very proud of, and justifiably so. Proactive people are value-based, as are Tilloo and Mazumdar. If they say they will give a call, they do so. They do not trot out excuses to tell why they were unable to.

Narayana Murthy is a vocal proponent of the value of honesty, integrity, honouring commitments, value-added performance, willingness to sacrifice for opportunities and so forth. Murthy has a right to speak about values—he said he would take his company public in ten years and actually did; when I was interviewing him for this book he unfailingly kept our appointments; he wanted to share wealth with his employees and that's what he's done.

'Not getting along' is a 'bad word' in Ronnie Screwvala's United Television. Says Ronnie, "All hell will break loose if interpersonal issues are not resolved. It is a cherished value with me that people must get along in my organization, I have no time for arbitration."

Dhanrajgir swears by his value-based upbringing. Not to flaunt wealth, kindness, hospitality and respect for guests and elders were the rules of his house. He thinks he is a better person because of these values. Ravi Khanna has mandated in his Control Group that people must treat each other, customers and visitors with courtesy. He exhorts employees to develop _madhurya_, a certain sweetness and grace in tone, speech and manner. His staff greet each other with 'Radhe Radhe' which means 'kindness kindness'. Bhau Jain similarly talks of values of integrity and truthfulness. His integrity was evident when he passed on the benefits of the pre-budget price to customers when the government increased the price of diesel from Rs 58 to Rs 85 in 1963.

HIGH ENERGY

High energy, or spiritedness, stamina. The secret of unbounded energy lies in intense involvement in the task at hand, in 'doing' things, in conceptualizing, in getting interested in work itself. It is your infectious spiritedness that gives you the stamina to listen, to speak, to persuade, to travel, to contribute without a break. All our role models are bouncing with energy; not only the youngest, Manoj Tirodkar (36), but even the oldest, Verghese Kurien (79). Pawar, Chitale, Jain and some others had heart attacks (Jain had as many as three), yet they remain spirited. Dhanrajgir battles the stress and strain of cancer, but his face doesn't show it. In fact, he radiates enthusiasm. All these leaders work non-stop. Vikram Tannan's stamina makes him say, "Work is the greatest high for me." Screwvala animates UTV with his very being. Says he, "You must love what you do."

LEARNING

Learning, or knowledge. One acquires knowledge or skill through proper study and experience. The result of learning is modification in behaviour, approach, attitude, perspective. One becomes more skilled and competent.

Dr Bakhle recommended a particular computer for the Drug Information Centre at J J Hospital in 1985. The Computer Research Society's secretary asked him what authority he had to make such a specific recommendation. In other words, he was challenged because he had no education or experience in computers. Bakhle learnt how to work on computers within a year and became a master. Aga learnt transactional analysis and become a counsellor. Chitale learnt from a neighbouring Kutchhi shopkeeper the art of cultivating customers. Tirodkar, at the age of 14, learnt the art of loading cargo ships by watching the marketing officer in his father's office; he learnt how to operate the telex because that's how the shipping business was then conducted. Tirodkar, who has passed only the 12th standard, studied telecommunication sales and after-sales service by reading literature on the subject and founded Global Tele-Systems. Says he, "If change is the only constant, then learning and listening are the other constants."

Chaudhari chose to work on the shop floor to learn from the workers. Calling it "hands down learning," he says it was "necessary grounding for becoming a real manager of men and machines." While scripting his career Chaudhari made deliberate efforts to learn sales, marketing and commercial skills before launching his independent venture, Praj Industries. He is an ideal example of a self-willed and self-made manager-entrepreneur. Tilloo has learnt Japanese decision-making and their way of thinking by closely watching their behaviour on the job in the course of some 50 trips he has made to Japan. Ratnaparkhi and Chitale swear they learnt immensely through participation in seminars, attending conferences and visiting industrial exhibitions.

These 22 executives have made special efforts to learn the art of management, the craft of product and service innovation, the skills in marketing and leadership competency. They learnt on the job, through books, meeting people and discerning observation. Most of them are voracious readers. They read anything and everything that they come across which could add to their width and breadth of knowledge—business magazines, financial journals, balance sheets and management classics. Screwvala subscribes to as many as 19 business magazines. Parekh picks up reading material for many of his colleagues relevant to their on-going concerns and tasks at hand, according to HDFC's public relations chief R Anand. He adds that this shows how Parekh keeps tabs on the work-in-progress and leads by providing pertinent inputs. Parekh's chamber, as all the participants', was strewn with books and the latest publications, not packed away in inaccessible shelves but close at hand. Learning constantly is a passion with all of them without exception. All of them said they learnt more by 'doing', by trial and error. It is the attitude towards learning that is instructive. More than learning skills and competencies, these achievers have learnt the art of strategic thinking, which has made them exceptional executives. It is their learning aptitude which they have leveraged for creating wealth and showing performance.

HUMILITY

Humility, or ego in check, modesty, unpretentiousness. Men and women of merit, outstanding achievement and soothing humility are an inspiration to people who are interested in self-development. Most of the role models are steeped in humility. They credit their achievements to colleagues, teams, family members and a fair bit of luck. They are unassuming and unpretentious. They are unwilling to take all the credit for their unrivalled success. Not that they do not appreciate moderate doses of praise, but they certainly shun flattery. When I probed, some of them modestly acknowledged their personal accomplishments, brave moves, creative forays, challenges successfully met, and skillful handling of difficult situations.

Their egos appeared to be in complete check. When lesser mortals like us brag about our run of the mill achievements, you feel humbled in reading about them, and all the more so meeting them. The uncommon characteristics of these 22 characters inspired me. I felt their presence, experienced the _Reiki_ from a close distance. I am sharing my joy with you.

Non-listening

To the question, 'Are you a good listener?' most answered, 'No', they are not good listeners. I was surprised. The pattern emerged: Many were definite non-listeners at the beginning of their careers but they became better listeners over time. Firmness is a quality, obstinacy is not. It was difficult to assess if their tendency of not listening led them to becoming obstinate, even obdurate. It suggests that these leaders may not be very open-minded. They might have become so when warranted by circumstances. It may be that as strategists they are being non-revelatory on purpose. What damage non-listening has done is a moot point. They confess it is not a good trait and they are decidedly the losers. On the other hand, non-listening may have helped by shielding them from distractions and allowing them to remain focused at crucial moments.

The Gestalt Works

What matters is the performance and creation of our exceptional executives. Kurien, Jain, Murthy, Khanna, Chaudhari, Mazumdar, Screwvala, Kanegaonkar, Jain and Soota created wealth out of nothing. They are creative people. Mihaly Csikszentmihalyi in _Creativity,_

Harper Collins, 1996, mentions the contrasting traits of a creative person:

- Aggression and cooperation;
- Playfulness and discipline; playfulness is the antithesis of doggedness, endurance and perseverance;
- High energy and yet very quiet;
- Imagination/fantasy and rootedness in reality;
- Extroversion and introversion;
- Humble and proud;
- Escape rigid gender role stereotyping between masculinity and femininity;
- Rebelliousness/iconoclasm and traditionalism/conservatism;
- Passionate and objective;
- Enjoyment and pain.

For this study, I did not feel the need to know the presence, absence and weightage of the contrasting characteristics. There are bound to be some idiosyncrasies. The fact that the positive aspects outweighed their opposites is motivating.

After I had completed most of my interviews, in 1999 I came across two books on British and American business leaders, respectively—*The New Alchemists* by Charles Handy and *Lessons from the Top* by Thomas Neff and James Citrin. I was delighted to find that the traits identified by me in our sample are also present in the foreign achievers. The characteristics are neither gender-biased nor racial. The ambience in which our role models grew up is not materially different from socialist Britain's economical, political and social environment at the macro-level, although if differs from capitalist America's. At the micro-level, however, there is a great deal of commonality between Indian, British and American values of honesty, integrity, education, training, influence of mentors and the role of critical events. These appear to produce identical characteristics as we have seen. Certain well-known cultural differences, like a very high value for independence, early separation of children from families, less respect for elders, and a questioning stance appearing to border on arrogance, are more prevalent in America. Our leaders stressed the family bond, the spouse's intelligent and unstinted support, respect for elders, mentoring, and courteous treatment as important ingredients of their success. Non-listening was a galling shortcoming.

The performing characteristics are amazingly common in these exceptional managers and extraordinary entrepreneurs. Gita Piramal in her bestseller _Business Maharajas_, Viking Penguin, 1996, found three characteristics shared by eight great Indian industrialists—Dhirubhai Ambani, Rahul Bajaj, Aditya Birla, R P Goenka, B M Khaitan, Bharat and Vijay Shah, and Ratan Tata. They all have high focus, a high level of energy, and they are obsessed; they are totally committed to their ambitions and work long hours to realize their goal. Says Gita, "You could call them stubborn, even bull-headed, and once an idea has germinated in their mind, they won't give it up easily." Some or all of these traits are found to some degree in all of us. It is the blending of characteristics that makes the difference. The intensity of application depends upon the quality of each person's substratum. As I reflected on these subjects for almost two years I started seeing some configurations, something that is born out of the alchemy of the nurturance syndrome, uncommon characteristics, performance, goals and creations. *The gestalt works.* The reflexive search led to spotting the source code, described in the next chapter.

Chapter 3

Glimpses of the Source Code

O nce I had identified the thought leaders' traits, my search acquired added focus. Since the mere presence of exalted traits does not lead to producing exemplary results, I was curious to find out what does. I spent long hours of reflection at my desk near the window in my study. I have a breathtaking view of the sea and the sky behind a cluster of beautiful trees.

While immersed in the thought world of each individual, I got a glimpse of the combinatorial use of traits, tools, methods, preparation, practice and unique self-expression. The success of these vocationally integrated executives lies in the strategic use of their assets. Their progression, I realized, is their journey from being to becoming through domains, which provides clues to the clusters, the accelerators. It is the purposeful use of clusters which accelerates the thinking process and velocity of action.

THE COMPONENT CLUSTERS

There are three clusters in the source code. All three interact and cohere to produce exceptional results. I call these clusters **Reflexive Search**, **Leveraging Through Domain**, and **Value-Added Branding**. The table below shows the components of each cluster:

Clusters of the Source Code

Reflexive Search	Leveraging Through Domain	Value-Added Branding
Conceptualization	Focus	Stand for something
Commitment	Learning	Self-expression
Persistence	Methodology	Persuading
Difference	Quality	Branding
Curiosity	Innovation	Positioning
Meaning	Preparation	Packaging
Reflection	Tools	Bonding

At the heart of the reflexive search is the desire to make a difference; leveraging through domain involves thorough preparation to optimise one's skills; and value-added branding is to demonstrate that one stands for excellence in one's field.

Howard Gardner, professor of education at the Harvard Graduate School of Education and adjunct professor of neurology at the Boston University School of Medicine, developed the theory of multiple intelligences (*Frames of Mind*, Basic Books, Harper Collins). Gardner proposed that human beings have evolved as a species to possess at least seven distinct forms of intelligences for solving problems: Linguistic, logical/mathematical, spatial, musical, bodily kinetic, and two personal intelligences oriented towards understanding firstly oneself, and secondly others. Subsequently, he added an eighth intelligence: The apprehension of the natural world (*Extraordinary Minds*, Basic Books).

Our first cluster of characteristics by and large puts to use personal intelligences—understanding oneself and others. The second uses logical/mathematical and spatial intelligences, and the third, linguistic intelligence. Their confluence produces extraordinary results, as we shall see.

I did not see the need to probe the relative use of the three component clusters. While discussing each cluster, I have given detailed treatment to Kurien, Murthy, Parekh and Mashelkar. In addition, six more leaders have been covered under each cluster to substantiate its wide use. It does not mean that Chaudhari, described under 'reflexive search', Khanna under 'leveraging through domain' or Mazumdar under 'value-added branding' have not used other clusters. Far from it. They all have their unique mix. In fact, it is a proposition of this book that one will not become an exceptional executive unless one accesses all the three levers (clusters) to unlock the source power. It is the discovery of the difference—the asynchrony—in each one that leads one to draw upon the clusters as the situation demands. It is the holistic approach which prevails. Let us now proceed to study each cluster in turn.

Reflexive Search

In the reflexive search the executive is looking to make a difference, looking for a conceptual breakthrough in unfolding a grand vision or enabling an idea to take concrete shape, or is just curious to find out what would work to move forward. He knows he has the power of thinking, appropriate skills to forge alliances, and the capacity to combine diverse resources that would make commercial sense. He persists in playing with unrelated ideas, unconnected issues, ambiguous situations. His insatiable urge to grow leads him to reflect deeply on the reality of business problems, obstacles and larger issues of conceptual growth. Our exceptional executive revisits his 'search' almost every few hours. He is not a mechanical worker, he is a knowledge worker. He gravitates to this cluster more often than ordinary executives.

In the metaphysical sense the reflexive search is a search for meaning, a search for self-actualisation through the medium of work. However, the subject under consideration for us is performance in the domain of creation of wealth. Let's take a few examples:

- Kurien rejected offers of employment from the Tata group and Union Carbide. He chose to stay at Anand because he knew there was so much to be done, he could try and make a difference. He knew that his independent contribution in established and structured organizations would not be as easily measurable. He wanted a virgin field, and he got one. He constantly conceptualized the issues, whether 'Operation Flood' or the spray drying of buffalo milk. His commitment to the farmers' cause was conceptually far superior to that of any of the known crusaders. Kurien was a visionary. He had a vision about a farmers' modern dairy. In searching for solutions he drew on the farmers' raw wisdom. To build an institution for them he used his immense organizational skills. His strategic thinking, command over English and daredevilry helped him to find meaning in an unsuitable environment.

- The speeches he made (*The Unfinished Dream*, Tata McGraw-Hill) over 50 years all over the world bear testimony to his deep thinking processes on every facet of farmers' cooperatives, dairy technology, management, and the far wider issues of global socio-economic change. "The central lesson of Verghese Kurien's professional life," says 1970 Nobel Peace Prize Laureate Norman E Borlaug in the foreword, "is that farmers who control their resources and hang together in mutual self-help organizations (cooperatives) controlled from their 'grassroots' can discover enormous political and entrepreneurial power. Indeed, so organized, Kurien believes that there is virtually nothing they cannot achieve." His reflection on his own dreams served as an indispensable aid in advancing his search for building the ideal institution that he built.

- Murthy's conversion from a die-hard communist to a powerful proponent of humane capitalism is a case of reflection on the fundamental value of creation of wealth. At a deeper level Murthy must have realized that unless the very fabric of his thought changed he wouldn't be able to create wealth. Anwar Sadat's reflection from his autobiography *In Search of Identity*, Random House, 1975, aptly proves the point.

  > "... he who cannot change the very fabric of his thought will never be able to change reality, and will never, therefore, make any progress ... but the fact that change should take place first at a deeper and perhaps subtler level than the conscious level was one I had established as a basis of action ..."

  Like Gandhi's famous 'experiments with truth', Murthy's 'experiments with values' in ethical behaviour, sharing wealth,

417

'walking the talk' while building a world-class infotech organization 'for the professionals, by the professionals, of the professionals' is a sure-shot recipe for success in the volatile IT industry. Murthy freely shares his vision, values and practices with audiences of all genres. The western influence on his thinking is visible in the terse rationale he provides to elucidate his actions.

The published material and conversations with me reveal his reflective search on the creation of wealth for eradication of poverty. Murthy's influence-set consists of the most impacting combination in eastern culture: The dazzling creators of phenomenal wealth, J R D Tata and Lee Kwan Yew; and the more sublime Mahatma Gandhi, caretaker of the poor. Murthy is trying to find meaning in his daredevil search in the highest end of technology. Murthy is orchestrating seemingly contrasting notes. His immersion in western classical music must be helping him to refine his reflective abilities.

- Parekh's venture is a classic case in providing affordable housing finance for the middle class, by the middle class (professionals) in the middle of the road socialist government. Over the years his vision has extended from providing housing finance to consumer finance to building a financial supermarket to include insurance, mutual funds *et al*. The fundamental principle is that excellence is not achieved by competition with someone else, but in competition with self-defined standards of performance and behaviour.

Parekh is a profound thinker, as the following statement proves: "Visions can be wrong, hopelessly off the mark, if they are not born from strong values, strengthened and nurtured by an analytical ability to constantly assess emerging environments and strategic alternatives." Parekh's expertise lies in connecting unrelated issues, seeing patterns, and being on the spot before others venture to even start. His reflexive search is for more and more value-added financial services for the spine of society—the middle class.

- Mashelkar made a difference to two science institutes, the National Chemical Laboratory and the apex Council of Scientific & Industrial Research (CSIR). He made a significant difference in domain by launching two IPR movements, Indian Patent Rights and Intellectual Property Rights. More than this, he has brought about a mindset change in our science fraternity, to make research commercially viable. To take a bold initiative in making research user-friendly and economically beneficial is a pathbreaking approach. He is the first visionary CEO of a government monolith who has proceeded in a highly professional manner to put a vision document in place through consensus. The entire document is saturated with the language of commitment, so vital for making the vision inspiring.

Mashelkar's key to success is his ability to convey the message in the language of the audience. He is a super salesman of his innovative concepts. As a research scientist, reflecting comes naturally to him. His reflexive strategic search for a brand new vision for himself led him to carve out new roles. On taking charge of CSIR, he called himself chief executive officer; now he prefers to be called chief information officer. These redefinitions of role demonstrate novelty of approach, non-obviousness and utility of the idea. From his innumerable speeches and interviews and our animated discussions, I felt his search is still on, to make an indelible mark on the national innovation movement.

- Anu Aga indulges in reflexive search all the time. Her thoughts, serialised in the Thermax house journal *Fireside,* bear eloquent testimony to her inquiring bent of mind. Her commitment to the employees of Thermax is exemplary. Even when Rohinton was running the show, she made the difference in HR practices by introducing a more humane and transparent approach. Her determination to stay loyal to her compassionate belief system is admirable. It is being tested by employees who want more weightage given to loyalty (their long years of service) rather than performance, as the market dictates.

  Anu's documentation of her thought processes in facing personal crises—the death of her husband, son, mother-in-law and pet dog—is a lesson in practical philosophy. While dealing with personal tragedy Anu is also responsibly navigating the fine ship Thermax, which is currently passing through rough weather. Her tenacious search to find meaning amid the bewildering pressures of life inspires you to launch a more piercing search in the critical incidents of your own life.

- Pramod Chaudhari's search is continuing on the premise that his customers must prosper as a result of taking his solutions and Praj Industries must become a global reference point. His choice for acquiring experience in different facets of organizational functioning to equip him to start his venture by the age of 33 shows that he was determined to find his own path. Having satisfied the urge for independent creation (Praj as a quality supplier of alcohol and brewery plants and equipment), he shifted his search to make a niche for it in the global market. Says Pramod, "Curiosity is at the heart of the growth model."

Pramod's intensive search to understand the embedded factors that make an organization a reference point continues. It is visible in his being and reflected in his writings in the house magazine *in-touch*. In the Praj brochure titled *'Pratham'* (which means 'first' in Sanskrit) the last stanza fleshes out Pramod's reflexive approach: *"Pratham* is a constant search, it is a discontentment with the latest gain—for it wants only, in the end, to be itself, the First."

- Bhavarlal (Bhau) Jain is an ideologue who put Jalgaon on the world map with rare dedication. His conceptualization of the agro-economic development of the quaint little town and his commitment to societal issues are visible when you visit Jalgaon. The difference he made to the life of that remote district headquarters and to the micro irrigation industry is exemplary. Bhau's entrepreneurship through social commitment has come out of deep thinking on Indian values and philosophy, Gandhian teaching and tenets of Jainism, and above all a quest to excel over western sophistication in the Indian milieu. I have accompanied him on his morning walks over the beautiful Jain Hills and the insights he shared are as refreshing as the morning breeze.

- Ravi Khanna's legacy of pride in the family, respect for elders, spirituality and bearing witness to the trauma of refugees has instilled in him a rare combination of entrepreneurial search. Ravi determinedly decided to build his controls and switchgear venture, making a humble beginning in his father's garage. His conceptualization of the Control Group's growth and resourceful people management made him a major player in the electrical and electronic industry.

Ravi's enthusiasm and presence make the difference. In the *Vedanta,* he has found an instrument for reflexive search. He has to a great extent succeeded in shaping organizational behaviour on the five principles of *Vedanta* which I have recorded in his profile. When impolite behaviour with customers is the order of the day, Ravi has inculcated in his staff a sense of *madhurya.* This is training in the basics of customer care and interpersonal ethics.

- Ashok Soota at the age of 57 co-promoted a new venture in order to be a player in the booming internet and electronic commerce market, propelled by "a growing urge to seek self-expression." When I met him in March 1999 I had sensed that he was searching for an opportunity to give fuller expression to his being. A rank outsider to the IT field, Ashok made a difference to Wipro Infotech by dint of his conceptualization abilities, hard work and determination to make the company a leader under the suave leadership of Azim Premji. Ashok's distinctive contributions have made him a more reflective thinker. He is able to accurately guess where opportunities are waiting to be tapped. He is adept at making meaning out of chance meetings and coincidences. Such search requires curiosity and a desire to find hidden meanings. We discussed coincidences, echoing identical thoughts about their significance in the scheme of growth. Ashok's reflective abilities give rise to an urge to discover a more independent niche for self-expression, and he found one. Let us see how he adds further value to Ashok Inc.

- Sudheer Tilloo has the uncanny art of showing that he has understood something by quoting the most appropriate thought of great management thinkers like Peter Drucker, Jack Welch or Kenichi Ohmae. In order to grasp management practices that work, he is a voracious reader of management classics and tries to meet stalwarts in the field. When he returns from an overseas trip he has something productive to tell about the insight he got. His obsession of looking at the performance of better companies and the best managers is, he says, "a touch-stone for reflection". Sudheer's new _mantra_ for performance deserves to be quoted again:

- Quarterly Results
- Monthly Progress
- Weekly Movement
- Daily Action

If reflecting is fundamental, then it must lead toward an examination of lessons from one's daily experiences, whether implicit or explicit. Sudheer's _mantra_ is making executives do precisely that. He has a moral right to coax them, since he himself is addicted to the reflexive search for superior perfor-mance.

Everyone in our sample is a deep thinker and a reflexive searcher on his role in the bewildering human drama of creation-perform-ance-meaning and the lasting contribution he can make and would like to make. The focus of these 'thought leaders' is on meaningful intellectual achievement in performance. They are curious to find solutions. Their creativity and aesthetic sensitivity give them the greatest joy. This is the difference between them and us; we avoid problems whereas they seek them out so they can be solved.

These brilliant managers push forward to find out 'what's there?' They recognize patterns, similarities and dissimilarities between events, in their thinking and that of others. All of them were searching for more and more information. Such search leads them to find out 'what leads to what' i.e. the chronological patterns, the sequence of events. These result-oriented executives are able to establish causal relationships, then focus there, and be the causal agents themselves. With such deep thinking they establish their control in given situations and pilot the enabling process to take progressive steps in the movement of men, money and materials.

Michael Schulman argues (*The Passionate Mind*, The Free Press, Macmillan, New York) that infants and Nobel laureates alike seek to discover the same four things: *What is out there, What leads to what, What makes things happen*, and *What is controllable*. These concerns underlie the scientist's search for knowledge, the artist's search for creation, the philosopher's search for truth, and the exceptional manager's search for excellence.

In all our participants I noticed shades of such a search garbed in different words and phrases. Through extensive reading, communication and innovative search techniques, they have advanced their thinking. These executives consciously and relentlessly reflect on their work. The reflexive search is based on a differential approach and the use of 'multiple intelligences'. They leverage their distinctive capabilities through their domains.

Leveraging through Domain

Leveraging means making your strengths more productive, more effective. Such executives have prior knowledge about (a) their strengths and shortcomings, and (b) their field of expertise. They gain greater professional and economic control by leapfrogging over their weaknesses. They leverage their combinatorial skills through tremendous focus on key result areas.

One of my most important findings is that all the managers and entrepreneurs are masters of preparation: Collection of data, checking, analysis, tests, trial runs, discussions, workouts, simulations, role play, you name it. Practice makes perfect, the saying goes. Such thorough preparation in thinking, doing and positioning is bound to produce results. Our subjects are obsessed with quality, innovation, and the use of modern tools and methodologies. The commitment to succeed is unwavering.

It is not as if these executives spend their time theorizing. They do get thrown into situations beyond their control. They pick signals for action in their interactions with the outside world. The triggers may come from anywhere. They are alert to all such stimuli.

If they have gone into unrelated diversification, like Bhavarlal Jain, they have failed. They focus and refocus on leveraging their strengths in their chosen vocation; that is their calling. Kelkar, with his nose for perfumes, won't venture into infrastructure leasing. He would like to restrict himself to his specific area of work. He would delimit his scope of work because he would like to 'stand for something'. These executives master reasoning techniques—diagnostic, inductive, tactical, mathematical and even symbolic.

Focus on one's chosen domain gives the ability to improvise, sharpen skills, and leverage them to advantage. Like the American brands Intel, Motorola, GE and Microsoft, our brands Tata, Wipro, Reliance, HDFC, TVS, Amul and Infosys stand for excellence in their own domains. There's a saying that there is a woman behind every successful man; we could say that *behind every successful brand, there is an exceptional executive.*

Let us now look at how our role models leveraged through their domains.

- Kurien strategically networked at the political, administrative and institutional levels. For solving technical problems and for technological upgradation, he depended upon his colleague Dalaya. Both of them innovated in spray drying buffalo milk. In building the National Dairy Development Board (NDDB) or replicating farmers' cooperatives on the Anand pattern, he prepared meticulously. Kurien relied on exhaustive data collection and analysis of information. He marshalled facts and presented them convincingly. He told me, "Before going for meetings I would role-play with Dalaya. We would anticipate arguments and objections, the difficulties we would encounter, and decide our responses in advance." How many of us do this?

  Kurien fought vested interests from the local to the global levels. He was a champion of the farmers' cause. How would he have fought the illiterate and inarticulate farmers' cause if he had not been competent enough to outmaneuver the opponents? He would demonstrate what he was capable of doing and delivering. In ensuring that the boilers reached on time, he knew exactly how transport logistics would function. This shows his systems thinking. Kurien's strengths are strategic thinking, phenomenal administrative skills, tremendous networking capabilities, foolproof preparation, and above all, a killer instinct to maul the opponents.

For political savvy, Kurien relied on his mentor Tribhuvandas Patel, and for wisdom, on the farmers. His ability to see patterns in the development of the dairy technostructure and network of farmers cooperatives is mind-boggling. The Anand (joy) pattern replicated throughout India is truly joyous. Kurien leveraged his strengths by co-opting help in areas where he was deficient. His ability to deliver predictable success in his domain, dairy development, is a lasting contribution to poverty alleviation.

- Murthy is outright a systems thinker. He may have perfected the art of thinking when he worked as chief systems programmer at the Indian Institute of Management, Ahmedabad. Murthy's strength is selecting the right person for the right job. His expertise in putting together a team with a mutually exclusive but collectively exhaustive set of skills, whether for a venture or a project, is remarkable. Murthy has demonstrated his expertise in creating an enabling environment, building customer relationships on trust, and spotting business opportunities globally in his domain, software development.

Murthy leveraged these strengths in putting systems in place in the husbanding of HR, from selection to retention, to the pathbreaking employee stock option plan (ESOP). Similarly, he instituted globally accepted best practices in corporate governance by following the GAAP system of accounting, publishing brand valuations, and adopting a global delivery model. With all these measures he increased predictability in deliverables. Systems thinkers are best at the use of tools, and in methodical work sequencing, scheduling, flow and output. They generally produce reliable results. Murthy's was a unique piece of conceptualization—thinking of software as a pure and simple HR business, taking the Indian expertise in mathematics and wielding teams to leverage collective value-added skills by cutting across time zones in record time in the global market. He is leapfrogging in his domain, HR husbanding and software development.

- Parekh's strengths are the ability to think big, financial acumen, banking expertise, networking, building customer relations, and creation of trust. A chartered accountant by training is more likely to be lost in details because by temperament he is inclined to see the devil in each and every figure, but Parekh soared high in the field of housing finance, leasing and banking without losing sight of the critical figures that made commercial sense. Parekh focused on inspiring customer convenience. He instituted customer-friendly, less bureaucratic procedures by simplifying the loan process. He reduced paperwork, speeded up approvals, computerised transactions, reduced the number of trips to HDFC offices and simplified the eligibility criteria. Parekh created enormous goodwill amongst his constituencies of customers, fellow bankers, the financial community, and with officials who were his fellow members on various committees and apex bodies.

Parekh himself is a veritable trust house. He leveraged his expertise in finance, networking and trust building to expand into infrastructure leasing, banking and now insurance, mutual funds, you name it. A bank is a bastion of trust, and a banker, a *repertoire* of customer confidence. I worked in a bank in Mumbai and London for over a decade. I know how an honest bank officer is helped by his reputation. Parekh capitalised on his personal assets—his capacity to think big, his high level of integrity and his trust—to make HDFC a powerful financial corporation.

- Mashelkar's domain is scientific research. His strengths are innovative thinking, marshalling evidence and selling concepts to scientists and the bureaucratic laity. He leverages these strengths with the acumen of a competent business manager, without having an MBA in marketing. Mashelkar convinced his colleagues at NCL of the utility of going in for patentable papers to gain entry into the international knowledge markets. He carried his conviction about the protection of patents and intellectual property rights to successfully compel the law-makers to amend the Indian Patent Rights Act. The turmeric victory shows how he prepared thoroughly and marshalled facts to jampack his case with irrefutable evidence. The 'Vision 2001 and Strategy' document again brings out the same strength (thorough preparation), which he leveraged to get CSIR laboratory chief executives to work through and own the new vision.

A convincing communication style comes later, first comes innovative thinking. Mashelkar ensures that his ideas pass the strict criteria of novelty, non-obviousness, and utility. As a research scientist, this comes to him naturally, and he leverages this root strength with tremendous dexterity. Enthusiasm, says Dr Norman Vincent Peale, makes the difference. Mashelkar's enthusiasm is visible and his solution-orientation stimulates his colleagues to act. Mashelkar leverages his ability to communicate in the language of the audience to forge the 'innovation engineering' movement.

A few more examples will further illustrate the point:

- Rajabhau Chitale's focus on customer tastes led Chitalebandhu Mithaiwale to consistently produce quality *mithai* over 50 years. Year after year, customers use the adjective 'pure' (*shuddha*) to describe Chitale products—pure milk, pure ghee, snacks made from pure ingredients. The secret for getting such word of mouth publicity lay in the Chitales' ability to prepare products of a certain standard with zero imperfection in mixing, blending, heating, frying or any other process.

  The tools they use, the methods of preparation, prior tasting and constant product innovation lead them to leverage through their domain. Rajabhau's learning has not stopped. Now it is more through doing, preparing, systematising, and perfecting the methodology with the help of modern equipment. And don't forget, Rajabhau is leveraging in the most perishable commodity—milk. Despite preservatives and refrigeration it is freshness, that customers value above all.

- Humayun Dhanrajgir's transferable skills are his immense persuasive power and strategic breakthroughs in crossing regulatory hurdles. He leveraged them in Glaxo and Kodak. He persuaded Glaxo chairman Sir Paul Girolami to allow him to introduce the number one anti-ulcer formulation Zinetac in India through third-party manufacturing. From conception to successful launch it took just six months, with Humayun ably crossing many regulatory hurdles.

  Kodak India faced stiff competition from Japanese products (it still does). In addition, the local distributors were playing tricks. To overcome this double problem, Humayun conceptualized starting a unit in Nepal. Here again, he leveraged his persuasive power with the directors of Eastman Kodak in Rochester, US. His skills in crossing innumerable regulatory hurdles came in handy while dealing with the Nepali and Indian governments. There is now a 100 per cent subsidiary of Kodak India in Nepal. Humayun leveraged his skills in two different MNCs, the domain being strategic management. That's why he is an exceptional chief executive.

- Bhausaheb Kelkar's domain is the creation of perfumes. He has excelled in it by leveraging his strengths, analytical abilities, blending skills and meticulous attention to detail and quality. Fragrances are deeply personal choices for people. To cater to innumerable demands requires a developed nose and the discerning capability to guess customer acceptability. The methods he uses and the tools he employs in his research laboratories or aroma plant are highly sophisticated. The fact that Bhausaheb has earned the respect of choosy Parisians for decades is in recognition of having maintained outstanding quality over the long haul. Bhausaheb has leveraged his durable values of quality through enchanting fragrances all over the world.

- Prakash Ratnaparkhi is a doer of the first order. He doesn't talk of doability, he does it. This 'doing' strength, which many of us lack, Prakash has in abundance, and he exploits it to the hilt. Prakash's super-focus for two years in experimenting with 67 ideas led to the development of a spark erosion machine. Prakash leverages his strong desire to innovate, to explore what is in store, collect exhaustive information and the tools to experiment on a new CNC wirecutting machine or a digital readout system. Prakash's mastery in teaching technical intricacies by demonstrating what the spark erosion machine does led him to develop hundreds of engineer-entrepreneurs who would sell those machines. When I asked Prakash what he would like to henceforth concentrate upon, said he, "R&D, HRD, reliability and quality". His unflinching commitment to his domain is abundantly manifest. Those are his strengths, his areas of reflective search for excellence and meaning. Prakash wants to devote the rest of his career to leverage his talents through his life-long vocation.

• Sartaj Singh's strengths are people management and he first learnt to leverage them in the British multinational Imperial Chemical Industries (ICI). That is his transferrable skill and domain. So whether in rubber or speciality chemicals at ICI, or later in Cargill Seeds, or now in FMC-Rallis in agrochemicals, Sartaj has learnt to understand the business by learning from specialists. This learning process in different businesses has provided him with tremendous insight into how people learn, get taught, motivated and influenced for higher performance.

In addition to leading by example, Sartaj spends a considerable amount of time training his people in value for money, cost-cutting, avoiding waste, attending to customers, negotiation and such other topics by giving live examples. It does not mean that he is only a skilled trainer. It means getting work done and showing exemplary results through on-the-job coaching, which of course is supplementary to leading from the front. The importance of 'coaching' is endorsed by none other than Jack Welch, the legendary CEO of GE, who recently told an interviewer: "With increasing transparency brought about by the internet, the CEO will increasingly be the orchestra leader of very bright people doing their thing, sort of cheering them on, coaching them." Sartaj is fully focused on the 'purpose-process-people' model. His initiative and sense of ownership for achieving the defined targets are exemplary.

- Vikram Tannan proclaims, "Work is the greatest 'high' for me." Curiosity, preparation and persuasive presentations are Vikram's strengths. Curiosity led him to pick up a bottle of pearl-like tablets in Mumbai's Crawford Market, opening up a grand vista of business opportunity in softgels. His determination to continue his father's challenging work led him to conduct experiments and trials to convince England's Seven Seas to offer him the technology.

  Vikram's detailed preparation and power point presentations convinced Banner Pharmacaps to part with their technology and later build a state-of-the-art plant at Bangalore. Vikram's methodology, use of proper tools, and religious commitment to quality helped him in two respects—to get a 'Good Management Practices (GMP)' certification from WHO, and loyal MNC clients for his quality products. Vikram has fully leveraged his persuasive power to communicate in techno-commercial language in his domain, softgel manufacturing.

All the managers in our sample are doers first and sellers next. They leverage their 'doing' skills and 'thinking' competency through performance demonstration in their field of expertise. They are neither preachers nor teachers, they are learners and demonstrators. They show what they have done, how they have done it, and why; whether it is conceptualization, conflict resolution, crossing regulatory hurdles, product idea, service innovation, technology tie-ups, or whatever. The critical variable between the non-exceptional manager and these exceptional leaders is that the latter leverage their strengths by sharp thinking, meticulous preparation, and doing. They avoid empty talk and evasion. They are loyal to their domains. They prefer to earn their laurels in their chosen vocations.

These managers are skilled thinkers. They use what Edward de Bono called a 'Carpenter Model' of thinking, which has three basic operations —*cutting, stitching* and *shaping* (*Teach Your Child How to Think*, Viking Penguin). A carpenter cuts only a portion of a log of wood. Cutting means you want to remove a part of the whole and concentrate on it. While taking a picture with your camera, you do the same thing; you cut out what you don't want and focus the lens on what you want to click. In problem-solving, a manager separates the wood from the trees. A competent judge picks up only the relevant portions from the mass of evidence produced before him. A skilled cosmetic surgeon cuts only the needed portion of skin for a graft.

The sticking operation involves pasting so that things don't fall apart. A carpenter makes very good connections. He sticks together pieces which match the design in his mind. Our thought leaders recognize connections and put things together for a purpose. It is the association of ideas that leads them to make a new pattern. They collage things and events.

The shaping operation is design thinking. A potter shapes a pot. Similarly, a creative manager has the ability to make new formulations, shape new scenarios, in addition to checking against existing shapes. Fabric designers, architects and sculptors constantly create new shapes.

Those who use computers are constantly cutting, pasting and shaping information they want for a particular purpose. Designer cars, clothes, handbags, watches, jewellery—all are born out of a designer mind. Similarly, institutions become best because of the leader at the helm, such as Kurien, Murthy or Parekh. Excellent products and excellent service are a creation of the designer mind.

Let us now see how our leaders add value and brand themselves.

Value-Added Branding

As I absorbed their images, I realized these thought leaders stand for something—Kurien for dairy development, Murthy for software development, Parekh for housing finance, Mashelkar for patents, Kelkar for perfumes, Chitale for mithai, Mazumdar for enzymes and so on.

In this becoming mode our artists 'show and tell' what they have done and what they stand for. They do not take a 'couldn't careless' stance towards the buyers of their concepts, craft, creation, products and services. They design and demonstrate the meaning of their 'doing', the utility of their offspring, the value of their contribution. They are interested in multiplying the takers of their value-added extension and expression of the self, and therefore they sell themselves. They have their detractors, opponents, jealous colleagues and branded non-doers wallowing in self-pity, but I suppose they learn to live with them or leave them.

In their becoming they have added value to themselves. Each one has carved out a niche for himself in the minds of his stakeholders. Their elegant packaging of their work and its strategic positioning is what creates value and wealth. They do not remain content only with creation. They need a fan club, approval from recognized professional bodies and a pat on the back from legends in the field.

Let us glance through our brands:

- Kurien stands for dairy development. The Amul brand displaced Polson in butter and gave stunning competition in *ghee*, milk, cheese, chocolate and so on to other manufacturers of these products. That is the brand for consumers. The designer and architect is Kurien. He expressed his creativity through the dairy network that he built across the country. He enlisted help and compelled donors to part with their commodity aid on his terms.

  Positioning himself as the saviour of farmers, Kurien pleaded their cause before the authorities but did not succumb as a supplicant. He packaged himself as a master strategist, organizer par excellence, shrewd tactician, a no-nonsense top class professional who had the guts and gumption to show amazing results. Gradually he became an accepted brand for results and leadership in the cowsheds of Anand, dusty Krishi Bhawan in New Delhi, the plush offices of the Food & Agriculture Organization (FAO) in Rome and at international conferences from Canada to the Philippines. His bond with farmers and consumers grew stronger with every fight he waged on their behalf.

- Murthy is the quintessential professional, selling world-class software made by Indian brainware. His packaging of middle class values, spartan lifestyle, and collection of competent professionals with a mutually exclusive and collectively exhaustive set of skills has won him the accolades of both professionals and the government. Murthy's immaculate record of deliverables meeting strict standards of global deadlines has positioned him favourably in the minds of his western clients. Emotional bonding with the software world at home and abroad is achieved with the heady brew he has concocted on his brilliant transactional calculus.

Having created a brand value of Rs 5246 crore for Infosys and 270 dollar millionaires, Murthy has positioned himself not only as a creator of wealth but also as a maker of wealth creators in the software marathon. Murthy's race for value-added global branding has begun.

- Parekh, as I said earlier, is a walkie-talkie brand of housing finance. Consumer product branding is relatively easy; the value addition is somewhat easily measurable by the user. That is not the case with finance, it is money; rupees, paise, one per cent interest differential, and marathon calculations, packaged by a bank or a trust house. Here it is the trust house called HDFC, but the man who built that trust is Parekh. He packaged it suitably for middle class habits and positioned it as such with phenomenal networking. Parekh is the redoubtable wizard of financial fund management. His persuasive skills have finally liberated insurance from government control. Parekh's value-added branding in financial matters is as strong as a bank vault.

- Mashelkar has taken a risk in positioning himself as a priest for the marriage between two incompatible partners, science and business. We are impressed with the results of his team with its turmeric victory and patents movement; and his contribution to business thinking which he is imparting to the research and science personnel. Mashelkar's networking makes the difference. His communication abilities, non-staid behaviour and his urge to excel in non-conventional areas have made him acceptable to the business barons and the politico-bureaucratic hornets' nest in Delhi. His movements in the seamless world of science, industry, bureaucracy and politics allowed him to create and add value to institutions. Whether he is branded as a 'knowledge peddler' or 'patents pilgrim' one thing is certain—he stands for both knowledge and patents. He is accepted as such by industry and that is what matters.

Let us see a few more examples:

- Dhananjay Bakhle stands for medical informatics. He is expressing himself eloquently in actively promoting the interface between medical research personnel, marketing staff, field personnel, and his doctor fraternity in establishing an understanding between these three constituencies about drug research and the effectiveness of new products. He positions himself as an 'information highway' of supply-chain management. Dhananjay's creativity in drug discovery, mastery in computers and expertise in medical journalism have given him a cutting edge image in the pharmaceutical and medical worlds. Dhananjay dresses immaculately. His insight in marketing helps him to stand out as an expert medical researcher who adds value to the bottomline of the company he works for.

- Deepak Kanegaonkar stands out as a restless entrepreneur in a hurry to make his mark in the perfume capitals of the world.

Having made Phoenix Alchemy a successful venture in speciality chemicals, he has positioned Urvashi in a silver flacon with cabochon in 24 carat gold in Paris and other European markets. Deepak expends a great deal of energy in persuading others to accept his viewpoint on the subject under discussion. He is an intense person. His personal value addition in the creation, packaging and positioning of his perfumes is tremendous.

- Kiran Mazumdar has style. Her voice eloquently conveys her convictions. An entrepreneur of solid achievements in enzyme research and manufacturing, Kiran has good chances of becoming the first global woman entrepreneur in her chosen domain, having positioned herself very thoughtfully in the niche enzymes and high-tech biotechnology market. She expresses herself clearly in simple words on all business and socio-economic issues.

  Kiran's presence at various professional seminars and social events has quite an impact. She has been getting impressive press coverage for her accomplishments in the last decade. Kiran bonds lucidly with intellectuals, and that matters in high-tech. She has collected the best talents in R&D and other functions in Biocon. Her retention record is outstanding. I was tremendously impressed by her response to my question on the secret of her success in HR: "I sold my colleagues the vision of Biocon and my own personality." I have not come across such a succinct display of value-added branding.

- Pratap Pawar is at heart a social worker. Whether he is running his Ajay Metachem, or a brewery, or the newspaper *Sakal*, his mind is engaged with issues of societal concerns. Whether it

439

be the Baramati farmers, the Mahratta Chamber members, the welfare of the blind or students, Pratap is ceaselessly thinking how he could improve their lot. Pratap has skilfully put across the work he has done to the elite of society. He mixes with them and learns from them. His grasp of wider issues has helped him considerably to add value to the deliberations of the different bodies with which he is associated. His bonding with cross sections of society places him in a unique position.

- If Ronnie Screwvala the talk-show master didn't know how to brand himself, who would? Ronnie undoubtedly stands for entertainment right from his college days. He has graduated in the same domain to the high-tech world of infotainment and audio-visual communications. He is simple and affable. Ronnie's casual wear, animated conversation and a speed of response meeting Bill Gates' criteria endear him to the mod jeans and T-shirt techies and artists of the entertainment universe. Ronnie didn't have to make any special efforts to package or position himself. Slipping into the new role of a creative infotainment entrepreneur came naturally.

- Manoj Tirodkar is himself a portal. His portly frame and incisive mind represent the software intelligence of Global Tele-Systems to their entire client network spread from New Zealand to Latin America. This non-graduate entrepreneur in the high-end of the high-tech business is a marvel of sorts. Manoj is an engaging conversationalist who is an icon for young Indians to venture into any field of business with imagination, deep study and the intense desire to become a millionaire. Manoj stands for doggedness in learning in pursuit of wealth. His unquestioned value addition earned him the India

Young Business Achiever award and also the World Young Business Achiever award. Impressive branding indeed!

These managers follow a simple principle—'show and tell'. This is a major difference between us and these exceptional people. You have to self-promote what you stand for. Most of us have a need to express ourselves, and for that you must first have a 'self' to express. When companies are fighting hard for brand positioning, it is incumbent upon exceptional executives to leverage their personal brand—Me Inc. This is a need of the e-commerce age. Voluntarily or involuntarily, our characters have done it effectively, whether openly or subtly. It's a win-win strategy. They and all their stakeholders are the winners, only their detractors are the losers; too bad. In any case, humility has not abandoned most of them.

THE HOLISTIC TRI-CIRCLE OF INFLUENCE

The manager's search for making a difference is the starting point which encompasses a mode, a circle called 'Reflexive Search' which includes characteristics like commitment, curiosity, etc. These are not mutually exclusive traits. In fact, these traits collectively _cohere_ to provide a river bed for reflection. The second circle, 'Leveraging Through Domain', similarly consists of characteristics like focus and learning, which together allow the executive to leverage his strengths in his domain, the primary field of engagement. The third circle, 'Value-Added Branding' has characteristics like packaging and positioning, which stamp the executive's value-addition with a brand name.

The schema of the interacting circles looks like this:

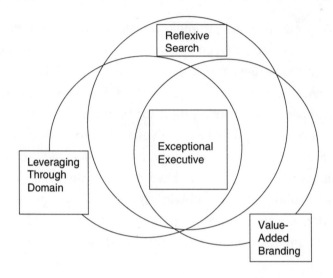

The three circles should be seen as interacting wholes. They over-lap. They are organic in character, therefore *holistic*. The more they co-mingle, the more they blend to produce an exceptional execu-tive. Such confluence *(sangam)* of the tri-circles creates the indi-vidual's catchment of influence. The larger the width of confluence of design, architecture and performance, the greater the influence. It determines whether he becomes a local, regional, national or a global brand. Each one of our exceptional managers is a brand by himself—a role model of sorts. His influence zone depends upon what he has decided to carve out for himself. There are no zonal restrictions. All of them have accessed the source code to reach where they have reached. The reach factor depends upon the vi-sion, creativity and the degree to which each one fine-tunes the component clusters. In the next chapter, I propose to validate the source code by reflecting on my personal experience.

Chapter 4

Validating Through Personal Reflection

*I*n this chapter I propose to validate the source code through my personal experience. As a human resources professional, self-introspection was always my *forte*. Work on this book over the last three years has led me to deeper personal reflection. I do not lay claim to scientific rigor or originality in the psycho-social field, but the findings are of great practical use. Perhaps my process of validation will help you in your own search.

At the beginning of my search, I did not yet know that there is a cluster of characteristics—conceptualization, commitment, persistence, difference, non-listening and meaning—which operates as a cohesive apparatus and vectors thinking to a higher plane.

As I met these stalwarts, studied the literature on relevant subjects and made dozens of drafts before the whole became greater than the parts, I was ruminating most of the time, particularly on morning walks, on the intricate amalgam of performance, excellence and exceptionality. I drew up exhaustive notes on my nurturance (quite loving and motivating); and systematically appraised my traits. My assessment tells me I had and still have in good measure many traits of our participants. Although I was a successful manager, I did not become an exceptional executive. Why, where did I miss out?

Navigating Through Turbulence

Let's start at the beginning: In the heyday of obstinate unionism and an ethos of distributive justice, industrial relations presented more challenging roadblocks than market competition, technology or customer care. One had to deal with multiple unions for workers and staff and officer associations. They represented numerous constituent interest groups spread across various divisions dispersed throughout the country. One had to interact with dozens of union leaders, from shop floor representatives to lawyers to leaders of national stature. Court judgements, the arbitration machinery, laws and government were all on the side of the unions. Unions were more united in their approach, strategy, study and demands.

Managements, on the other hand, were splintered. Inter-personal rivalries and ego clashes were a common feature. Productivity and performance lay on the wayside because there was room for loading the customer with additional wage costs, in the 'control and rationing' raj of the external government and the reflection of the same governance mode in the internal government of many organizations. The bureaucracies of most private sector organizations were rule-bound, status quoist and non-cooperative, and did not share information. Informal organizations and the grapevine played important roles. Once their job was done, scapegoats were periodically sacrificed by the management.

I was successful in making bold, innovative and productive experiments in volatile industrial relations, organization culture change and communications. I produced exemplary results when the companies I worked for were in dire straits. This is not to discount the contribution of bosses and of many colleagues holding different positions in various divisions across each company. The contribution of task teams in successful outcomes is acknowledged without a grain of reservation. My conceptualization of the issues on negotiations, charter of demands, charge-sheeted and dismissed employees, strikes, transfers, recognition of unions, frauds, individual ego clashes, broken promises, low trust levels, productivity, performance, officers associations' demands, etc. was holistic. My unwavering commitment and determination to succeed led to marvelous success. With special communication drives, training, seminars and meetings, I could help to bring about a change in the organization culture. The 'win-win' strategy always won. Naturally, I incurred the wrath of game players. In the major events that occurred in different organizations I improvised in every combat, bringing more order out of disorder occasionally bordering on chaos.

THE SEARCH WITHIN

Patchy reflection led me to ignore the reality of the power holders' egos and their conjoint malevolent impact on my progression. I had influential contacts in political and administrative circles, but I chose to keep away from them. If I had used them discreetly, as I had done in some matters earlier in my career, I would have benefited immensely.

In order to avoid divisional friction I refrained from influencing certain officer constituencies within some organizations. Had I done that, I would have considerably widened my circle of influence and checkmated non-cooperative peers in their habitats. Despite feedback and suggestions from well-wishers to penetrate such divisional bastions, I chose to do nothing. I took on role fights but I scrupulously avoided personal skirmishes of the Kurien tactical variety, and that was my undoing. I did not develop the protective cover to checkmate the professional politicians and therefore avoided battles of wits. I paid dearly for that omission.

Without assessing the competency, intentions and interests of the person I was talking to, I indulged in excessive sharing of my values, concepts and belief system. That did not necessarily result in either better understanding or a cordial relationship. Others were more interested in temporal transaction-based relationships. Murthy has systematised such relationships as a code of conduct. I learnt transactional analysis like Aga, but did not use it like her with practical wisdom. To the extent I succeeded it was because I had set my own standards for performance like Parekh; and like Mashelkar I had command over language and communications. The degree of my commitment was lower than Jain's 24-hour addiction. I digressed from life goals, hence I did not become a reference point like Chaudhari. I did not develop the 'madhurya' of Khanna or the perceptiveness of Soota to look into the meaning behind coincidences. Although I have probably read more on management and social sciences than Tilloo, I did not sufficiently imbibe the messages of profundity and therefore the underlying themes did not translate into action as seen in his behaviour.

In sum, I did not engage myself in reflexive search—a regular conscious consideration of the events of daily life in the light of my long-term aspirations. I did not draw apt lessons from some turning points of life although I thought I had done so. Consequently I lost the learning opportunity to discern the clues to proceed differently in future. I was trapped in unidirectional thinking; I did not shift into the process view of thinking. Our thought leaders resort to reflexive search as a habit of life, whereas my analytical thinking froze me into pondering separately on each characteristic—conceptualization, learning, communication, etc. Although I was using matrix thinking almost religiously in problem solving with tremendous success, I did not use it in reflection. In other words, it was essential to internalise experiential learning for personal growth. It would have helped to develop integral competence. The result: I was competent but did not become exceptional.

LEVERAGING STRENGTH

I have assessed my strengths and weaknesses against focus, learning, tools, methodology, quality, innovation and preparation, which together help the manager or entrepreneur leverage through his domain to exceptionality.

Like Kurien and Parekh I am excellent at resourcing and networking, but the use of these assets has been somewhat patchy. I prepare well like Kurien and Tannan, but I did not use role play techniques to prepare for meetings or trial runs for presentations. I had great success at building trust with most of the union leaders, but on the creation of one-to-one trust with bosses, colleagues and subordinates success was inconsistent. On the selection of the right person for the right job, I yielded to power play against my better judgement. I am good at creating an enabling environment like Parekh or Murthy, but my record on durability or maintaining such a facilitative environment could have been better. I am not a systems or logistic thinker like Murthy or Dhanrajgir. I am methodical but my use of tools is poor. Like Dhanrajgir my capability to cross regulatory hurdles is pretty good. I have in ample measure the analytical ability of Chitale and Kelkar, but not their blending skills. Over time my skills in getting things done have considerably improved, with simultaneous impoverishment in actual 'doing'. Whenever I revert to actual 'doing', like Tannan, I add more value to myself. I state my views unambiguously, forcefully and with conviction, like Ratnaparkhi does. Like Singh, I am an impact-making trainer.

On reflection, I find that I succeeded when I prepared well and that is one of the most significant factors in the achievements of all the thought leaders. I have leveraged my strengths in HR by focusing on learning, training, innovation, preparation and communications. I skirted my weaknesses in actual arithmetical calculations, the methodical study of rules and regulations, and the use of tools like calculators and computers by getting this work done by others.

In complex IR situations also, I used my scholastic strengths (language and personal abilities) and went past my limitations in the arithmetic of wage costs and productivity link-ups. I was able to do so because the managements did not have the willpower to face any disturbances on the shop floor, and there were no convincing formulae which could neatly fit into the mindset of all the stakeholders. I could take a 'prism' view of multiple representations and reconceptualize the issues, leading to major breakthroughs in IR imbroglios and consequent changes in the organization culture.

I am an effective speaker. I leveraged the fundamental competence of holding spellbound audiences of workers, supervisors, staff, officers and managers on the themes of unity, cooperation, collaboration, dialogue and quality of life, at seminars and group meetings. The syllabi were designed largely by me. The conduct of sessions on different topics to colleagues or consultants was delegated very sparingly. I knew that the personality of the trainer matters. Simultaneously, practical issues were settled out of court in face-to-face meetings with a great sense of timing, giving unions positive strokes in action and results. The resolution of issues was strategically positioned alongside the seminar schedules so as to increase individual confidence, interpersonal trust, and credibility of the seminar messages like 'I am ok, you are ok'. Many structural changes could take place in the composition of union committees and leadership. Dependence on outside lawyers, advisors and leaders was reduced. The mindset became more constructive and the atmosphere enabling. It was surcharged with hope and reasonable expectations which were responsibly fulfilled. I am not claiming I was the saviour or taking credit for all the beneficial changes, but as a catalyst, I was blessed with success and satisfaction. Such leveraging of unique strengths in the IR and HR domain produced exemplary results.

Unutilized Contribution

Assessing oneself on value addition and branding is difficult for a functional executive. In our sample we have only one such example, Dr Bakhle, who stands for medical informatics. With his focused efforts and conscious study of marketing techniques he packaged himself as an authority on drug research, utility and delivery. Bakhle positioned himself strategically at the interface of R&D, the marketing staff and the doctors' fraternity with considerable impact. I was uniquely positioned at the interface between unions, management, government and society, but neither did I read much on marketing nor press the advantage of my value addition to the different constituencies.

Although I made a significant difference, I did not leverage my differentiating brand. I should have sold my unique perception, action and results to widen my circle of influence. Now I realize how strategic it is to 'show and tell' what you have legitimately achieved.

Unlike Kurien, the saviour of farmers, or Rusi Modi, the caretaker of Jamshedpur's workers, I did not get a special image, I was not the chief executive. That certainly was a role restriction but that is no excuse. Faced with jealousy, temperamental incompetency retired me to my shell.

Here, I have to go back to what I wanted to become, my ambition. I wanted to become a result-oriented top management HR executive, and I did. This is confirmed by feedback, including that from my detractors. I am aware of my shortcomings and failures. I made mistakes, committed blunders. In the process, I might have unknowingly and inexcusably hurt some people.

Initially I made conscious efforts to package and position myself in various symposia and through occasional writing for journals and newspapers. I added value through such participation but did not pursue it. It was necessary to push further, especially in circles that matter. Here again, my reflective search on 'Who am I?' was not concrete despite reading dozens of books by Paul Brunton on Raman Maharshi and his central inquiry 'Who am I?'

SOURCE CODE VALIDATED

A word about the methodology of this reflection: I am aware that an individual has a tendency to rate the outcome of a situation higher if he knows that his input was solicited. He also tends to take greater credit whether or not his influence has a significant impact on the situation or the outcome. I am possessed by neither illusion because:

(a) No special input was either expected or requested. Neither was there any document clarifying role/responsibilities/expectations, nor any written or oral communication in this respect. One could have taken a proverbial political route and solved puzzles. Whatever I conceived and implemented was my input. If the experiment had failed, it would have been my funeral.

(b) I accept others played their roles positively or negatively. I believe in the contributions made by unseen forces, coincidences, luck, et al.

This personal reflection suffers from one limitation, viz. I have not preserved back-up data, and no opinion survey or proper study was conducted. It was a common malaise that many managements were not interested in studying episodes for reflection and guidance. In any case, I am validating the presence and utility of the source code by looking outside the box.

The quintessence of this personal reflection on the source code and its three component clusters has given me unbelievable satisfaction on three counts:

1. It has validated the presence of the source code which one needs to decipher to become an exceptional executive.

2. It confirms that executives with diverse backgrounds and varied competencies become exceptionally successful because they access the source code (*'sutra'* in Sanskrit) and use it innovatively.

3. I realized that competence alone does not lead to becoming exceptional.

Whether such executives access the code consciously or unconsciously is a moot point. We now know its presence and the way to sensitise ourselves to reach similar heights of excellence and prosperity. One of the best ways to sensitise ourselves is through exposure to role models. To conclude, we shall dwell on the influence wielded by our thought leaders.

Chapter 5

Thought Leaders Influence

With the advent of the knowledge economy the need for alchemical leadership to lead organizations to a predictable degree of success has soared. The *business* of business has become exceedingly complex. The congruence of information technology, media, and the *lingua franca* of young business India requires leaders of extraordinary influencing capabilities.

Exceptionality is most likely to develop if our ambitious executives are exposed to exceptional models. All of us, including those of us who are non-exceptional, will have the opportunity to ponder over the lessons embodied in such contemporary thought leaders' exemplary life histories. We can adopt proven thinking practices and leverage our strengths. It is for each of us to script our own success.

Remember, it is neither a formula for success nor an atmosphere congenial to growth which alone matters. It is the alchemical drive to attain great heights in one's chosen domain which counts.

Revolutionaries like Gandhi, scientists like Bhabha and Sarabhai, geniuses like Mozart and industrialists like Jamshedji Tata are visionaries. These are extraordinary people with extraordinary energy. Their commitment to their mission in life is awe-inspiring. An extraordinary leader's whole life is a message. His extraordinariness lies in his state of being. Such exemplary personalities always influence us positively.

In the business field we derive inspiration from exceptional leaders like J R D Tata, G D Birla or R P Goenka in India and let's name a few recent heroes from America like Jack Welch, Bill Gates and Andrew Grove. However, our thoughts on management have been durably influenced by the great management thinkers like Tom Peters, Kenichi Ohmae and Peter Drucker, to name a few.

Drucker introduced many new concepts like 'management by objectives' or 'managing for results'. I would say his art lies in asking the right questions to make the questioner 'think' about the right answer. It means Drucker 'does right things right'. When he says, "Yes, you want to manage for results. But what do you mean by results?" he is making the client rethink if he is talking about the correct results. Take another question, "What business are you really in?" This made executives think about core competencies. Such original questions and new concepts led him to influence millions of managers for nearly five decades. Drucker is a firm believer in "What gets measured gets managed."

In our thought leader's thinking process we found a confluence point in the source code between three variables: 'Reflexive search', 'leveraging through domain', and 'value-added branding'. These are their context and time-invariant attributes which they use with speed, imagination and excellence in execution. The degree to which these attributes are used depends upon each leader's leanings. Each leader's exceptionality is determined by his quick reflexes and his simultaneous play with these three thinking modes. When he reaches the state of 'flow', he creates. The longer he remains in the state of 'flow', the greater the value-addition.

We have cracked the value code of the intangible asset, the 'thinking leadership'. We now know the dynamics of its play. The value addition must begin at the top of each organization, big or small.

Let us visit the leadership site and look at what I call 'infrattitude', or infrastructure of attitudes. We find there is a leaders' club of managers and entrepreneurs of various hues whose infrattitude is quite promising. Each one has a unique mix of traits, core competencies and life goals. This is an 'aware' society, a professional association of knowledge workers, each one of whom would like to sensitise himself to exceptional performance. Whether through education, training or experience, they already know enough about leadership. They function in strategic posts, decision-making slots and leadership positions at the 'difference' making level. These leaders might like to look at the framework of exceptionality, understand the source code, and master the thinking practices of thought leaders.

Many of them, like Narayana Murthy or Azim Premji, know that the 'New Age' is about velocity, the speed of business and the speed of change. They are on the frequency of Bill Gates' _Speed of Thought_. They have designed their infrastructure around information flow. Gates says that "Knowledge management is nothing more than managing information flow ... The goal of business is to make business reflex nearly instantaneous and to make strategic thought an ongoing, iterative process—not something done every 12 to 18 months, separate from the daily flow of business."

The 'killer application' is evident with Premji's and Murthy's impressive global spreadsheet. The manifestation of their digital nervous system competency is a reflection of their access to and use of the source code. The alchemy of the source code remains in flow for large chunks of time.

All our thought leaders access the source code. If I had included more celebrities like Azim Premji, Ratan Tata, Rajendra Pawar, Anji Reddy, Kumarmangalam Birla, Keki Dadiseth, Gautam Singhania, Pratap Reddy, Karsanbhai Patel, Anand Mahindra, S Ramalinga Raju, Anil and Mukesh Ambani, Subhash Chandra, R Ramraj, Ajit Balakrishnan, Vineet Jain, Kalanidhi Maran, Rahul Bajaj, Mallika Srinivasan, M V Subbiah, Narottam Sekhsaria, Brijmohan Munjal, Hemendra Kothari, Xerxes Desai, etc. this compendium would have become richer but it would also have taken another couple of years to complete.

All our thought leaders have understood the need to manage interdependence. You can no longer resolve issues only by applying cold logic and mathematical formulae, or by linguistic mastery. You have to make far more use of personal intelligences in understanding yourself and others, because performance now largely depends upon management of interdependence. You need to develop a deeper understanding of yourself and others to expand your sphere of influence. You know you can only succeed through others.

While writing on managing oneself, Drucker advocates the use of 'feedback analysis' to measure performance and remedy bad habits: "Feed-back analysis soon identifies the areas where intellectual arrogance causes _disabling ignorance_. Far too many people—and especially people with high knowledge in one area—are contemptuous of knowledge in other areas or believe that being 'bright' is a substitute for knowing" (_Management challenges for the 21st century,_ Butterworth-Heinemann).

In such self-study one might realize that one has most of the characteristics of the exceptional leaders one knows of, and yet one has not reached the exclusive club. This is because of lack of knowledge of the source code. Access to the source code can lead to success in any vocation, even if here it has been derived from the vocation of business management and entrepreneurship.

A common complaint has been the lack of a facilitative environment. However, things are slowly changing. We now have in place a global, national, organizational and individual framework for performance in the creation of wealth, quality products and efficient services. India has a vision document in place, prepared by distinguished scientist Dr Abdul Kalam, _India 2000—A Vision for the New Millenium_ (Viking Penguin). In a link-up with the world's top wealth creators, prime minister Atal Behari Vajpayee signed a vision document with US president Bill Clinton for fruitful collaboration in various fields. Controls are being lifted, markets opened up. The socialist armada is under attack. The creators of wealth are being cheered instead of reviled.

Our executives may have reservations about wholeheartedly embracing Ayn Rand's philosophy of excessive objectivism (_Atlas_

Shrugged, Penguin) but they have gathered its essence: That man as a heroic being is responsible for his own happiness, with productive achievement as his noblest activity.

The global Indian diaspora leverages software and entrepreneurial skills to give Indians new pride and a positive brand image. Two other skills which promise great returns are yoga and our inborn emotional intelligence. The practice of yoga has spread throughout the world and can help build a network of relationships. Emotional intelligence, meanwhile, didn't enter the picture until Daniel Coleman put it into focus with his best-selling book by that name. The western rational thinking model was thought to be the best business model until Coleman brought home the fact that rationality alone does not help business growth; emotional intelligence is required. We Indians knew this all along but did not bring out a model for adoption in daily business practice. This is an example of how we miss out by failing to conduct research into our ancient intellectual practices and then codify them in modern terms. However, we are better equipped to take advantage of our expertise in yoga and rapport-building for cultivating productive interpersonal relationships and developing business. Such leveraging has excellent global reach, since our thought leaders treat man and woman—customers in their multitudinous manifestations—with dignity and affection.

As Indians the chances are on our side, according to Joel Kotkin. In *Tribes* (Random House, New York—a must read), Kotkin says the five global tribes—British-American, Jewish, Japanese, Chinese and Indian—will run the globalised economy. This is because of their common characteristics, which are *a sense of strong origin* and *shared values, geographic dispersion, belief in scientific progress,* _mutual dependence;_ and a global network based on _trust, passion for technical knowledge, open-mindedness, ethnic identity, thrift, education_ and _family_.

People at the top are said to be lonely, our thought leaders are not. They are not recluses. They claim to have maintained an equilibrium between work, leisure and family. But they have certainly lost the luxury of unplanned relaxation and idle moments in their ever-deepening obsession with life goals. In pursuit of their mission they might often lose friends or family contacts who do not fit into their work world, or do not share their zeal for intellectual growth and self-development.

What is creditable is that they have not only survived, but prospered. They have shown exemplary performance without recourse to the licence raj's permitted greasy routes. Kurien, Murthy, Parekh and Mashelkar contribute to shaping the policies of the government by participating on various committees connected with their respective industries. They operate on a wider horizon. All 22 have done well in the post-liberalised decade. It shows their knack for spotting opportunity.

The personalities and thoughts of these 22 leaders have possessed me. Whether Manoj Tirodkar, "I can be a billionaire only if my colleagues become millionaires"; or Sudheer Tilloo, "I need every one; nobody needs me"; or Pratap Pawar, "Transform the 'aware' society into a 'commercially aware' society"; or Kiran Mazumdar, "I sold my colleagues the vision of Biocon and my own personality"; or Verghese Kurien, "We must build on the resources represented by our young professionals and by our nation's farmers. Without their involvement, we cannot succeed. With their involvement, we cannot fail ..."; or Deepak Kanegaonkar, "I am an inde-fatigable optimist, difficult to demoralise"; or Ravi Khanna, "Lack of resources makes you resourceful"; or Narayana Murthy, "It is better to under-promise and over-deliver"—they all held me spellbound.

These thought leaders made me reflect on my own life. This helped me validate the presence of the source code. It also threw light on the career path I could tread hereafter.

I found the 22 participants' awareness about the power of per-suasion to be high. They were persuasively selling their vision, con-cepts, goals and targets. They were addictively engaged in constant reengineering of attitudes, knowing full well that unless those are changed they won't get superior performance. These leaders reframe issues, reinterpret the meaning and recreate the passion for achievement. They do all this through the spread and persuasive spell of their thoughts.

There is much more that I would like to know about the source code. For that, however, one has to scan the inner chambers of the mind. One would need far more time for such a thorough exercise. Although some questions remain unanswered, I have come thus far in this first effort to provide some tools and strategies to become a successful thought leader.

I am passing this thesaurus of thoughts to you. Reflect on it, and you could well be transformed into a thought leader. I was warned that I would feel empty after I had finished writing. On the contrary; I am feeling full, replete with the differentiating thoughts of thought leaders.

Annexure 1

Data Sheet

Classification	Entrepreneurs	7
	Entrepreneur-Managers	6
	Manager-Entrepreneurs	3
	Family Entrepreneurs	3
	Exceptional Managers	3
		22
Business Profile	From low-tech *mithai*-making to high-tech information technology, dairy, biochemicals, softgels, pharma, imaging, engineering, science.	
	Organization structures: Informal to highly-structured.	
	Ownership: Family, co-operative, government, public, and MNC.	
	Turnover: Rs 52 crore to Rs 2200 crore.	
	Number of employees: 150 to 26000.	
	Spread : Regional to global.	
Main Location	Gujarat (Anand)-1; Karnataka (Bangalore)-3; Delhi - 2;} Maharashtra (Mumbai - 9, Pune - 6, Jalgaon - 1) 16. }	22
	Urban - 20; Rural – 2 — —	22

Annexure 2

Data Sheet

Age Profile	Youngest - 35	Between 35 & 40	- 8	Male	- 20
	Oldest - 79	Between 51 & 65	- 11	Female	- 2
	Average - 54	65+	- <u>3</u>		
			22		**22**

Qualifications	Undergraduate	—	—	
	Graduate - Com/Eco/Arts/Law		—	
	Science	—	—	1
	Engineering - Civil/Mech/Elec/Metallurgy		—	7
	Medical	—	—	3
				10
				<u>1</u>
				22
	Postgraduate - 6; Management - 3; }			
	Foreign Education - 6; Others - 7. }		—	**22**

Family (Economic status)	Poor - 3; Middle Class - 13; Upper Class - 6 —	**22**

Regional Origin	Kannada - 1; Malayali - 1; Telugu - 1; Marwari - 1; }	
	Punjabi - 4; Gujarati - 4; Marathi - 10. }	**22**
	All converse and conduct transactions in fluent English; Most speak well in Hindi.	

Community	Sikh - 1; Christian - 1; Hindu-Muslim - 1; }	
	Jain - 1; Parsee - 2; Hindu - 16. } —	**22**

Annexure 3

Data Sheet

Main Family Influence	Father - 13; Mother - 7; Others - 2 — 22 Generally, the parents' influence is very strong, followed by that of teachers and siblings.

Family Values	Ethical values (Honesty, integrity, hard work,
	                  commitment) — — **Very high**
	 Learning — — — Very high
	 Favoured domain skills - Arithmetic, reading,
	    writing and communication — — Very high
	 Education — — Very high
	 Independence, ideas, doggedness, High
	    self-confidence-
	    discipline/freedom — — Balanced
	 Choice of career — — Total freedom
	 Atmosphere — — Open
	 Risk-taking/Safety - Emphasis slightly tilting towards safety
	 Outdoor activities/games — — Fair
	 Adventure — — Poor

Bibliography

Abdul Kalam, Dr A P J and Rajan Y S, *India 2000—A Vision for the New Millenium*, Viking Penguin, 1998.

Coleman, Daniel, *Emotional Intelligence*, Bantam, 1995.

Csikszentrinihalyi, Mihaly, *Creativity*, Harper Collins, New York,1996.

de Bono, Edward, *Teach Your Child How To Think*, Viking Penguin,1993.

Drucker, Peter F, *Management Challenges for the 21st Century*, Butterworth-Heinemann, USA,1999.

Gardner, Howard, *Extraordinary Minds* (1997) and *Frames of Mind* (1993) Basic Books, Harper Collins, New York, 1997.

Gates, Bill, *The Speed of Thought*, (Free Microsoft ® Windows Media Player),1999.

Handy, Charles, *The New Alchemists*, Hutchinson, Random House, London, 1999.

Kotkin, Joel, *Tribes*, Random House, New York, 1992.

Kurien, V, _The Unfinished Dream,_ Tata McGraw-Hill,1997.

Neff, Thomas J & Citrin James M, _Lessons from The Top,_ Doubleday, Random House, New York, 1999.

Piramal, Gita, _Business Maharajas_, Viking Penguin,1996.

Rand, Ayn, _Atlas Shrugged,_ Penguin Books, USA Inc, 1957.

Sadat, Anwar, _In Search of Identity,_ Random House, New York,1975.

Schulman, Michael, _The Passionate Mind_, The Free Press, Macmillan, New York, 1991.

Self-Made Impact Making Entrepreneurs, Entrepreneurship Development Institute of India, Gandhinagar, Gujarat, 1998.